# PHENOMENOLOGY OF LANGUAGE

# PHENOMENOLOGY
# OF LANGUAGE

BY
REMY C. KWANT, O.S.A., PH.D.

DUQUESNE UNIVERSITY PRESS
Pittsburgh, Pa.
Editions E. Nauwelaerts, Louvain
1965

## OTHER TITLES OF IMPORTANCE

REMY C. KWANT, *Philosophy of Labor*, $5.25

REMY C. KWANT, *Encounter*, $3.25

REMY C. KWANT, *The Phenomenological Philosophy of Merleau-Ponty*, $5.25

WILLIAM A. LUIJPEN, *Existential Phenomenology*, $6.25

WILLIAM A. LUIJPEN, *Phenomenology and Atheism*, $6.95

ALBERT DONDEYNE, *Contemporary European Thought and Christian Faith*, $5.75

Forthcoming titles:

*Phenomenology of Social Existence*, REMY C. KWANT

*Phenomenology and Metaphysics*, WILLIAM A. LUIJPEN

Library of Congress Catalog Card Number 65–12528

# Table of Contents

# Preface

WE may begin this preface by indicating why and for whom this book has been written. Of old, language has been the object of all kinds of scientific studies. Among the Greeks and the Romans the study of grammar and rhetoric occupied an important and even dominating place in education; classical logic often devoted attention to problems arising from the structure of language; the traditional European gymnasium and the corresponding types of American schools are based upon a great awareness of the value possessed by language. They want to educate young men and women by introducing them to the meaningful speech of the past and the present.

The historical origin of our languages has become a topic of scientific research. Much is known today about the genesis of languages, although the farther we penetrate into the past, the greater the obscurity becomes. How intense the study of language is appears even from a simple glance at the language departments of leading universities. They are well staffed with numerous experts and assistants in important and exotic languages, busily engaged in linguistic research projects as well as teaching.

Philosophers also show great interest in the phenomenon of language. The philosophy of linguistic analysis devotes itself largely to the analytic study of the structure of language. Since man wants to throw light on reality by speaking, he cannot justify his thought without justifying also his speech.

These few examples should suffice to show that language today is the object of much scholarly inquiry and reflection. In one way or another many students at universities pursue linguistic studies and outside the realm of the universities there are also numerous people who are systematically concerned with language. This situation is hardly surprising. Life is a being-together with our fellow-men; hence the art of living is to a large extent the art of encountering our fellow-men. The means *par excellence* to encounter the others is language. One who wants to prepare youth for life has to introduce them to language. This introduction begins at a tender age in the family, is then pursued in elementary education and continued in all other forms of schooling. Consequently, it is inevitable that many people make language the object of their daily occupation.

Language, unsurprisingly, is also a phenomenon that is taken for granted. We grow up in it just as we grow up in the world. It is not a phenomenon that makes everyone stand back and wonder. Many, even of those who are *ex professo* occupied with language, never wonder about it. Understandable as this absence of wonder is, it is also to be regretted. It is understandable because linguistic sciences take the phenomenon of language for granted as something given. Like all positive sciences, they presuppose the existence of their object, and they restrict themselves to studying the structure of language and the laws of its development. Genuine wonder about the phenomenon of language as such arises only by way of philosophical reflection. It is regrettable that many linguists devote little or no attention at all to the philosophy of language. For this neglect means that they omit to pay due regard to the fundamental questions arising in connection with the object of their studies. True, one can be an expert in the positive sciences of language without worrying about the fundamental philosophical questions raised by the phenomenon of language. The positive sciences are not unqualifiedly dependent upon philosophy. On the other hand, it is true also that this phenomenon could come alive again in a new way for them if they would reflect upon it philosophically.

This book does not intend to make any detailed examination of specialized problems in the philosophy of language or to present a survey of the discoveries made by this philosophy. Its aim is to introduce the reader to the fundamental problems regarding language. By means of the living reality which language itself is, this book wants to arouse the reader's philosophical wonder concerning the phenomenon of language. It would like to take away the unquestioning obviousness with which language is accepted and make the reader ask himself: How is it possible that there exists such a phenomenon as language?

It stands to reason that the author occupies a certain standpoint in the writing of this book. No one, unless he limits himself to writing a history of philosophy, can divest himself of his philosophical orientation when he wants to write, as Husserl says, about "the things themselves." The philosopher does not find his insights "ready made," but has to proceed laboriously along the road to understanding. It is inevitable that the road he has followed will influence his approach to the problems about which he speaks and writes. For the past decade the author of this book has devoted himself mainly to phenomenological philosophy. Thus it should not be surprising that this work approaches the phenomenon of language from the phenomenological standpoint. Those who follow a different trend of philosophy, e.g., that of linguistic analysis, would undoubtedly approach the problem of language in a different way. They will not always be able to agree with what is offered in this book. Nevertheless, I may express the hope that the fruitfulness of the phenomenological perspective will reveal itself in the way in which it throws light on the phenomenon of language. Experts in contemporary philosophy will have no difficulty in recognizing the influence of Merleau-Ponty on this book.

Let me emphasize once again that this book is written not so much for the benefit of the few philosophers who specialize in the philosophy of language as for the many linguists who are interested in that branch of philosophy and would like to possess a work which raises the problems of the philosophy of language in such a way that even the non-philosopher can fruitfully study it.

University of Utrecht　　　　　　　　Remy C. Kwant, O.S.A.

The American edition of this book has been adapted where needed to fit the public for which it is intended. Subtitles have been inserted to improve its readability. Indexes have been added, as well as a bibliography. Our thanks are due to Mrs. Betty Connelly for improving its style and suggesting a few slight modifications. The translation has been read and approved by the author.

Duquesne University　　　　　　　　Henry J. Koren, C.S.Sp.

CHAPTER ONE

# A Faulty View About the Function of Language

WHENEVER the phenomenon of language is discussed by philosophers or linguists, there is always a tendency to underestimate the function of language. In this first chapter we will draw attention to this strange fact and try to discover the reasons for this tendency.

## 1. INTERIORIZATION

In his recent work, *Critique de la raison dialectique*,[1] Sartre constantly uses the term "interiorization." It is proper to man, says Sartre, to interiorize the world in which he lives. By using this term, Sartre does not intend to introduce again a distinction which he had previously rejected as an "illusion of immanence." In the past people often made a sharp distinction between the external world of bodies, including that of man, and man's so-called interiority. They described this human interiority as the "place"—improperly, of course, for interiority is not a place—in which man's perceptions occur and in which there are images and ideas.[2] This interior world would be, as it were, a mirror of the external world. Sartre continues to reject such an interiority

---

[1] Vol. 1, *Théorie des ensembles pratiques*, Paris, 1960. 755 pages. Sartre defines human praxis, which is the topic of this volume, as follows: "Praxis is a transition from one objective situation to another by interiorization" (p. 66). The term "interiorization" is used throughout the whole book.

[2] The localization of knowledge and affections in a human interior is a very striking feature of Locke's works. He analyzes this interior almost as medical science analyzes the human body.

1

as illusory. Man, he says, is wholly bound to the world. His existence is always orientated to the world and runs its course in this world. His existence is a dealing, an interchange with the world, an interplay of giving and taking with the world.

What, then, does Sartre mean when he speaks about "interiorization"? By using this term, he wants to express that, living in the world, we make this world have meaning for us, we appropriate it, as it were, as a field of meaning. Sartre calls every individual a "totalization" of the world. The individual human being makes the world a whole extending around himself of which he himself is the center. Man cannot experience the world, including other human beings, in any other way than as his own field of existence, which lies around him and of which he is the center. At the same time, man knows very well that the other human beings likewise experience themselves as such centers. Just as I experience others as elements pertaining to my field of existence, so do the others experience me in their fields of existence.

Strictly speaking, all this is already implied in the fact that man is a "subject." True, man is also part of the giant causal interplay of forces which we call the "cosmos." Like houses or trees, men undergo the force of the wind. When a bomb explodes, he is exposed to its destructive power. When many human beings are together in a small space, each contributes through his respiration and body heat to the resulting suffocating atmosphere. We are part of the cosmos and its enormous interplay of forces. However, we are more than just that, for as "subjects" we make the world and everything contained in it be meaningful for us. We are a part of the world and at the same time a center of the world as a field of meaning. This is what Sartre means when he speaks of "interiorization."

According to Teilhard de Chardin, all matter is fundamentally characterized by a tendency to interiorization. Precisely because matter tends to ever increasing interiorization, its evolutionary process ultimately tends to man, in whom this interiorization reaches a provisional summit. Whether Teilhard's all-encompassing view is true or not is a question which we do not have to decide here. What is true, however, is that man interiorizes the world, i.e., he makes the world have meaning for himself. According as man becomes more human, that is, according as man reaches a loftier plane in the history of his development, this interiorization also increases. In a primitive society the individual's existence merges with that of the group. The primitive is more characterized by belonging to a group than we modern men are. Biographies of individuals are appropriate in a developed society rather than in a primitive group. There is a greater and a more differentiated wealth of existence in a developed society than in a primitive group. The developed society possesses more knowledge, more skills and higher levels of skills. This wealth can be preserved only in persons, for mankind exists only insofar as human beings exist. If, then, the total wealth of existence increases, the persons must make a greater effort to appropriate it. The individual members of a developed society have to devote greater attention to the development of their knowledge and skills. This effort leads the individual person of necessity to a higher level of interiorization: he has to put himself forward in his individuality, in his subjectivity, and he experiences himself more as a center of a world of meaning.

In our era with its enormous total wealth of existence and the manifold forms of this wealth, we often speak about the loneliness of the human person. Although all of us form part of a giant socio-economic community, each one is in it in his own way.[3] As a society grows and develops, the proper character of

[3] Only when the individual surrenders his own mode of existence within the group may one speak of the group as a "mass." This happens, for example, when many individuals merge into a cheering or jeering mass and let themselves be carried away by its collective mood. In our opinion, however, it is not correct to refer to man's existence in our contemporary technological order as a "massified" or impersonal existence. Although this order contains very many individuals, they exist in this order with their own thoughts, problems and feelings. It is a sign of intellectual pride to speak too readily of "massification." One who refers to the others as the "mass," places himself outside the group, makes the group an object of his stare, and reduces his fellow-men to a single homogeneous object.

the different modes of existence also becomes more differentiated. Many contemporaries, for example, devote their lives to the pursuit of a particular science or a particular form of art. If the individual wants to get somewhere in our modern world of work, he has to occupy a function; and there are innumerable different functions. Such a diversification of existence is, of course, not found in a primitive society. The more complex a society becomes, the stronger also each one feels that he has his "own place" in the whole. True, our existence remains a participation in a common life, but each one participates in it in his own way and knows that he has his own mode of sharing in that common life. The growth and development of a society causes differentiation and therefore leads to a kind of isolation. Precisely, however, because this isolation occurs within a whole and is due to the whole's development, it is accompanied by the need for communication. The more this isolation increases, the greater the problem becomes to maintain communication. For this reason man devises constantly new means of communication.

## 2. LANGUAGE AS MEANS OF COMMUNICATION

Thus it is not surprising that we experience language as a means of communication. Reading books about language, one is struck by the fact that language is always described as a means of communication. Language, so the facts seem to claim, is the means of communication *par excellence.* The various means of communication invented by man are largely based on language. Mail, for example, serves to make our words known to distant people. Telephone and telegraph are for the same purpose but in a quicker fashion. Radio and television are powerful means to make man's words known simultaneously over large areas. He has built world-wide networks of communication, all of which lie in the line of speech. Language, so it seems, is *par excellence* a means of communication.

*Language and Thought.* A means of communication serves to

make our thoughts known. Language, therefore, is a means to exchange thought. This exchange is, of course, fruitful also for the development of thought itself. By becoming acquainted with the thinking of others, we are able to enrich our own thought. Despite our increasing isolation, we have not yet lost the awareness that we need a dialogue with others to form our own ideas. We have been forced, however, to cast this dialogue into new forms. As long as people lived in relatively small social groups, they were able to enrich one another's ideas through a life dialogue between bodily present persons. For instance, the philosophies of Plato and Aristotle grew from such life dialogues. We are too numerous now to limit ourselves to the dialogue of bodily present persons. For this reason we were obliged to create means of communication. These means made it possible for one to speak or write and for many to listen to what is said. One who makes a special study of any particular science is thereby obliged to become acquainted with what the most prominent people in the field have to say about it. However, he cannot do so by consulting them in person, for otherwise he would make it impossible for himself as well as for those prominent scholars to lead their own lives. For this reason dialogue assumes here the form of consulting the works written by these persons. One who undergoes academic training, therefore, must learn how to find the works relevant to his field of study and how to assimilate them profitably. In this way it becomes possible for him to enter into dialogue with others even in a world as complex as ours.

Accordingly, we experience language as a means of communication, i.e., as a means to make our thoughts known to one another. This statement does not mean, of course, that language has nothing to do with the world in which we live. Our speech cannot be disconnected from that which we speak about. But that of which we speak is the world in which we live. Each one of us makes the world be his field of meaning. Each one is in his own way—and to a limited extent, of course—a synthesis of the world. When we speak of the world, we speak of it precisely insofar as we have made it a field of meaning for us, insofar as we have made it our own or, in Sartre's words, insofar as we have interiorized it. We speak of the world which we experience and upon which we reflect. Language, therefore, is a means of communication through which we make the world of our experience and reflection accessible to one another. Each one of us is an "interiorization" of the world. We have to aid one another in this interiorization; we have to make one another's efforts to do so fruitful; we have to collaborate because of our specialization and the inevitable limitation of each one's own interiorization. All this means that we have to communicate with one another, and the means helping us to do that is language.

*Presuppositions of Language.* It is more or less natural for us to think that that which is spoken of existed already before it became a topic of our speech. When, for example, we visit the dentist, we tell him that we have a toothache and try to indicate through words where it hurts. The affected tooth and our feeling of pain existed before we spoke of them, and our speech changes nothing either in the condition of the tooth or in our feeling of pain. Again, when we want to take action in connection with an intolerable social condition, we first talk it over with others in order to get a clear picture of the situation. This situation exists already and its intolerable condition is an objective fact. Whether we speak about it or not, whether we discuss it intelligently or not, it exists. To use a third example, the scientist faces the object of his study in the same way: molecules, atoms, electrons, protons and nuclear energy exist in the physical world independently of our speech. Our intellect penetrates into these existing realities and, when we have understood them, we express them in formulae. These formulae may be to the point or miss it, but whether they do so or not, does not change anything in reality itself.

Three phases, so it seems, should be distinguished. First of all, meaning exists in the world; it exists in the physical world or in the social world, but at any rate it exists. This is the first presupposition of speech. Secondly, we have to interiorize this meaning, we have to understand it, feel it, or whatever other term one wants to use to indicate this phase. We have to make the given reality be meaning for us. Speech comes only after this, in the third phase, in which we express the interiorized meaning in language in order to be able to communicate with others and arrive at a fruitful exchange.

*Accessory Character of Language.* Language, our means of communication, thus seems to possess a more or less accessory character. There exist many languages in the world. These languages indicate the same thing by means of very different words. What ours calls "table" others refer to as "Tisch" or "mensa."[4] The term seems to be merely a means of expression in the most divergent languages. It often happens that the same book is published in many languages. This fact does not change the reality of which the book speaks nor the ideas which it expresses.

The inner meaning of reality is characterized by necessity, and this necessity is mirrored in the interiorization through which we appropriate the meaning to ourselves. For we feel that we are not permitted to think differently from the way we are doing it because our thinking is governed by the compelling necessity proper to the object of our thought. Language, on the other hand, is not characterized by the same necessity, for one and the same thought can be expressed in the most divergent languages. Moreover, the language which we speak has a strongly historical character. It has *de facto* developed in a particular way but could undoubtedly have developed also in a quite different fashion. Although linguists try to discover the laws governing the evolution of the various languages, these laws do not hold with absolute necessity. Latin, for example, has developed in different ways into Italian, Spanish, French and Rumanian, but what reasons caused the variety of this evolution? We face here the contingency of history. True, certain laws operated in the process,

---

[4] For this reason scholastic philosophers sometimes refer to words as "arbitrary signs," in opposition to concepts as "natural signs." The two are radically different. Cf., e.g., Joseph Gredt, *Elementa philosophiae aristotelicae-thomisticae,* Freiburg i.Br., 1937, vol. 1, pp. 11 and 20.

but these laws do not explain everything. Strictly speaking, they explain nothing at all in a wholly compelling way.

Language is undoubtedly connected with a world of light. Our words enlighten others. When we listen to a talented speaker, he introduces us to a world of light. By means of his words, we penetrate into that world of clarity. For language is a means of communication, enabling us to share with others the light which we ourselves possess. Nevertheless, the light imparted by means of language seems to be essentially independent of our language. Language points to this light but itself does not produce it. Let us illustrate the matter through an example.

In his voluminous and important work Karl Marx pointed to the influential function of the economic infrastructure and argued that this structure determines the whole of life. Whether or not this function had found expression in words, it was present in the reality of life. One could say that the function in question was not at all dependent upon its verbal expression. Words tried to indicate something that already existed before them. Such a verbal expression may be correct or not correct, depending on whether it expresses matters as they are, exaggerates or underestimates them. In the case of Marx his expression went too far because he ascribed to the economic infrastructure a fully determining character. He went beyond reality. His words, which were intended to express reality itself, did not fully succeed in doing so.

*Pre-Existence of Meaning.* The idea behind this description may be expressed as follows: the meaning intended by speech precedes speech itself and is presupposed by it. To clarify this statement, let us explain first what is meant in this context by the expression "the meaning of speech." As anyone knows, disconnected words do not say anything. If I enumerate the words "paper," "room," "cigar," "garden," "city," and "car," I have not yet stated anything. At most a psychologist could investigate why I have chosen these particular words. Words begin to say something when together they constitute a sentence. This happens when together they have a coherent signification, when they "make sense" and indicate something. When I say, "An ash tray stands on the table," I have really stated something. These words constitute a sentence because together they give expression to a reality. When we speak here of "the meaning of speech," we want to refer to that which is brought to light by speech. This meaning can be a truth, a desire, an order or any other of the many forms which meaning can have. For our question, the differences between these forms are unimportant.

A sentence does not result from the simple observance of certain grammatical rules. One can join a subject, a verb and an object in such a way that the whole remains meaningless. Words constitute a genuine sentence only when together they have meaning, when together they give expression to something. A sentence may be grammatically incomplete and nonetheless remain meaningful because, within the context, the listener himself is able to supply what is needed. A simple "Yes" can be most eloquent. The "meaning of speech" is that which is given expression by speech.

The meaning of speech, so it seems, precedes speech. In the above-mentioned example of the ash tray on the table, that ash tray stood on the table before the sentence was spoken and the presence of the ash tray was wholly independent of the speaking. Contemporary sciences make all kinds of statements about atoms and molecules or the composition of matter. Here, too, one would be inclined to say, matter was already composed of atoms and molecules before man spoke of it.

It becomes somewhat more difficult to maintain that view when there is question of literature. A novel, for example, does not speak about pre-existing matters. In general, its characters, as well as their lives, their actions and words, are fictitious. One could object and remark that a novel is good only if it is true to life, if its fictitious characters express real life. Only when this is the case will the novel be successful. Even though such a novel does not unqualifiedly speak of real life, the reader realizes that it is "real." Literary fiction somehow manages to remain in touch with the reality of life. Even the litterateur has to express life, although he may do it in a way that is entirely his own and by means of fiction.

The same applies to wishes and commands. The wish must express a real need; the command, to be good and appropriate, must express something that really must be done, something demanded by the objective requirements of the situation. Wishes and orders may not be purely arbitrary.

For this reason one who speaks feels that he is not entirely free. True, he arranges his words in his own way, for everyone has his own way of speaking. Nevertheless, he feels that he should speak as he does because he wants to express a meaning that exists prior to his speech. Speaking is the expression of what is and is therefore bound to reality.

Everyone occasionally experiences that he has spoken wrongly. He wanted to express a certain form of meaning in words, but his words failed, as it were, to catch the matter. His speech was meaningless because his words did not touch the real meaning. Such a failure can occur not only in a theoretical explanation but also in literary fiction and even in humorous remarks. For one can think that there is something funny in a matter which afterwards appears not to be funny at all. Speech, then, is governed, so it seems, by a meaning which precedes our words. If our speech touches this meaning, it is good; if it fails to touch it, it is wrong. In other words, speech does not contribute to the very existence of meaning. It may be important to communicate the known meaning to others but it does not make the meaning be. Our speech depends on the meaning because it indicates that meaning. As an indication, a sign, it is inconceivable save in relation to that which is signified. The opposite, however, is not true, for meaning exists independently of speech.

*Speech as Non-Creative of Meaning.* All this, so it seems, can be readily verified by paying attention to discussions. It happens occasionally that someone opposes a current way of speaking.

10

For example, at the time of Galileo everyone said that the earth was the center of the universe. The earth was supposed to be immobile and the sun to revolve around it. Galileo opposed this way of speaking and claimed that the earth revolved round the sun. He experienced great opposition, especially from clergymen. This opposition, however, was not offered in the name of current speech but in that of "the things themselves," of reality. Man is always inclined to consider his speech an accessory indication of relatively little importance. The important matter are the things spoken about. These things impose themselves with binding force on our speech. We speak as we do because reality is as it is. The necessity of things affects our speech. What we have to respect in the first place is these things and not speech itself.

Speech serves to communicate the known meaning. Our speaking brings this meaning to light also for our own consciousness. However, speech does not make the meaning be. Speech, we could say, accepts meaning, it does not give or create meaning. By speaking, we make an existing meaning our own; but as soon as we change anything in it, we falsify the meaning, so that our speaking is no longer true speaking. As soon as our speech wants to give meaning, it is false.

*Realistic and Idealistic Development of This Conception.* This conception of speech can be developed into two opposite directions, one more realistic and the other more idealistic. The more realistic view starts from the supposition that that of which we speak is ultimately always the real concrete world in which we live. We simply speak about the world, about reality. It would not be right to say that we speak of our own thoughts. It is true, of course, that we are able to speak about reality only because and to the extent that we have thought about it, and we must therefore admit that we always speak about a thought world and thought reality. Our thoughts, however, converge on the world and reality; they do not have the character of a center which demands attention for itself. The meaning, therefore, of which we speak and which governs our speech is the meaning

11

of reality, of the world itself. The realistic view will ultimately always refer to reality when it considers the motivation of speech.

This view is rejected by the more rationalistic or idealistic conception of speech. We do not speak, its representatives claim, about a brute given world but about a world of light. But the world is not a light of itself. The world becomes a light by virtue of our concepts and ideas. The world offers at most the subject matter of knowledge, but our concepts and ideas give clarity and transparence to that matter. This clarity comes from the man who understands and not from the brute datum. Accordingly, we ultimately speak about our field of thinking, about thought reality, and not simply about reality.

Nevertheless, in both views speech continues to have a purely secondary character. Whether the meaning is given in the real world or originates in man's understanding, in both cases the meaning of speech precedes speech itself, either as the real world or as a concept or idea. In both cases speech serves to express a light which precedes our speaking and to which speech has to adapt itself. It is then of secondary importance what further interpretation is given to that light. The word is only an accessory sign. Language is a means of communication and transmits the light which it itself does not create. Speech is denied a creative character. Does not experience itself confirm this standpoint? Isn't it true that we know from experience that speech expresses something which precedes our expression?

Accordingly, a distinction is made between the meaning of speech and speech itself. This distinction is continued by a further distinction between knowing and speaking. For if meaning, the content of speech, precedes its verbal expression, it is possible to know this meaning or content before one speaks. Like students sometimes say during an oral examination, "I know it, but I cannot say it." Speech is a secondary, arbitrary expression, needed for communication, but not for knowing itself.

*An Antiquated View.* The conception of language sketched in the preceding pages is no longer accepted by the most current

12

forms of contemporary philosophy of language. One has to go back to the past to find it defended. Contemporary philosophy of language developed in a struggle against this view. This is the reason why we did not want to omit it entirely from our study. Moreover, it cannot be denied that one who begins to philosophize about language is still inclined to take that standpoint.

Speech is a creative force which, as we will see, produces meaning. At the same time, however, speech makes this meaning so "natural" that one is inclined to consider it simply as given and to disregard the creative power of language. Speaking, especially in its common form, makes the meaning which it produces appear so natural and obvious that it is easy to lose sight of its origin in man. The view which disregards the creative force of human language has been sketched in these pages. It is time now to throw light on the creative power of speech, to devote attention to speech as the origin of meaning.

CHAPTER TWO

# Language and Existence as Giver of Meaning

At the end of the preceding chapter we said that we would study language as the origin of meaning. Strictly speaking, this expression is not entirely correct. Language is not an autonomously acting reality; hence it would be better to say that we will consider speaking man as the origin of meaning. Man is the origin of meaning in his speaking, but not only as speaking but also in many other ways; for instance, as playing, as working and as feasting. Speaking, then, is one of the many ways in which man gives meaning. For this reason we face here a twofold task. First of all, we must try to clarify what is meant by existence as giver of meaning, and secondly, we must show the particular way in which we give meaning in our speaking. In this chapter we will consider the relationship between language and our existence as giver of meaning.

## 1. The Compenetration of Language and Human Existence

One could ask why we want to speak here first of our existence as giver of meaning in general. Is not this work supposed to speak of a special topic, viz., language? Why, then, should we first pursue more general matters instead of coming directly to the point?

The reply is that the suggested direct approach is not possible,

14

for the simple reason that language is interwoven with the whole of our existence. Our speaking is not an isolated event, but functions within the whole of our existence as giver of meaning. This total compenetration does not manifest itself with all desirable clarity when we pay attention to specialized ways of speaking, such as those of the various sciences. In all sciences man brings reality to light through speaking. The development of scientific life, however, which continues to run its course, has given rise to many specialized sciences and the majority of these have little to do with man's ordinary life. A glance at a university catalog suffices to show us a list of such sciences. If we want to see how life and speech are interwoven, we should not direct our attention primarily to these greatly specialized ways of speaking. For the more a human occupation, whether that of speaking or that of acting and doing, is specialized, the farther it is removed from ordinary life.

*Compenetration of Language and Existence in Ordinary Life.* Man's ordinary life very clearly reveals to what extent speech and existence are interwoven. Playing children offer a striking example. Body movements have an essential role in their play, for man cannot play with the things of the world without playing at the same time with his body. Yet his attention goes out to the world and not to the body. All kinds of shouts and cries, of warnings and indications, play a role in the games of children. The schoolyard is full of children's bodies running in all directions, but at the same time filled also with shouts. Speech is an integral part of play. One who would forbid children to speak with one another during their games would really stop them from playing. In their games the children have to give a certain meaning to the space around them and to the things in this space. For example, in "Run, sheep, run" a certain area is the prison, which rescuers have to invade without being caught by the guards. The meanings which things have in the children's play have to be defined and for this reason speech plays an irreplaceable role within the context of play.

15

Speech has a similar role wherever human beings work together; for example, when mother and daughter together clean the house, when the farmer tills the land with his sons, when mechanics together repair a car. They talk while they work and sometimes interrupt their labor to consult one another. True, the topic of conversation may be irrelevant to the work; they may talk about the latest football scores while fixing the car. However, this is not always true. Talking together may be an integral part of working together, for the work requires co-ordination and this co-ordination is supplied by means of speech. When many work together one will have to be the leader, either officially or unofficially, and he leads the others by means of speech. Even if speech seems to be unrelated to the work, it still belongs to it in one way or another. For example, the work is performed in an atmosphere of mutual understanding which finds expression in speech or is perhaps created by it. If, on the other hand, speech leads people who work together to profound disagreement, their work will suffer from it.

The compenetration of language and man's total existence reveals itself also in the difficulties experienced by deaf-mutes. Unable to participate in speech, they feel greatly out of touch with life unless, as happens now, they are aided in special ways to re-integrate themselves again in life. This aid consists partly in making them participate again in speech in a way appropriated to their condition.

*Language Itself as an Example.* The compenetration of language and total existence manifests itself even more strikingly in language itself. A glance at a dictionary suffices to show that many words are connected with regions of existence distinct from those of our speech.[1] Such words are wholly unintelligible and useless for anyone who does not live in the regions in question. For instance, a man who does not live in the region of

---

[1] As is well known, Heidegger often investigates the most original sense of words having philosophical importance. He usually wants to show thereby that this original sense manifests itself as a being-attuned to the fundamental situations of human existence.

visual meaning because he has been born blind cannot understand the proper sense of terms referring to visual meaning, such as words for colors and shades, for differentiations of illumination, for distances perceptible to the eye. These words, moreover, are often used metaphorically, but one who does not understand their proper sense will likewise be unable really to understand such metaphors.

Other words are connected with taste; first of all, of course, all words indicating the various tastes. But this connection can go beyond mere taste. The French language, for example, is full of terms derived from the taste of wine. Other words again belong to the world of odors or that of sounds: for instance, the language of music. In addition, there are numerous terms with a strictly motoric sense which would be unintelligible if the world were not the field in which man moves. Finally, there are innumerable words connected with spheres of activity, such as sports and games. Any form of occupation gives rise to many terms. For this reason there are numerous words which are hardly ever used by one who does not concern himself with the activity to which they refer. A person, for example, who casually enters a carpentry shop, a garage, or a marine workshop will hear many expressions which he does not understand. The language spoken in these places is fully dependent on the corresponding sphere of action. Likewise, the language spoken in the everyday life of an isolated village is permeated with the daily cares and occupations of the villagers. Thus it is not surprising that when a new form of work or a new occupation comes into existence, it enriches our language with new words and new expressions.

There are, moreover, many words, expressions and ways of speaking which somehow are connected with sex life.[2] One who has no experience whatsoever of his sexual being would be unable to understand our language in this respect. A confirmation of this assertion may be seen in the fact that when adults speak to children in terms of this sexual language, their words are given

---

[2] Freudian psychoanalysis finds here a fruitful realm of research.

a quite different sense by these children. The latter do not know, for example, what is meant by "unchaste" because the sphere to which the term refers is still unfamiliar to them. Hence they attach all kinds of strange meanings to it.

Finally, there are many terms and expressions based on space and spatial relationships. They can be understood only from the standpoint of the way in which man exists in space. High, low, distant, close, right, left and other such terms are meaningful only on the basis of man's situation.[3] One can speak of a horizon only when one's field of vision extends indefinitely. "Space" itself indicates first the world insofar as man has freedom of movement in it and insofar as it provides room for the things needed by man. From this original concept man has gradually developed more abstract concepts of space.

*Reciprocal Dependence of Language and Existence.* The preceding examples clearly show that our language is to a large extent intelligible only on the basis of our existence in the world and specifically on modes of existence which precede speech and are, in part, independent of speech. If we were to try the impossible and isolate speech from our total existence, speech would become largely unintelligible, for the meanings which are given expression in speech arise mostly in other zones of our existence. Speech, therefore, is not autonomous or self-contained.

Human language is not the language of an absolute consciousness but of an "existing" consciousness. For a being which does not "exist" as man and is unable to think in terms of man's situation, human language would be wholly unintelligible. Language is connected with the total structure of human existence.

It would be erroneous, however, to think that the dependence

---

[3] Investigating our way of speaking, one would find that we are inclined to think in a spatial and localizing fashion even when there is question of realities which cannot be localized. This way of speaking has occasionally led to misconceptions. For instance, the view was put forward that our knowing and perceiving take place in our so-called "interior." Thus the question arose of how this interior was to "contact" reality outside us. Existential phenomenology rejects this question because it is based on an erroneous preconception.

in question is unilateral in the sense that language would be dependent on other zones of our existence and not vice versa. An example may serve to illustrate the reciprocal character of this dependence. Words and expressions indicating flavors, such as sour, sweet and bitter, are meaningless for one who has no sense of taste. They depend on our taste. The opposite is also true. Because we express different flavors in our language, we become conscious of them and their differences, which has the effect of making us able to taste better. Again, words connected with a particular field of action can be understood only on the basis of this field. Conversely, our speaking of such words helps us to improve and expand our field of action. We will revert to this question in subsequent chapters.

The preceding remarks show sufficiently that language constantly interacts with our whole existence and all its zones. Our speaking is one of the functions of this existence and, as such, wholly interwoven with the whole. We do not want to answer here the question whether this statement applies to language in its entirety, but merely claim that our speaking is to a large extent interwoven with other functions of our existence. In other words, our claim does not exclude the possibility that man's speech may sometimes rise above its dependence on other aspects of his existence.

Briefly summarized, our speaking is interwoven with our whole existence, first, because language often gives expression to a meaning which originates in another zone of our existence; secondly, because our speech often serves to orientate us in our practical situation in the world.

## 2. OUR EXISTENCE AS GIVER OF MEANING

As we have stated, our speech often expresses a meaning originating in another zone of our existence and, moreover, positively contributes to that meaning. Speaking, therefore, is an aspect of our existence as giver of meaning. For this reason it

19

will be necessary for us to reflect upon meaning-giving existence as such.

*Existential Phenomenology and Positivism.* The term "giving meaning" is used mainly in existential phenomenology although other trends of thought often also make use of it. Existential phenomenology is a reaction against certain realistic and positivistic ways of thinking.[4] These trends of thought are characterized by their tendency to maintain that meaning is simply found by man and that our consciousness does not make any active contribution to the origin of meaning. Our world, they claim, is a field of meaning of which we simply become aware. Such a view does not necessarily imply that meaning is simply reality itself. Hardly anyone today would still admit that, for instance, colors, odors and flavors simply exist in reality. There can be question of color, odor and flavor only by virtue of a certain interaction between objective stimuli and the human body. Eyes, tongue and nose are "touched" by certain stimuli, and as a result of this, there arise impressions which we indicate in terms of color, flavor and odor.

The interaction, however, which gives rise to these values is a purely causal process which is wholly independent of our consciousness or subjectivity. This causal process leads to a field of which our consciousness becomes aware without contributing anything, so it is claimed, to the origin of this field. According to the positivistic view, meaning is an objective datum, whether it belongs to a real world that is entirely independent of us or originates through a causal interaction between body and world. Meaning is originally found by man as a consciously living being, it is not "projected" by him. Hence we should not speak of giving meaning but of accepting or registering meaning.

It is not easy to describe the view which existential phenomenology takes with respect to these matters, hence its standpoint

---

[4] For an excellent treatise of existential phenomenological thinking see William A. Luijpen, *Existential Phenomenology*, 3rd impr., Pittsburgh, 1963, especially Chapter Two (Phenomenology of Knowledge).

is sometimes misrepresented. It is wrong, for example, to say that existential phenomenology makes consciousness the source of all meaning. The existential phenomenologist will reject such a characterization for two reasons. First, he regards the human subject rather than consciousness as the source of meaning; secondly, the human subject is never the source of meaning by himself but only in his dialogue with "the other," that which is not this subject himself. Let us elaborate these two points.

*The Subject as Source of Meaning.* According to existential phenomenology, the human subject is the source of meaning. It would be less correct to say that consciousness is this source. But, one may object, is not the human subject consciousness? We cannot simply answer this question in the affirmative. True, in a certain dimension the human subject is self-conscious. We are beings who designate ourselves as "I." We know ourselves, for instance, when we think or make decisions.

However, there are in our subjectivity also dimensions of which we are not conscious. Consciousness is concerned with a certain zone of our existence but not with our entire existence. Our feelings and emotions originate in a zone of existence in which consciousness does not penetrate. We are unable to penetrate through our consciousness into the dimension of ourselves in which arise dark moods and joyful moods. Our desires originate in a kind of semidarkness, sometimes even in complete darkness. We do not know why certain associations present themselves to our mind and we are astonished by the surprising combinations which we make in our dreams. There is, then, an unconscious or preconscious dimension in us which nonetheless really belongs to our existence.[5] Even where our existence is conscious of itself, we may not unqualifiedly identify our being with being-conscious.

Many forms of meaning are experienced in a conscious way. Yet, strange as it may seem, it is very difficult, we may even say

---

[5] Cf. Remy C. Kwant, *The Phenomenological Philosophy of Merleau-Ponty,* Pittsburgh, 1963, pp. 11–30.

21

impossible, to point to a single form of meaning which can be explained solely and entirely on the basis of consciousness alone. We experience it as meaningful to look at the world on a day of beautiful sunshine, to enjoy a good meal, to be together with friends, to listen to a brilliant speech or beautiful music, and to arrive at understanding after laborious study. We seek these and other forms of meaning consciously, i.e., we situate ourselves in such a way that we exist in these forms of meaning. We ourselves are in part the source of these experiences of meaning. Yet on the basis of our consciousness alone we cannot fully explain why all this is meaningful for us. The meaningful character of all meaning cannot be wholly explained by an appeal to the fact that man is a conscious being, a being endowed with reason. Ultimately we will have to say: I happen to be constituted in such a way that watching a sun-lit world, a tasty meal, the company of friends, listening to a brilliant discourse or beautiful music, and arriving at understanding are full of meaning for me. It is something which we can never fully explain. Ultimately we have always to accept it with gratefulness that meaning exists for us.[6] From experience we know that the meaningful is full of meaning and we have to accept this experience without ever being able fully to account for it.

For this reason we must say that not consciousness, but our existence, is the source of meaning. Even as pre-conscious our existence is the source of meaning, and when existence is conscious, meaning is never fully explained solely on the basis of consciousness.

*The Subject in Dialogue as Source of Meaning.* Secondly, existence alone is not the source of meaning. Our existence gives rise to meaning in interplay with the "other," with that which is not the subject, so that this "other" plays an active role. This idea is implied in the fundamental concepts of existential phenomenol-

---

[6] For this reason it is very dangerous to plan an order for life fully from the standpoint of aims pursued by reason. Man is a manifold searching for meaning. If reason plans the whole of life by itself, certain aspects of man may fail to receive due regard.

ogy. The central idea of existential philosophy is the concept "existence," which indicates that our being is essentially and always openness to the other. A central idea of phenomenology is that of "intentionality," by which is meant that our consciousness is always consciousness-of-something, i.e., it is interwoven with the other. Precisely because these fundamental ideas are common to existentialism and phenomenology, these two streams of thought have been able to merge into a single stream as existential phenomenology. This philosophy, therefore, asserts that human existence is never the one and only source of meaning. All meaning is to be understood on the basis of man, but no form of meaning can be understood solely on that basis.

As we mentioned in the preceding paragraph, there is an interplay between our existence and the "other" and this interplay gives rise to meaning. We must now try to explain more accurately what is meant by "interplay" or "interaction," for only then will it be possible to understand the characteristic position of the phenomenological view. When the terms "interplay" or "interaction" are used, one thinks spontaneously of a causal process running its course in two directions. When, for example, we place a bottle of cold milk into a basin of warm water, there is interaction. The warm water heats the cold milk, and the cold milk cools the warm water. This process continues until it reaches a state of equilibrium, in which both liquids have the same temperature. Both influences occur simultaneously, but they can be understood separately. The water exercises a warming influence on the milk, and the milk exercises a cooling influence on the water. However, the causality of one does not cause the other, the cooling influence of the milk does not cause the warming influence of the water. One physical process encompasses both these actions which do not cause each other and which can be understood separately. This is the kind of interaction which we find especially in inorganic nature and which we study in physical science.

When existential phenomenology claims that meaning originates in the interplay between existence and the "other," it does not at all refer to that kind of interaction. On the contrary, it most emphatically excludes such a view. For this reason phenomenologists often say that meaning originates in a "dialogue" or an "encounter" between existence and the "other." These expressions are obviously of a metaphorical nature and make some people wonder why phenomenological writings so consistently appeal to them.

Let us see, therefore, why these metaphors are used. In a genuine colloquy, which is not a disguised monologue, the two interlocutors influence each other. It is not sufficient to say that at the same time one influences the other and the other influences the first. There is more, for, when $A$ at a given moment makes a valuable contribution by a bright remark, he is able to do so because $B$ raised a very pertinent question or formulated the problem with all desirable clarity. $A$ makes a contribution, but in this contribution he is dependent on $B$. There is question not only of an influence in two directions, but the two partners are also the cause of the influence which they exercise on each other. In a successful colloquy the participants urge each other on to higher levels, they stimulate each other to make a contribution and to active participation. After a successful colloquy between partners of equal rank it is wholly impossible to separate that which one contributed from that which the other contributed, for they have also caused each other's contribution. The two contributions are so interwoven that it is impossible to unravel them into two separate strands capable of being understood separately.

The same consideration applies to a genuine encounter between two human beings, for instance, between betrothed. Occasionally philosophers refer to this kind of interaction as "circular causality": one partner is the cause of the influence which he undergoes from the other, and vice versa.[7] The causal relations

---

[7] Phenomenological philosophy often speaks of circular causality, but before it, Gestalt psychology had already drawn attention to this kind of causality. The Gestalt is characterized by this that everything in it is influenced by everything else. The phenomenologists make grateful use of that psychological viewpoint in order to throw light on the relationship

appear in the form of circles reverting to the same point. Existential phenomenology thinks that the giving of meaning takes place in a circular causality between human existence and the "other." Because this circular causality reveals itself most strikingly in the dialogue, the encounter between human beings, the existential phenomenologist likes to use these terms to indicate how the giving of meaning takes place. Those who want to conceive the interplay between man and world after the model of interaction in inorganic nature will borrow their terms and images from simple processes occurring in nature. The phenomenologist, however, derives his images from a different sphere, in which the relationships are so complex and so circular that they defy unravelling. This procedure, the others object, makes analysis impossible. The phenomenologist replies by simply accepting this reproach, for he precisely wants to exclude the possibility of analysis. What the others reproach him with as something to be blamed he considers to be precisely praiseworthy.[8]

Accordingly, the phenomenologist rejects two extreme positions: first, the idea that meaning arises wholly out of the subject himself; secondly, the view that meaning lies entirely outside the subject and is wholly independent of meaning-giving existence. Meaning originates within a dialogue, an encounter, an interplay between subject and the "other." However, this thought pattern of the phenomenologist is far from homogeneous. The interplay between existence and the "other" can assume the most divergent forms within this fundamental pattern. Man gives meaning to the world through agricultural and industrial labor, but in the latter kind of work man is more active than in the former. The

---

between man and the world. As Merleau-Ponty correctly remarks, phenomenology has radicalized the fundamental idea of Gestalt psychology.

[8] Phenomenologists are somewhat suspicious about analytic thought. Of course, they do not want to reject every form of analysis. On the other hand, they refuse to accept that the whole can be understood on the basis of elements disclosed by analysis. The whole, the Gestalt, is primary. Analysis can merely disclose aspects of the Gestalt which should be understood in relation to one another and to the whole.

mathematician and the geologist pursue science and in both cases there is a dialogue between man and the "other," but in mathematics the human mind is more active, more creative, than in geology—to such an extent even that it becomes very difficult to indicate here man's dependence on the "other."

*Inseparability of Giving and Accepting Meaning.* As should be clear from the preceding considerations, phenomenology claims that with respect to meaning we should always speak of both giving meaning and accepting meaning. For man is at the same time both active and passive in regard to meaning. According to the phenomenologist, it is wholly impossible to separate these two aspects. We cannot isolate that which comes from us from that which comes from the "other." Such an isolation is excluded in principle because in our very activity we are passive and in our passivity also active.[9] Our activity is co-produced by the "other," and we ourselves likewise co-produce the "other's" activity. Unravelling the two aspects is impossible in principle because, as we have explained, the causality involved here is of a circular nature. A single example may serve to illustrate the point. When we eat we are at the same time both active and passive. We are active because we ingest and assimilate the food; we are passive because we undergo the action of this food. Both aspects are inseparable. The food itself stimulates the active processes by which it will be consumed, but our organism enables the food to exercise this activity. We may even say that it is due to our organism that the food is food. Food is not a purely objective datum, but a reality-for-us, which is inseparably connected with our organism.

The inseparability of our activity and passivity is the reason why, according to the phenomenologist, it is impossible to indi-

---

[9] Many are afraid that this standpoint will lead to subjectivism. All meaning coheres, indeed, with the human subject. Thus the interpretation of the human subject is of decisive importance. If the subject is only particular, all meaning will be likewise particular. If, however, the subject is universal in its particularity, the meaning also will be universal, in spite of the particularity. For this reason Heidegger makes a distinction between *Subjektivität* and *Subjektität*.

cate anything in our world of meaning which is not at all reality-for-us. Man wants, of course, to know reality. He sometimes desires to know pure reality, pure objectivity, on which we, as meaning-giving existence, would not exercise any influence. But the fulfillment of such a desire is not possible, says the phenomenologist. He does not want to deny that we "accept" meaning, but wishes to affirm that accepting meaning is always permeated with the giving of meaning. Reality manifests itself to us, but always because we make reality appear to us, and the way in which we make it appear influences the way in which reality manifests itself to us. Meaning can never be isolated from our existence as giver of meaning. Meaning is always connected with reality as well as with our existence as giver of meaning.

It lies beyond our scope to develop this fundamental idea of phenomenology more fully. Yet we could not fully omit it because we want to look at language in the light of this perspective.

## 3. LANGUAGE AS A MODE OF MEANING-GIVING EXISTENCE

After considering the way in which language and our entire existence are interwoven, we have stressed that our existence is a giver of meaning. These ideas lead to the conclusion that our speaking is a certain way of giving meaning and, therefore, also a certain way of accepting meaning. For to give meaning and to accept meaning are always inseparably connected, even though their mutual relationship is not always exactly the same.

In considering language and existence two dangers are to be avoided. First, we may not isolate language from the whole of our existence as giver of meaning; secondly, we should take care lest we disregard the proper character of language. Both of these dangers need to be considered somewhat more in detail.

*The Danger of Isolating Language from Existence as Giver of Meaning.* It is not entirely superfluous to point to this danger. Language itself is an aspect of our existence as giver of meaning,

27

but this aspect has attained a large measure of independence especially in modern times. In literature as well as in science man pursues meaning-giving speech for its own sake.

To realize the truth of this assertion, one should keep in mind that thinking and speaking are not isolated from one another, as we shall see more in detail later. We think in words. In our speaking, whether with others or merely in our mind, we make the meaning be in a new way, we bring reality to light. Man is so convinced of the power possessed by speech to bring reality to light, to give meaning, that he has deliberately pursued the culture of speech. Speech has more or less detached itself from life as a whole and has become a pursuit in its own right. We may refer to it as an "autonomous culture of the word." In a primitive society speech is integrated into the whole of life. In our modern society, with its sciences and literature, speech has developed into a more or less independent domain. A striking sign of that is the fact that many sciences possess their own technical language, which is not used in ordinary life and which is unintelligible to any outsider.

If a philosophical reflection upon language would start one-sidedly from such an autonomous culture of the word, one would no longer see that speech is a way of giving meaning which is inseparably connected with other ways of giving meaning. Such a procedure would make us lose sight of the continuity which speech has with other aspects of our existence. One of Merleau-Ponty's great merits is precisely that he has drawn attention to this continuity.

Very often, we may even say nearly always, our speaking brings to light a form of meaning that existed already before we spoke, even though it is true that this meaning begins to exist in a new way for us in our speaking. This point is rather evident. We realize that, no matter how much our speaking is creative of meaning, it is governed by a normative meaning which is more or less independent of our speech. However, this fact is sometimes misinterpreted. Some are inclined to explain it in a realistic or

28

positivistic sense and claim that the meaning is given in a world existing independently of us, in an objective field. As should be evident from the foregoing, the fact in question must be interpreted in a different way. The meaning which through speech begins to exist for us in a new way does not unqualifiedly belong to a real, objective world. It has arisen, independently of speech, on another level of the dialogue between the world and our existence as giver of meaning. We say "another level," for it would be dangerous, however, to refer too rashly to a higher or a lower level in this context.[10]

*An Illustration.* Let us clarify the matter by means of an example. Psychology and psychiatry often speak of sexual meaning. In his speaking of sexuality, man depends, of course, on a reality which precedes his speech. However, this reality which is prior to speech is not a purely objective world, but a field of meaning which arose within a different form of dialogue between world and existence as giver of meaning. Man is not only a speaking subject but a sexual subject. As sexual subjects, we give rise to the sexual field of meaning in dialogue with the "other." How we do it is a matter about which, despite all scientific research, we know very little. Our speaking about sexuality is evidently dependent on this field of sexual meaning. We may distinguish two types of dependence.

First of all, the speaking subject is at the same time a sexual subject. Because all aspects of our existence are interwoven, our speaking is therefore unconsciously influenced by the field of sexual meaning. For example, psychological investigations have led to the conclusion that the homosexual's way of being in the world manifests itself even in his choice of words, metaphors and images. While it is beyond my personal competence to affirm or deny the correctness of this conclusion, it does not surprise me at all. To give another example, when a man addresses an audience

---

[10] As Viktor E. Frankl correctly points out, it is possible to speak of unconscious spirit. Cf. his work, *Der unbewusste Gott,* Vienna, 1948. The "unconscious" is not always the "lower."

of ladies he will not do it in the same way as he addresses a male audience. The emotional tone of one's speech is likely to be connected with the sexual zone of our existence. Again, it is undoubtedly not an accident that hurricanes and technically very complex machines are given women's names by men working at tasks with which women generally do not concern themselves. Man's sexual dimension unconsciously or preconsciously affects his speech. We may add in this connection that, as has often been pointed out, mystical writings are full of images borrowed from the sexual world.

Secondly, our speaking depends on the field of sexual meaning when we make the latter the theme of our discussion. When we do so, we must be guided by, and follow the norms of, the reality itself of our field of sexual meaning, for we make this field the object of our speech. We are able to do that because we live in that field.

A third point should be added to these two. As we noted above, man's sexual dimension unconsciously influences his speech because the different zones of his existence are in constant interaction. The reverse is also true. The way in which we are accustomed to speak of sexuality influences the way in which we live in the field of sexual meaning. This influence likewise runs its course in an unconscious or preconscious fashion. There was a time—it is not yet wholly past—when certain Christian circles spoke about sex with a kind of anxiety, fear and even condemnation. St. Augustine, who has exercised a profound influence on Christian thought, wrote about sex in a way which continues to affect Christian speech even now.[11] This way of speaking has

---

11 According to St. Augustine, man's sexual impulses were fully controlled by his reason before original sin. He considers the fact that sexuality has become independent and imposes itself on reason and freedom to be the major sign of man's sinfulness. Without identifying concupiscence and original sin, he connects the two very closely. Although these ideas are found also in other Christian writers, St. Augustine managed to unite them in a clear synthesis. Through his influence they became commonplace among Christian theologians. At present theologians are rethinking these matters.

greatly influenced the way in which the Christian lives in the f
of sexual meaning, although he does not cle

This illustration shows sufficiently that
speech from other modes of giving me        Our speaking is a
way of giving meaning which constantly       ts with other ways
of giving meaning. One who thinks              speaking is ever
wholly independent forgets that everything is permeated with
everything else in our existence.

*Uprooted Speech.* The way in which Karl Marx regarded practice clearly shows how much this philosopher was aware of the
compenetration of language and existence. He lived at a time
which saw beautiful and coherent theories formulated while real
life became more and more disorganized. The theories glorified
the ideals of liberty, equality and brotherhood of the French
Revolution, while reality was characterized by a great lack of
freedom for the masses of laborers, by an unacceptable economic
inequality and by class struggle. Marx realized how much speech
can be uprooted. Our speaking is uprooted, he says, when it is
not rooted in practice, when it does not give expression to practice. By "practice" Marx meant the whole of life as it runs its course
in reality, no matter how harsh reality is. Practice is found, first,
in labor, which makes life possible. It is found also in man's
dwelling in common in the world which his work has made useful. Everyday practice makes real history. Sometimes man tries
to escape from practice in his speech. This means that he runs
away from reality to dwell in a dream world. His speaking is
meaningless and estranged from reality. Speaking is meaningful
only if it gives expression to practice and contributes to the
latter's development. It is not in line with Marxist thought to
make speech independent.[12] Marx called uprooted speech "idealistic," that is, a flight from reality to ideas.

*The Danger of Denying the Proper Character of Speech.*

---

[12] Theoretically, speaking is wholly subordinated to practice according to
the Marxist. In fact, however, it is difficult to conceive a system in which
practice is subordinated as much to theory, i.e., speech, as is the case in
Marxism.

Above, we have pointed out that there are two dangers to avoid when we consider the relationship between language and existence. The first of these is that of isolating speech from the whole of our existence as giver of meaning. The second, which we will consider here, is to emphasize the bond between language and existence so much that the proper character of speech is denied. As a rule, meaning does not arise from speech because, independently of speech, it had already originated in other zones of our existence. However, through speech meaning begins to exist in a new way for us. By being spoken about, meaning receives a new mode of being.

We experience this new mode very clearly when we listen to an excellent speaker who throws light on an aspect of life which we have never thought about or heard discussed before. While he is speaking, we have the feeling that we really knew already about the topic of his speech, but on the other hand, we also really experience a new light in that matter. We knew what he said but, nonetheless, we begin to know it in a new way. The new mode of being which meaning obtains through speech will have to be considered more in detail in one of the following chapters.

As we have said, as a rule, meaning does not arise from speech, yet speech does not leave the meaning unaffected. It would be wrong to claim that all meaning is wholly dependent upon speech. Once, however, a meaning is discussed, it is no longer fully independent of speech. Our existence as giver of meaning makes meaning exist for us. When we speak of this meaning, we make this same meaning exist for us in a new way, so that the meaning which first existed in this way now exists in that way. Our speaking about the meaning is not at all a harmless pointing to meaning from without, but does something to that meaning.

*Illustrations.* Between two persons there can exist a conflict which has never been put into words and upon which they have not even consciously reflected. Once, however, such a conflict has found expression in words, it begins to exist in a new way. If it erupts in words as a passionate confrontation of fixed standpoints, the conflict will become more acute and disturb our consciousness. If, on the other hand, we quietly discuss it and in our discussion realize the relatively small importance of our conflict, it will lose much of its vigor. In the nineteenth century, for instance, social conflicts and tensions existed even before Marx spoke and wrote about these matters. The way, however, in which he expressed them greatly contributed to the mode of existence proper to the social problem. His writings made them more acute. By saying that speech merely gives expression to a pre-existing meaning, one underestimates the power of speech.

Some people are dangerous for society because their way of speaking makes any existing problem more acute. One cannot say that they are wrong in everything they claim, for as a rule the problems of which they speak are real. Yet the way in which they tackle them serves to make these problems greater and to render them more insoluble. Others likewise speak of the same problems, but the way in which they do it is such that their discussion shows the road to the solution.

Precisely because our speaking gives a new mode of being to meaning, it possesses a margin of freedom with respect to the pre-existing meaning, which nonetheless governs it as a norm. It is governed by this norm in such a way that at the same time it contributes to the way in which this meaning will develop. Our speaking is guided by the pre-existing meaning, but as a rule, it is not determined by it. Speech participates in the power of our existence to "project" meaning. It is an expression of that which is, but in a way which makes it at the same time a project.

## 4. The Central Place of Language in Our Existence

We have repeatedly emphasized that language is interwoven with the whole of our existence and that it is but one of the ways in which we give meaning. This emphasis could easily impress the reader with the idea that language is not a central phenomenon of man's life. To counteract this wrong impression, we want now to draw attention to the central position of language within the whole of life.

*The All-Encompassing Character of Language.* Although language may be said to be one of the many ways in which man gives meaning, it is at the same time a way of giving meaning which encompasses all other ways. By this assertion we do not merely mean that language influences all other ways of giving meaning. Every way of giving meaning somehow influences all other ways; hence such an assertion would not indicate anything special about language as giver of meaning. As we have mentioned, our existence has the character of a Gestalt, and the typical element of the Gestalt is that everything in it influences and is influenced by everything else. The Gestalt is characterized by the circular causality mentioned in the preceding section of this chapter.

Language, however, extends to all other forms of giving meaning in a very special way: it can make all the others the theme of speaking. Our speech can make all other forms of meaning the object of its consideration and therefore is able to give them a new mode of being. It is impossible to point to anything in life which cannot be spoken of in some way. Language, then, is a way of giving meaning which encompasses all other ways in a very special fashion. Through speech we create, to use Merleau-Ponty's expression, a "universe of discourse." Every meaning can be incorporated into this universe. True, as we have pointed out, our speech must let itself be guided by the previously given meaning and is governed by this meaning. However, our speech is not determined by that meaning and enjoys a certain amount of freedom in its expression of meaning. For this reason language possesses a certain power over the way in which all meaning appears to us. It is one of the most powerful factors in the sphere of giving meaning. We will revert to this point later.

*Decisive Role of Language in the Origin of Meaning.* Moreover, language is a means of communication. Above we have denied that language is nothing else but a means of communication and we have objected to a philosophical approach which would consider language merely from the standpoint of its communicative value. All this, however, does not take away from the fact that language is by far the most important means through which we enter into contact with one another. By being discussed, meaning is integrated into the process of exchange. All meaning becomes "communicable" through language. This communication is fruitful for the persons involved in it. It is not merely a mutual exchange of what is already given, but also the common development of meaning. For this reason, although language is only one of the many modes of giving meaning, it plays a decisive role in the origin of meaning. A brief consideration of history may serve to clarify this point.

Modern man is more than ever aware of the fact that human existence is characterized by historicity, that mankind's common history is endowed with a creative power. Until recent times people projected the cultural man, as they knew him, back into mankind's grey past. They could not think of man in any other terms than those of cultural man. The book of *Genesis*, for example, speaks of the first men as beings who speak, engage in agriculture and cattle breeding, build towns, work with metals, manufacture musical instruments, etc. Briefly, it presents cultural man as the man of all times. In the past it was difficult to do otherwise because man's horizon was too restricted for a different view. Our contemporary horizon, however, is somewhat larger. We have become acquainted with very primitive modes of existence in isolated corners of the world, and we have penetrated more profoundly into history and prehistory. We are vaguely aware of what a primitive existence is and of the distance mankind had to travel before that primitive mode of being developed into man's modern existence. No single individual can claim that he has traveled that distance relying on his own forces alone. We can live in the way we live now by virtue of mankind's common history. Man possesses the power to pass on to others that which he himself has achieved. This is the reason why common progress is possible, the reason also why there can be history. Alone among all living beings man has a history. History is possible only on condition that there is communication. This communication is brought about mainly through language. For this reason language plays a decisive role in the development of common meaning. Language makes all forms of meaning communicable, thereby making them dynamic and capable of development.

Language brings all other forms of meaning to light in a new way and makes them communicable. Language makes it possible for us to be mutually fruitful and to work together at the development of meaning. It enables our existence to be an existence by means of one another. Language, therefore, is really a central phenomenon in our lives. Anthropologists are right when they make language a norm of man. When they find skeletons and try to determine whether these are human or animal remains, they investigate whether or not these skeletons indicate that the organism was sufficiently developed to make speech possible. If the answer is in the negative, they tend to the conclusion that the remains in question are not human.

*Language as the "Locus" of All Meaning.* It is proper to man to express all meaning in language. Therefore, although language is not unqualifiedly the "locus" of all meaning, it is nonetheless true that in a certain sense language is such a "locus." Nearly every meaning can exist, at least in a primitive fashion, without being dependent upon language; nevertheless, all meaning can acquire existence in language.

Moreover, there are several levels on which meaning can exist in language. A distinction is to be made here between pre-scientific and scientific speech. Speech becomes scientific by being subjected to a very critical inquiry, by being critically refined, by a very deliberate and careful choice of terms. Man has only gradually learned to give expression to meaning in speech. In a primitive society there are still many forms of meaning that have not yet been expressed in speech but continue to exist in a latent way. Modern man has learned to embody many forms of meaning in language. We have even learned to speak about very many forms of meaning in a scientific way. It is no longer possible to indicate any form of meaning about which there exists no science. This is the reason why today there are so many sciences.

By being embodied in speech and especially by being expressed in a scientific way, meaning is objectivized. This term indicates that a meaning which was originally only "lived," which surrounded us as a kind of climate or sphere in such a way that our existence fused with it, now becomes the object of our consideration. We continue to live in that meaning, but at the same time we place ourselves at a distance from it. This objectivation is a powerful means to help us seize that meaning, to manipulate it. More than ever before, modern man has acquired power over his world of meaning. This power is due to his speech, especially to his scientific discussion of this world of meaning. Speech, therefore, is certainly a central phenomenon of our life.

*"Lived" Meaning and Spoken Meaning.* It is important, however, to keep in mind that the spoken meaning, the meaning that is discussed, is not *per se* faithful to the "lived" meaning. It is true, of course, that in speaking of meaning we intend to make our speech the expression of the "lived" meaning. But it can happen that the spoken meaning merely seems to express the "lived" meaning. Discussing a meaning should open our eyes to that meaning as it is "lived." Yet it can happen that it does just the opposite. The "universe of discourse" should be an expression of the "lived world," but we have no guarantee that it will be that. Speech is an exceedingly precious gift, but it can also become an exceedingly dangerous power. It is possible for our "universe of discourse" to be unfaithful to life; we may get lost more or less in that universe, so that our view of life and reality becomes very obscure. Recent history offers several examples of that danger. During the Nazi regime in Germany, the party's "universe of discourse" made innumerable people blind to the reality

37

of life and changed men into monsters. The same occurred in the Russia of Stalin, as is now openly admitted by that country's new leaders. Collective speech blinded men in these countries. Speech is a powerful gift but also a great danger.

Another factor has to be considered here. Not all forms of meaning let themselves equally be expressed in speech. Let us compare, for example, mathematical meaning and the meaning of music. Mathematical meaning lends itself very easily to expression in speech, at least once man has invented a special kind of language for this form of meaning. This mathematical meaning cannot be isolated from the mathematical language which is adapted to it. It is much more difficult, however, to express musical meaning in words. True, it is possible to discuss this meaning; there exist musical sciences and one can even obtain a Ph.D. in them. Likewise, many people write about music, and numerous dailies and weeklies have regular columns about music. Nevertheless, all such speaking about music remains very inadequate and continues to be wholly dependent on a different form of knowing musical meaning, which itself is largely independent of its discussion in speech. Little children, who are unable to make or understand theoretical considerations of music, may nonetheless have a great feeling for music and in exceptional cases even be able to produce high level music. Although speech is important for music and greatly helps in its development, it should be clear that our speaking of music is a very inadequate way of approaching the reality of music.

Another pertinent example is religious meaning. This meaning also is primarily experienced. Despite the great development of the sciences of religion, we still know very little about the nature and roots of religious experience. Religious meaning also is difficult to put into words. The same applies to the relationship, or rather the many forms of the relationship, between man and wife in marriage. Much has been said and written about this matter, but in spite of everything the meaning of that relationship remains something which greatly transcends speech and does not lend itself to expression in words.

*Ineffability of Meaning.* As we have said, we live in a period in which meaning is discussed more than ever before. More than ever we make the "lived" meaning appear in the form of a spoken meaning, even in the form of a scientifically discussed meaning. It is not at all an imaginary danger that an excessive homogeneity of speech will fail to do justice to the heterogeneity of meaning. Our "universe of discourse" is inevitably somewhat superficial with respect to the variegated wealth of the "lived world." We say "inevitably" because language is unable to express all the subtle variations of the world of meaning. As long as man is aware of this defect, no great harm is done. However, it can happen that man forgets the inadequate character of his speech and consequently no longer worries about it. Thinkers who base themselves authentically on life are sharply aware of the inadequacy of our speaking. They are, of course, obliged to think in words and try to express themselves as correctly as possible. Yet one can hear them over and over again complain that meaning is really ineffable.

One who does not feel and experience this ineffability has already underestimated the true character of both the world of meaning and speech. He no longer realizes that there are many ways in which we can approach meaning and that meaning appeals to us in manifold forms. It is not only through contact with God that we come to the realization of this ineffability, although that contact is, of course, most powerful in making us aware of ineffability. Even our contact with the world can give us that awareness. One can be struck, for example, by the remarkable structure of a landscape, by the freakish but consistent outlines of trees visible in winter time; he will see these things better according as light falls on them in a more striking way. He will then try to express what he sees, but experiences that he is confronted with the ineffable. His gaze reveals to him a wealth, an order and harmony which he cannot put into words. He experiences how poorly his words express what he wants to say. Life is full of examples illustrating how ineffable reality is and how far words fall short from expressing its meaning.[13]

It sometimes happens that, penetrating through all functional relationships to a fellow-man, we establish contact with him in a way which we would have thought impossible. In such a profound encounter we feel what intersubjectivity means: we compenetrate each other in a way that cannot be expressed in words. True, we can talk about it, but our words do not indicate its depth. For these same words used to indicate the most intimate contact are used also to refer to a more ephemeral and more superficial contact between human beings. One who, in his very effort to give expression to meaning, does not from time to time experience the ineffable does not really know many forms of meaning. One must have experienced ineffability to know the limits of speech. It is difficult, of course, to indicate these limits. These limits are not so much of a material nature, for there is no matter, no form of reality, no form of meaning, which wholly resists expression in speech. These limits touch depth, intensity, that which brings man into ecstasy and carries him "out of himself."

*The Spoken Meaning as Danger for the "Lived" Meaning.*
Speech occupies a central place in our existence because everything can be made a topic of speech. This central position can become a great danger, for man may make speech the absolute norm of all meaning; he may make the "spoken meaning" unqualifiedly the norm of the "lived meaning," forget that speech is inadequate and consider it unrestrictedly the manifestation of all meaning. Speech is an attempt to express meaning, and this attempt extends to all meaning. However, the meaning expressed by speech reveals itself also in many other ways, and the expression which speech gives to meaning is inadequate as a revela-

---

[13] See, e.g., J. Linschoten, "Over de humor," *Tijdschrift voor Philosophie,* vol. 13 (1951), pp. 603–666. The dominating idea of this article is that humor is a reality which manifests itself very clearly in our experience but which is extremely difficult to put into words.

tion of this meaning. Speaking is the transposition of all meaning into a single sphere. This transposition is a great good because it objectivizes the meaning and makes it communicable. The same transposition, however, becomes a great danger if one fails to realize how defective it can sometimes be, if one forgets that the things which are expressed in the single sphere of speech belong to essentially different spheres.

It is not difficult to illustrate this danger by concrete examples showing how speech may tend to homogenize heterogeneous meanings. We will offer here examples of scientific, Marxist, and theological homogenizing tendencies.

*Scientific Homogeneity.* As we have mentioned, man lives now in a period in which the verbal expression of meaning occupies a greater place than before and in which we attempt especially to express meaning scientifically. From the preceding considerations it should be evident that man does not always have the same success in his attempts to express meaning scientifically in every realm. Most successful in this matter are the mathematical and physical sciences as well as technology, which lies in the same line as these sciences. These disciplines display a very striking form of rationally justified speech. Thus it is not surprising that this most successful form of speech is often presented as the norm of all verbal expression of meaning. In these sciences man knows exactly what he says. He is able to remove all inaccuracies from his language. He can stress as the ideal that no concepts or terms are to be used unless one has first established, or rather agreed upon, their exact sense. If, however, one claims that the mode of speaking proper to these sciences is the norm of all speech and that speech is the norm of all meaning, one reduces the heterogeneity of meaning to a homogeneity which, despite its striking character, is altogether unacceptable.

Yet it is easy to see that such people want to impose such an ideal. A glance at the past suffices to show that intolerable inaccuracies occurred very frequently in the speaking of former generations. Many faulty ways of thinking arose from careless

41

and defective ways of speaking.[14] They gave rise to all kinds of needless misunderstandings. Wherever possible we must indeed endeavor to speak "hygienically." However, if under the spell of this ideal one wants to impose a certain uniform pattern of being-scientific upon all forms of speech, one disregards the heterogeneity of meaning. Such an attempt is blind to the fact that many forms of meaning can be expressed in words only in a very inadequate fashion. It fails to take into consideration that our speaking has many different forms of relationship to the many different forms of meaning. The attempt to impose a uniform way of speaking impoverishes our "universe of discourse" in an intolerable fashion. Demands which may be correctly imposed in certain realms of speech cannot simply be transferred to other realms. In some realms univocal speech is a necessity; in others it is impossible to speak at all unless one uses analogous terms. Sometimes one is right in demanding a rigid rationality, and sometimes one has to recognize that such a rationality is impossible.

*Marxist Homogeneity.* Another example of homogenizing tendencies is provided by Marxism. Marxism discovered a new way in which social reality can be approached. It saw that the entire social reality can be seen in the light of the economic infrastructure. The economic infrastructure is found wherever human beings work together to wrest a living from the earth. Everything is conditioned by that economic infrastructure. This is true, of course, for our life is always a question of using the world and presupposes therefore that the world is usable. We ourselves have to make it usable; hence the economic infrastructure makes itself felt in everything. Marxism has placed itself in this perspective and has created a special language for the purpose. This perspective helps it to explain many things. However, Marxism goes too far when it wants to make this approach an absolute philosophy of life, a philosophy capable of making all

---

[14] Cf. G. Nuchelmans, "De kritiek op de metaphysica," *Wijsgerig Perspectief,* vol. 3 (1963), pp. 134–146.

meaning intelligible. It wants to integrate all sciences, literature, arts and everything else into this philosophy of life.[15] This attempt creates a deadly homogeneity, which artists and litterateurs especially find suffocating and which large segments of the population consider extremely boring. Marxism will have to discover that life is richer than its doctrine. This discovery is already being made, as is evident from the recent more liberal attitude assumed in the U.S.S.R.

*Theological Homogeneity.* A third example is provided by the philosophico-theological approach which until recently strongly prevailed in the Catholic Church. The sixteenth century break which separated Protestantism from the Catholic Church resulted in a reaction which made theology rather rigid. This rigidity became even stronger later when all kinds of modern trends of thought began to exercise influence within the Church in the form of so-called modernism. To counterbalance modern philosophies and the confusion to which they gave rise, Church authorities sought support in the past and imposed the philosophy and theology of Thomas Aquinas as a norm. Meanwhile Thomism had been reduced to an imposing but nonetheless rather closed system. In this way the theologians of the Church developed a perspective in whose light they regarded the problems arising in life.

Existing as she did in our modern time, the Church was forced into a confrontation with the special problems of our day. Her theologians approached them all according to the same abovementioned Thomistic pattern of thought. The result was a homogeneity of speech which failed to take into consideration the heterogeneous character of meaning. A narrow philosophy of science, for example, did not permit them to pay sufficient attention to the diversity of modern sciences. The special character and structure of technology and modern work escaped recognition. Ethical problems were studied on the basis of a concept of nature that was too rigid and too unreal, so that man's historicity was dis-

---

[15] Cf. G. Paloczi-Horvath, *The Writer and the Commissar,* London, n.d.

regarded. With respect to marriage, theologians spoke too glibly in terms of the categories of means and purpose. An exaggerated emphasis on the purpose of life caused them to regard life too much as a synthesis aiming at this purpose. This view led to an extremely rationalistic theology. Its rationality, however, differed greatly from the rationality proper to the sciences in the modern sense of the term.

All this gave rise to a tiresome homogeneity of speech within the world of Catholic thought. This speech no longer did justice to the rich inspiration of the Gospel. The homogeneity of speech built a rigid doctrine, a striking synthesis, which led theologians sometimes to the illusion that they knew all the answers in theological matters. The trouble was that their synthesis failed to do sufficient justice to the genuine wealth of life or to that of the Gospel. At present we witness a break-through of these narrow bonds. This break-through flows from two sources: a return to the rich inspiration of the Gospel and an awareness of the complexity of real life. It is no longer possible to maintain the homogeneous way of speaking which until very recently was current in Catholic literature.

*Collective Light and Collective Blindness.* Speech brings meaning to light in a new way and makes it communicable. For this reason the world that is spoken of is *par excellence* a common world. One could say that speaking "socializes" the world of meaning. Speaking therefore can greatly contribute to the dawn of a common light. One can easily observe this. All kinds of things appear quite obvious to us, but they were not at all obvious to people in the past. This obviousness is a result of speaking with one another about these things. The reverse side of the medal, however, is that our speaking with one another can also lead to a collective blindness. It is possible that a particular form of meaning is simply disregarded in our speaking with one another or even positively denied. Communist countries try to eradicate religious meaning in this fashion.

44

*The Crisis of Metaphysics.* It is interesting to consider the contemporary crisis in metaphysics in the light of these ideas about speech.[16] It cannot be denied that metaphysics is in a state of crisis. True, there are still relatively many thinkers who remain willing to leave room for metaphysics. However, there are very few left who consider themselves able to say meaningful things within this dimension, at least insofar as they do not repeat systems of the past. Two interpretations of this fact are possible.

First of all, one could say that the metaphysical systems of the past have been unmasked one by one as false or as having no basis, and add that modern man's critical sense has therefore discovered the impossibility of making any meaningful statements in this matter. This interpretation implies that metaphysics is considered to be impossible. It credits modern man with the discovery of this impossibility. In this way the crisis of metaphysics is an asset, a victory over a past which has outlived its usefulness.

Secondly, one can say that the crisis is due to a collective kind of blindness. Man, so claim the defenders of this view, has become so used to a certain kind of rationality that he no longer knows how to proceed in the realm of metaphysics. The contemporary crisis therefore is not a sign of victory or strength but rather of modern man's weakness. We have to learn again how to move in metaphysical matters.

At any rate, it should be evident that our collective way of speaking can make us blind and no longer open to certain forms of meaning. For this reason collective speaking can not unqualifiedly be offered as a norm. Such a way of speaking may be dangerously one-sided, and this one-sidedness can be overcome only by a return to our "living" of meaning. However, only the greatest geniuses will be able to correct collective speaking through such a return to "lived" meaning itself.

---

[16] Concerning this crisis see *Wijsgerig Perspectief,* vol. 3 (1963), no. 3, which is entirely devoted to metaphysics. It speaks of metaphysics, but does not offer any. The way in which it speaks of metaphysics shows how great the crisis is.

## 5. THE AMBIGUITY OF SPEECH

*Ambiguity.* The preceding pages have shown that our speaking is ambiguous and full of paradoxes. The use of the term "ambiguous" in this connection demands an explanation. We speak of a reality as ambiguous if it exhibits at the same time many aspects which seem to be opposed to one another, but in such a way that the unity of these apparently opposite aspects constitutes precisely the reality of the matter in question. To understand an ambiguous reality, one has to see the apparently opposite aspects together and in connection with one another. For it is precisely in their connection that they constitute the reality in question.

A simple example of ambiguity is provided by so-called "puns," which play with the different senses of a single term. One who does not at once see both senses does not understand the pun. If it becomes necessary to explain the pun, its humor is killed in the process. A more philosophical example of ambiguity is man himself. He is, for example, at the same time both particular and universal. He cannot really think without thinking in the name of all. When I make a judgment, I cannot assume the attitude that the judgment is true only for me but probably not for others. If I doubt whether it is valid for the others, I doubt also about its validity for me. I doubt the judgment itself, so that it is no longer a judgment. Nevertheless, the judging "I" is of necessity a particular "I." I judge as this particular person on the basis of this particular situation. Man himself is a wonderful unity of particularity and universality. One who divorces these two aspects from each other loses sight of man as he really is.

After these brief remarks about ambiguity, let us return to speech, which, as we have mentioned, is highly ambiguous and full of paradoxes. Some of these may be enumerated here.

*Meaning as Intrinsic and Extrinsic to Speech.* First, our speaking is the "locus" of all meaning; yet almost all forms of meaning exist originally outside speech. Speech puts us into contact with all meaning but is not the original contact with meaning.

Meaning is at the same time both intrinsic and extrinsic to speech.

*Speech as Contact with, and Distance from, Meaning.* Secondly, on the one hand, speech brings us into contact with a meaning, but on the other and at the same time, it puts us at a distance from that meaning. It puts us into contact with the meaning because the meaning is that which is spoken of and speaking is, of course, connected with that which is spoken of. At the same time, speaking puts us at a distance from the meaning because it makes the meaning an object and therefore removes us from the immediate experience of this meaning. If, for example, two people in love begin to talk about their love, they place themselves somewhat at a distance from their existence-in-love. At the moment when they experience their love most intensely, they will speak words of love but will not speak about love. Again, it can be a disturbing sign that the meaning of life is the topic of many discussions, for that could easily indicate that too many people do not forcefully experience life's meaning. As someone has not incorrectly remarked, the values which are most discussed are usually those that are most lacking.

*Speech as Approach to, and Separation from, Truth.* Thirdly, speaking leads us to the truth of the matter discussed, but at the same time there is a danger that it will separate us from that truth. Speech is intended, of course, to bring the matter discussed to light. To accomplish this intention, we have to place ourselves at a certain distance from our immediately "lived" experience of the reality in question. We approach it by objectivation, by making it an object over there, at which we look. This putting ourselves at a distance can, as we have seen, contain an unfaithfulness to reality. Our speaking nearly always eliminates the immediacy of our experience of the reality under discussion, so that it becomes possible for us to be unfaithful to our experience and even to stray away from authentic experience. Our speaking intends to be a new mode of making the reality in question our own, but it can happen that our very speech lets this

47

reality escape our grasp. We sometimes experience this in a concrete conversation. The discussion started because its participants were under the spell of a problem, a problem that had really arisen from life itself. After a time, however, we have the impression that the matter under discussion has simply evaporated and is no longer present in our field of vision. It happens sometimes then that someone will ask: Does anyone know what exactly we are talking about?

*Speech as Critical Tool and as Danger of Being Uncritical.* Fourthly, speaking provides us with a new instrument to develop our critical sense.[17] At the same time, however, speech exposes us to the danger of uncritically collectivizing our thinking. Language makes meaning exist for us in a new way because we objectivize meaning. This objectivation places us at a distance and therefore better able to assume a critical attitude. We see, for example, that when certain social conditions which were first taken for granted as normal are made the subject of discussion, they easily come to be regarded in a critical fashion and lose their allegedly normal character. However, we borrow the language which enables us to criticize from the speaking community to which we belong and easily take over the way of speaking proper to our group. Thus this common way of speaking will present us with new "normal" conditions, which sometimes we again accept in an uncritical fashion.

*Speech as Road to Communication as Well as Isolation.* Finally, language is both a road to communication and a road to isolation. It puts us into contact with others, but at the same time it promotes interiorization. It is obvious that language leads to communication and contact, for we borrow our speech from the speaking community to which we belong. Yet the same language is also the means *par excellence* for interior reflection. In reflection we generally make use of words. In the sphere of action, for instance of work performed in common or of playing

---

[17] Cf. Remy C. Kwant, *Mens en Kritiek*, Utrecht, 1962, especially pp. 43–53.

together, we also communicate with others, but this kind of communication lends itself less easily to the transition to interiorization. Speaking, on the other hand, makes interiorization much easier. For this reason man can easily make the passage to reflection in our modern world in which speaking occupies such an important place. Communication is greater and more encompassing than ever, but at the same time one can not incorrectly speak of modern man's isolation.

These are some of the paradoxes which we find in our speech. Man's speaking, therefore, really is an ambiguous reality. We should be on our guard against theories of language which are too simplistic. Language is an exceedingly complex reality, whose manifold aspects are to be respected.

The preceding pages have shown us the relationship between language and human existence. Man's existence gives meaning. Language is interwoven with our entire existence. It is a very special way of giving meaning, and many other ways of giving meaning exist in addition to language. Language, however, occupies a central position because all meaning can be given expression in our speaking, all meaning can become part of our "universe of discourse."

We must now devote our attention to the very special way of giving meaning which is proper to our speaking. Although it may be clear to us now that language is a special way of giving meaning, we do not yet know in what its special nature consists. The following chapter will attempt to discuss that matter, which is one of the most difficult problems faced by anyone who philosophically investigates language.

# CHAPTER THREE

# Language as the Giving of Meaning

As we have indicated at the end of the preceding chapter, we will now begin to reflect upon the specific way in which, while speaking, we give meaning. First, however, certain terms need to be clarified and rendered more precise.

## 1. LANGUAGE AND SPEECH

*An Objection: the Distinction Between Language and Speech.* This book is supposed to speak about the philosophy of language. Yet in the preceding chapters we dealt sometimes with language and sometimes with speaking. A few readers may have noted this and become annoyed with the apparently irresponsible way in which we passed from the one to the other. We must, they say, make a sharp distinction between language and speaking. Language presents itself as an objective datum. The vocabulary of any language is, or at least can be, neatly listed in a dictionary. Its structure can be scientifically examined. A first step of such a scientific analysis is the grammar and syntax of the language, but this examination can be carried on and made more profound in every respect by further scientific research. A language originates by a long process of historical development, and this process also is subject to scientific inquiry. True, this inquiry will ultimately always terminate in darkness because we have to reconstruct the past from still existing data and will eventually reach a point where further data will be lacking. Nevertheless, we can gaze far enough into the past to see that the development of any language is subject to all kinds of laws. Many of these laws have already been discovered, and man continues zealously to search for the others.

Speech, the objection continues, makes use of a pre-existing language. We must make a distinction between language as a useful and pre-given entity and the actual use that is made of it. In the same way we make a distinction between fertile soil which man can use and man's actual use of this soil. It is possible that the soil of a given country is very fertile, although its farmers make a very poor use of that soil. In the same way it is possible that a language is very rich, although it is very poorly utilized.

*Reply to the Objection.* While we do not want to deny the alleged distinction completely, we doubt that it is as important as is claimed. The comparison with fertile soil is deceptive. Land is indeed a fertile soil and as such useful to man. But it is more than this. Its usefulness for agriculture is only one of the many possibilities offered by a region. Many others exist in addition to it. The region may be a forest reserve, hunting grounds or recreational area. Its agricultural usefulness is only one aspect of a reality which possesses many. Language, on the other hand, cannot be divorced from its usefulness. Language is encompassed by its usefulness, i.e., usefulness belongs to the very essence of language. If we mentally eliminate the farmer who wrests a living from the soil, if we abstract from every agrarian aspect, it is no longer meaningful to refer to land as fertile. Nevertheless, the same land remains meaningful in other ways. On the other hand, if we abstract from man as using language, language loses all meaning and ceases to be language. Language becomes really language only in man's speaking.[1] Divorced from the speaking man, language is nothing else but lifeless and meaningless material.

---

[1] "The causes of linguistic changes do not lie in language as such but only in the speaking man. The mysterious life of language itself which is allegedly a kind of natural organism simply does not exist." F. Kainz, *Psychologie der Sprache*, vol. 1, *Grundlagen der allgemeinen Sprachpsychologie*, Stuttgart, 1962, p. 15.

It is true, of course, that language has a structure. This structure, however, has arisen out of living speech and continues to change within living speech. The structure of a language can be studied as an objective datum but only on condition that we always include the speaking man in our consideration. When we study the structure of a language, we always presuppose our familiarity with speech, with the speaking man. The same is true in the study of any kind of instrument: we always keep in mind the man who uses them, and if we do not do this, we can no longer consider these instruments as instruments. In the case of ordinary instruments, it remains true that these instruments, divorced from their instrumental character, still remain pieces of matter and therefore can be considered as such. If, however, we abstract from the instrumental character of language, hardly anything remains. One could at most point to a few sounds, but even this is questionable, for we cannot conceive these sounds without including a human being who produces them or hears them. As a physical reality, language is almost nothing. It becomes a reality within man's speaking.

*Dead Languages.* One could object that there exist dead languages, i.e., languages which are no longer spoken, and which nonetheless are the object of studies. In a sense this statement is true, but it is not quite correct from every point of view. The human beings who spoke those languages are dead, but in a certain sense they are resurrected in us who know their language. Man has the wonderful power to keep the past alive. Plato lives and speaks no longer. Yet Plato revives in a certain sense and continues to speak when someone reads his works in an understanding fashion. Plato continues to exercise influence in history. It is not at all excluded that in the future, under the influence of Plato, a new form of Platonism would come into existence.

These assertions sound strange and they really are full of wonder. Yet, strictly speaking, the same wonder occurs whenever we speak with one another. When someone has formulated a certain thought and communicates it to someone else in the course of a conversation, the thought of one man begins to live in the other. By listening to someone, we make him live in ourselves. The thought which was active in the speaker now becomes active also in the listener. It may even happen that this thought becomes more active and more fruitful in the listener than it was in the speaker. The same happens when we read, but now without the living contact of persons who are bodily present with one another. Although not bodily present, the writer makes the reader think. This influence can continue even after the writer's death. Plato, Aristotle, St. Augustine, Descartes, Hegel and Marx are still active in history. As long as a so-called dead language continues to be known and read, it is not entirely dead. It continues to exist as a language. Those who have expressed themselves in that language are still active in history through their works. Hence we may not claim that the language still exists, although those who spoke it have entirely disappeared, and use this claim to isolate language from the speaking man.

*Wealth of Language and Poverty of Speech.* One could search for other arguments to distinguish language from speech and say, for example, that language is much richer than the speaking of concrete man.[2] A child who is taken into a speaking community will at first use its rich vocabulary very poorly because he knows very little about the wealth contained in its language. Moreover, most adults become acquainted with only a fraction of the wealth contained in a language. The wealth, therefore, of a language exceeds, it seems, the speaking man, so that we are justified in distinguishing language from man's speaking.

In reply we may point out that we are willing to admit truth in the starting point of this argument but that its conclusion is wrong. The language which I speak is not exclusively my prop-

---

[2] "Man therefore has at his disposal elements which are at the same time too rich and not numerous enough. They are not numerous enough, for the words, the types of reasonings, and the methods are only there in a limited number; between them there are gaps and his nascent thought cannot find an appropriate expression. They are also too rich: for every word brings with it the profound meaning which the epoch has given to it." J. P. Sartre, *Critique de la raison dialectique,* p. 75.

erty, but a common possession of wealth. By calling it "common" we do not mean to say that language exists apart from all the human beings who speak it. It is not present somewhere in a space of its own. Language exists only in the speaking of many men. It exists in a richer way in some than in others. But it does not exist anywhere as a thing in itself. A great thinker of a literary genius enriches language. They make a language say something which it had never said before. Reading their works, we realize how rich a language is. Yet this wealth is due also to the work of these speaking men. My language exceeds me, not because it exists somewhere all by itself, but because it exists also in the speaking and writing of other men, because it manifests in them possibilities which remained concealed in my speaking.

*Bond Between Language and Speaking Man.* We may not divorce language from the speaking man. It is not even possible to do so. When we think of language, we always include also the speaking man. If we would try to abstract from man—which we cannot do—language itself would disappear. Obviously, we are using here the term "speaking" in the broadest sense. Speaking refers primarily to the talking of human beings in one another's bodily presence. But we speak also interiorly, for our thinking assumes the form of a dialogue with ourselves. Our writing also is a kind of speaking. Even when we write, we address ourselves to others by means of language. There exisits no other language than language which is used. Language comes into existence through use. It exhibits, of course, certain structures which can be studied as objective data. Yet these structures exist in real language, in the language that is used. Such structures are capable of development, but their development takes place in man's living use of the language. For this reason a philosophy of language is of necessity a philosophy of speech. Hence there is nothing strange in the fact that we refer here sometimes to language and then again to speech. Speech and language are one and the same reality.

It was necessary to explain this identity here before we consider language as giver of meaning. The giving of meaning takes place in the use of language, in living speech. The question, then, which we face here is the following. We human beings give meaning in many ways. Which of these many ways is found in the use of language, in speech? Once again, the distinction that can be made between the many ways of using language, of speaking, is not of decisive importance. We are concerned with speaking in the broadest sense of the term. Even the formulæ language used in mathematics should be considered to be a real language. This language is an extension of "ordinary" language, as appears from the fact that to the most elementary mathematical data there correspond words as well as symbols, such as figures. On a certain level of mathematical development "ordinary" language can no longer be used and then the mathematician invents a special language. Although this mathematical language has a character of its own, it does not cease to be a form of language.

We must see now what kind of giving of meaning there is in man's speaking.

## 2. SPEAKING AS "POINTING"

In his article *Travail et Parole*[3] Paul Ricoeur endeavors to find a notion which can be used as a counter pole for work. He points out that the term "work" is now used in a very broad sense.[4] This fact is very disturbing, Ricoeur says. A term which can have many senses ultimately means nothing at all. A term can have a definite sense only if it has a limited application, i.e., if it certainly does not mean certain aspects of reality. He then proceeds to oppose work to speech.[5] In developing his thought, Ricoeur could have made use of a distinction which psychologists make and

---

[3] *Histoire et vérité*, Paris, 1955.

[4] Cf. Remy C. Kwant, *Philosophy of Labor*, Pittsburgh, 1960, pp. 23 ff.

[5] His attempt is made particularly difficult because speaking itself has in many cases become work. The solution will probably have to be sought in this that certain aspects playing a role in work at the same time transcend work.

which, it seems to us, is very important—viz., the distinction between "grasping" and "pointing." We will develop that distinction here in connection with the giving of meaning.

*The Giving of Meaning as Revelation of Man's Possibilities.* As we have stated repeatedly, all giving of meaning takes place in a dialogue between existence as giver of meaning and the "other." We use here the vague term "other" and not the clearer term "the world" because we do not want to exclude man's dialogue with the transcendent, which is one of the main topics of Karl Jaspers' philosophy. It is evident, nevertheless, that the giving of meaning occurs mainly in a dialogue between existence as giver of meaning and the world. For this reason any form of giving meaning may be called a revelation in a twofold sense. It is, first, a revelation of human possibilities and, secondly, a revelation of the possibilities implied in the "other" to become meaning for us.

The giving of meaning is a revelation of human possibilities. Man is called "existence," "intentionality," which means that he has the possibility to enter into a dialogue with the "other." This one expression "the possibility to enter into a dialogue" contains a wealth of aspects. The progress of history may be described as a progressive revelation of man as a possibility to enter into dialogue with the "other." When in our thought we go back, insofar as that is possible, to man's primitive state of life, we find there a human being entering into dialogue with the "other." The forms of this dialogue, however, were poor and without much development. For us modern men it would be difficult, if not impossible, to "exist" in those forms. In the modern world we have grown up in such a way that we are accustomed to a rich and variegated dialogue with the "other." As a dialogue with the world we have progressed too far to fit in with the life of primitives. Even our body and our stomach have outgrown such a life. The forms in which man's modern dialogue with the "other" takes place have reached such a stage that no one man is able any longer to make them all his own. No one is able to

56

acquire all skills, to practice all arts, to study all sciences, to engage in all kinds of sports and games, to perform all kinds of work, or to become efficient in every form of functional dealing with other human beings.

All this causes a difficult problem in modern education. Young men and women have to prepare themselves to occupy a position in society and therefore must train themselves in all forms of dialogue with the "other" which are demanded by that position. Education and especially training must have an orientation and this implies that a selection has to be made. At the same time man must aim at a fully human existence and may not be one-sidedly immersed in a certain orientation toward a position. It is very difficult to establish a sound equilibrium between professional orientation and broadness of education.

The man who learns something, no matter in which sphere, always discovers a possibility implied in his existence as giver of meaning. Man is a very rich and very differentiated possibility of giving meaning. This possibility should not be strangled. The oppression of human beings always consist in this, that their rich possibility of meaningful existence is restricted and forced into too narrow a framework of giving meaning. The nineteenth century social problem can be expressed in terms of meaningful existence in the following way: the proletarians were forced to live in such a narrow framework of existence that it was no longer possible for them to do justice to their human dignity. Marx has analyzed that problem in a very sharp way, although not in the same terms. One should not try to put the blame for the proletariat's situation too much on individual persons. The decisive factor was a structure of life and society which was accepted as "natural," but which nevertheless was kept in existence by human beings. Even in our modern era there are still innumerable human beings who cannot assert their existence as givers of meaning but are forced to live in a condition that is unworthy of man.

*The Giving of Meaning as Revelation of the "Other."* The giving of meaning always also reveals a possibility that is present in the "other," a possibility to become meaning for us. We are less creators of this possibility than its discoverers. For this reason all giving of meaning contains always also an aspect of accepting meaning, although these two, the giving and the accepting of meaning, as we have mentioned before, cannot be separated. Man therefore always also experiences his giving of meaning as an un-concealment of what is given. Realism finds its truth in this fact, but incorrectly absolutizes this aspect of our existence by separat-ing it from the aspect of giving meaning.

It is very difficult to arrive at clarity regarding the innumerable possibilities of giving and taking meaning contained in our exist-ence and in that with which we enter into a dialogue. Neverthe-less, the distinction between grasping and pointing allows us to acquire a measure of understanding of this richly variegated and fathomless realm.

*"Grasping" and "Pointing."* In both grasping and pointing, we are dealing with modes of giving meaning which run their course in our contact with the "other." When we grasp reality around us, we have an aim in mind and want to realize something. The housewife who grasps the objects in her dwelling wants to ac-complish something; people who together prepare a hall for a meeting grasp the hall's furnishings to realize something, viz., a certain type of orderly arrangement. By grasping the world, we give a meaning to it, a meaning which is, of course, implied in this world as a possibility.

When we point to something we also give a meaning. A child who points to a person as his attacker makes that person known as the guilty one. When passers-by ostensively point to us, we look at ourselves to see why we draw so much attention. By point-ing to something, we make it the center of our own field of vision and that of others. In both cases, in grasping and pointing, there-fore, we give meaning.

However, the ways in which meaning is given differ consider-ably. By grasping we enter into bodily contact with reality, but not so by pointing. Pointing is even unthinkable unless there is a distance between the pointer and that which is pointed at. By grasping we make the meaning a reality which continues to exist even after we have grasped things. When, for example, we are ready with the preparation of a lecture hall, we cease our work precisely because the hall is ready now. By grasping we make a meaning become a physical reality. The meaning depends on our grasping for its origin but not for its continued existence.

In pointing, on the other hand, reality is not seized in a physical fashion. The meaning, moreover, does not continue to exist independently of our pointing. If someone is no longer pointed to by anyone as the culprit of a crime, he ceases to pass as such in common consciousness. In pointing there occurs a giving of meaning which is quite familiar to us but which nonetheless is difficult to describe. Pointing makes something happen, but the sphere in which this happening occurs is not unqualifiedly the sphere of physical reality. Yet something really happens. Pointing gives rise to a meaning; all of us know this meaning, but it is exceedingly difficult to analyze the mode of being of that meaning.

It should be evident now why in this study of the philosophy of language we had to speak about grasping and pointing. Our speaking is a way of pointing. We can point with the hand, a finger, our face, or a glance. Yet these ways of pointing offer only limited possibilities. They can refer only to things that are here and now bodily present. Moreover, there are all kinds of refined variations which escape these ways of pointing. Speech, on the other hand, is a "pointing instrument" which raises man above all these limitations. With words we can point to what is near and far away, to the present, the past and the future. When we point by means of words, we are no longer limited to bodily present reality. Words are the "pointing instrument" *par excellence.* If we want to understand the proper mode of giving meaning which is implied in speaking, we must reflect upon the nature and function of pointing.

*Pointing, Space, and Field of Meaning.* In its original form

59

pointing, like grasping, takes place in space. It gives rise to meaning in that space. Let us consider, for example, a traffic policeman who gives signals. He erects, as it were, barriers which one cannot pass. He provides a passage for the cars coming from the other direction. He exercises influence on everyone who passes his crossing, but does not seize anyone bodily. If he sometimes has to seize someone bodily, he stops giving signals and traffic comes to a halt. He causes all kinds of meanings to arise for us. He creates a field of meaning, an orderly image. The forms of meaning which he creates really exist. When, for instance, I approach the crossing, I find there either a blocked space or a free space.

In what sense do these meanings exist? The scope of this question reveals itself more clearly if the traffic agent has been mechanized, i.e., replaced by traffic lights. Let us assume that I have to wait for a red light at a moment when no traffic is coming from any direction. I then find myself before a free space, but on the other hand, I face a blocked space. I can drive through the red light without any physical danger, but not without getting a ticket, at least if a traffic policeman is nearby. We have here the strange fact that the space before me is both free and not free. The indications given by the traffic light fill space with meanings which are there but which are not of necessity. Other indications could be given and they would fill the space with other meanings. Man organizes space by means of his indications, his "pointings." To a certain extent he is free in doing this. The free space is made unfree by the traffic light, but it remains free in other senses. The meanings which are created here do not strictly exist of necessity. They are, of course, meanings which are fairly obvious, for otherwise the traffic signal system would be ineffective.

The meanings which arise by our pointing, our signals and indications, exist in space, in the world. They really exist, but only for man. The field of meanings created by the traffic agent or the traffic lights does not exist for a dog which happens to pass the crossings. Our pointing takes place in a world planned and organized by man. Or rather, by pointing we plan and organize a world. Our pointing takes place in an intentional field, i.e., in a field that is inseparably connected with human intentions, with man's giving of meaning.

The temptation is great to think that we must make a distinction between such an intentional field, that is, our planned and organized space, and another, more real field, a real space which precedes the intentional field. Real space seems to be prior to the intentional space which is connected with our intentions. Yet this is not really true. This so-called "real space" is always a perceived space, i.e., a space which we see, in which we hear, or touch. A space which would precede all perception simply does not exist for us. Now, even our perception is already an organizing of space. When we really see and do not simply gaze, we look at something. That which we look at plays the role of a figure, and the rest becomes a kind of horizon. The same applies when in darkness we grope for the light switch. Perception itself is an organizing of space. We place something in the center of our field and make the rest "surroundings."[6]

It should be evident now that even our grasping takes place in an intentional space, in a space which we have made into a field of meaning, no matter how true it is that grasping makes meaning be a reality, a reality which even continues to exist after our grasping. In the space in which we work some objects are important and others unimportant. But a field of "importance" is an intentional field. We do not know any other space than the one which we have organized by existing in it. In this organization we have a certain latitude of freedom. We do not of necessity have to make this particular thing the center and the rest "surroundings." The intentional field can be understood only from the standpoint of a human being who possesses freedom of movement even in his seeing, hearing and groping. Our work also always takes place in such an intentional field.

*Pointing as Giving a New Mode of Being to Meaning.* What,

---

[6] Cf. C. A. van Peursen, "L'Horizon," *Situation*, Utrecht, 1954, pp. 204–234.

then, happens when we point? By pointing, we make a certain form of meaning, which is present in our intentional world, exist in a new way. We bring a certain form of meaning to our own attention and to that of others. Even in perception that which we look at or to which we listen functions as the center of a field. It comes to the foreground. By our pointing it comes to the foreground in a new fashion. We have freedom of movement in the world because we are able to bring meaning to light. By pointing to that meaning, we bring it to light in a new way. When, for example, someone dresses ostentatiously, he draws everyone's attention. All eyes are on him. The situation becomes even worse if people start pointing at him and making remarks about him. A cripple cannot hide his infirmity; he cannot prevent others from seeing his deformity. Yet he can demand that others do not point to his deformity or speak about it in his presence. If they do it anyhow, his deformity begins to exist in a new and more striking way both for himself and for others. Pointing raises a meaning out of its relative concealment. It gives that meaning a new and more explicit mode of being.

Man, as we have said repeatedly, is a meaning-giving existence. He makes meaning be. Meaning is conceivable only as meaning-for-us. All meaning exists therefore in an intentional field, i.e., in the world which we have made to be the present world, in the world which for us and through us has become a "field of presence." Note that it is the world, reality itself, which becomes a "field of presence." This world is a field, and all meaning appears in this field. Meaning begins to exist in a more striking way for us when we bring it to light in that field. By pointing to a meaning, we bring it to light in a striking way.

The way in which we do that is rather peculiar. It consists in a process of "placing at a distance," which has a twofold aspect. First, we detach the meaning somewhat from the field, giving it a certain autonomy. We do this by drawing attention to the meaning in question. Secondly, we detach ourselves from our existential permeation with the meaning. Our acting always takes place in a field of perception, but in our acting and perceiving we ourselves are wholly immersed in, and a part of, the field of meaning. When, however, we point, we detach ourselves also to some extent from this field. Pointing demands "placing at a distance." If we want to arrive at greater clarity, this twofold distance is needed, we have to detach both the meaning and ourselves to a certain extent.

*Speaking as Pointing.* The twofold distance which exists in an elementary fashion when we point with our hand or finger reaches a higher level in speech. Speaking, we have said, is a kind of pointing. The shape of our throat, palate, teeth, tongue and lips permits us to produce many sounds. Even when there is not yet question of any human initiative, these sounds may express the condition in which the organism finds itself. A baby, for example, can crow and cry, expressing thereby the condition of its body. These sounds help its mother to determine what has to be done or not done. Even in the animal world such sounds are used to make contact with other animals. As recent research has shown, animals establish that kind of contact more frequently than was hitherto suspected.

Man has developed the marvellous power to make those sounds serve to indicate meanings which he experiences. Language has become accepted so much as a matter of course that we can no longer imagine how language came into existence. Yet in a certain sense this process still takes place before our very eyes. A baby's sounds are not yet language but gradually develop into language. This development is very gradual, for we cannot point to any particular moment when its sounds become language. We are able to indicate when that is certainly not yet the case and when it certainly is the case, but the transition takes place in a gradual way. It is extremely difficult if not impossible for us to think ourselves into the child's psyche. If child psychology could help us here, we would perhaps be able to know more about the origin and development of language. As long as we do not know more about it than we do now, we are forced to think about the matter on the basis of developed language.

By speaking we point to a meaning. The twofold distance which exists in an elementary fashion in pointing with the hand assumes a much clearer form in our speech. "Lived" meaning then becomes spoken meaning. This meaning is lifted out of the field in which it originally existed. It becomes the thema of our speaking. If, for example, a thunderstorm threatens, it reveals itself in the oppressive character of the air, in the shape of clouds. We feel it coming, as do many animals. We can begin to speak about it, referring perhaps to certain thunderstorms of the past. We talk about thunderstorms as such. In doing this, we place ourselves at a distance from the threatening phenomenon that is about to break loose. Sometimes we even manage to forget what is actually going to take place until a loud thunderclap brings us back to concrete reality.

There is something paradoxical in pointing and therefore also in speaking. On the one hand, our contact with reality becomes less firm, but on the other, it becomes stronger. It becomes less firm because it puts us at a distance. As a consequence of this, it is possible that our pointing or speaking will deviate from reality. In grasping we can make a mistake, but because we remain close to reality, such a mistake will manifest itself at once. If we fail to grasp what we wanted, it does not take long before we are aware of it. In pointing, however, we place ourselves at a distance and may therefore fail to point correctly. If that happens it does not always manifest itself immediately. It is possible for us to persevere in our mistake. Life teaches us how easy it is to fail to come to the point in our speaking.

On the other hand, however, our contact with reality also becomes more firm, for its meaning begins to exist more significantly for us. By pointing and especially by speaking, we reach a higher level of meaning-giving existence.

64

## 3. The Primacy of "Pointing"

In the preceding section we have drawn attention to two forms of giving meaning, namely, "grasping" and "pointing." Which of these two, one may ask, is more important for our human existence? This question may sound rather abstract and academic, yet it is of the greatest importance for our era. It is one of the most crucial questions dealt with in contemporary thinking.

*Two Forms of Culture.* The two fundamental attitudes indicated by those two terms lead directly to two forms of civilization which we may initially refer to as the "culture of grasping" and the "culture of pointing." Man has developed his grasping of, as well as his pointing to, the world to a high degree. The term "culture of grasping" is a primitive but clarifying way of referring to our civilization based on work. In our work we grasp the world to transform it into a human dwelling place. Work gives rise to meaning and makes this meaning be a reality in our world. The fruits of our work continue to exist even when our work comes to an end.

The "culture of pointing," on the other hand, has developed, as we have pointed out, especially in man's speaking. At first our speaking about the world was interwoven with our acting, but it soon became less closely connected with action and even independent of it. Man cultivated his speaking about the world, his universe of discourse, separately. We could speak here of an "autonomous culture of the word," in the sense that our speaking about the world has become a separate activity which is pursued for its own sake, for instance, in science and literature. This autonomous "culture of the word" has developed into an imposing whole, which still continues its process of growth.

Without raising the problem in the way it is done here, Western philosophy has generally assigned primacy to "pointing," to speech. The reason probably is that in this way meaning is more pregnantly brought to light because man places himself here more at a distance from meaning and realizes his freedom more

65

than by "grasping."[7] Man's life of the spirit manifests itself most of all in his "pointing." Yet the nineteenth century saw the birth of a philosophical view which assigns primacy to man's grasping of the world. This philosophical view, which is known as Marxism, places full emphasis on man's work and claims that the development of production means is the decisive aspect of history.[8]

*Reasons for the Primacy of "Grasping."* One can certainly present several reasons which favor the primacy of "grasping" the world over that of "pointing" to the world. Our grasping of the world, i.e., our work, is an effect of our needs and therefore characterized by an absolute necessity. We need the world for everything and through our work we ourselves have to make the world which we need. Work, then, is a condition of our entire existence. We always make use of the fruits of our labor, and the possibilities of our life are conditioned by the development of man's ways of working.

Moreover, the meaning which we bring to light by "pointing" and speaking is at first, as a rule, always a meaning that is connected with the "grasping" of the world, with work. As we have pointed out previously, many of our most elementary words are connected with our active dealing with the world. By "grasping" the world, by working, we create the indispensable basis of our life. Without this basis, everything else collapses. Therefore, one would be inclined to say, it would appear that the development of this basis is the decisive factor of history.

*Critique of These Arguments.* For several reasons, however, the preceding arguments fail to convince us. First of all, our "grasping" of the world, our work, reaches a higher level precisely through our "pointing" to the world. Human work implies that

---

[7] "Darwin regarded any expression of the inner intention with respect to a particular object as a natural action which is degraded by evolution. 'Pointing' was supposed to be a 'grasping' reduced to powerlessness, and the closed fist a relic of a defense which originally consisted of seizing the attacker." Louis Van Haecht, *Taalphilosophische beschouwingen*, p. 80.

[8] Cf. Remy C. Kwant, *Philosophy of Labor*, Pittsburgh, 1960, pp. 94 ff.

man is not limited to the world, the situation, in which he finds himself. Man's work is precisely a re-creation of the situation in which he is. Work, therefore, implies a certain freedom with respect to the situation.[9] Animals do not have this freedom and cannot work in the strict sense of the term. Work can be understood only because man, while living in a situation, is able to put himself at a distance from that situation. This statement is confirmed by the fact that work becomes more effective according as man is better able to put himself at a distance from his situation. This distance is realized especially in "pointing," in speech. Modern work is performed in the light of science, i.e., in the light created by placing oneself at a great distance from man's situation. Primitive man was much more immersed in his situation and for that reason his work also was very primitive. To reach a higher and more productive level, man had to rise higher above such a primitive immersion. In other words, the progress of work is conditioned by the distance implied in "pointing," in speaking about the world. It stands to reason, therefore, that the core of being-man should be sought in his power to place himself at a distance, to disengage himself from his situation rather than in his immediate dealing with the world which we call "work."

A second remark needs to be made. While it is true that the distance implied in "pointing," in speaking about the world, helps to raise the level of man's work, the placing of oneself at a distance is certainly meaningful also in a different way. Work serves to make it possible for man to live. But the man who places himself at a distance from his situation, from his immediate dealing with the world, will perforce ask himself what the meaning is of his working existence itself. Through his work man raises himself above total subservience to his needs. However, what is the meaning of an existence that is raised above that level? Placing oneself at a distance from one's situation itself is a

---

[9] Marx realized the truth of this statement when he undertook his concrete analysis of work. He saw in that analysis that work itself implies a certain freedom, a certain placing-oneself-at-a-distance from nature.

form of freedom and, in addition, it contributes to the satisfaction of needs, i.e., to liberation. This liberated existence itself must have an inner meaning. A prisoner desires to be free, because he experiences being-free as something having an inner meaning. Colonial peoples desire independence, obviously, because they recognize being-independent as a meaningful way of being. The very fact that work makes our existence possible indicates that the meaning of our existence transcends work. By virtue of a freedom belonging to the core of man's being, man is able to perform liberating work. It is impossible that the meaning of freedom is totally encompassed by the work which makes man free.

As a matter of fact, we notice that the most profound problems of existence arise only when, thanks to the progress of work, man rises above the level in which he is wholly immersed in satisfying his needs. People who have to wrest a precarious way of living and are barely able to satisfy their needs do not easily ask any question about the meaning of existence. Once, however, man rises above that level, this question is asked. In the U.S.S.R. people have devoted themselves enthusiastically to the development of work. Now that they have accomplished much in that direction, many ask themselves what the meaning is of their existence, the meaning of their work. People who by dint of much work have secured a margin of freedom with respect to man's prime necessities inquire about the meaning of their liberated existence. When the needs of man's material existence are satisfied, a more profound need often manifests itself.[10]

Pointing to the world, speaking about it, makes it possible to elevate man's work and to liberate him from the material needs of his existence. At the same time, however, it transfers man to a different dimension in which new problems arise. Marx's

---

[10] This phenomenon reveals itself in the literature of Russia. The question regarding the meaning of life is raised by many young Russians, and this question includes also the meaning of work and the entire social order. There are Russian writers who want this question to be taken seriously.

writings contain passages in which he clearly shows his awareness of this new dimension.[11] Yet Marx did not develop this perspective. He lived in a period of extreme need and pointed out a way in which this need could be overcome. The questions which would arise when this need had been eliminated did not occupy much of his attention.

From all these considerations we may conclude without any doubt that man's "pointing" reveals a more profound dimension of his being than is manifested by his "grasping."

## 4. FROM MEANING TO SIGNIFICATION

We are investigating the special way in which our speaking gives meaning. We began by observing that language cannot be divorced from man's living speech. Next, we saw that our speaking is a form of "pointing." It places us at a distance from the immediately "lived" meaning. We assigned to "pointing" the primacy over "grasping." However, we still have not yet arrived at a clear reply to the question of how our speaking gives meaning.

This section bears the title "from meaning to signification." This title could easily be misunderstood. It could give rise to the impression that by speaking we change meaning into signification, as if signification would not be meaning. Such an impression would be entirely erroneous. Signification is not something other than meaning but rather a new way in which meaning exists. Hence signification is not opposed to meaning but is a new form in which the meaning appears. We ourselves give rise to this new form of appearance. Instead of saying that meaning changes into signification, we could also say that meaning comes to be signification.

*Analytic and Synthetic Character of Speech.* As long as a meaning is still only "lived," it presents itself within a field of meaning. In this field the meaning always has many aspects. For instance,

---

[11] Marx speaks of the realm of freedom, which will come when man's needs have been overcome. He indicates that in that state man will come into his own, although this new mode of being will have its own problems.

a common meal is meaningful. This meaning is found, e.g., in the taste of the food that is offered. But in an appetizing meal many flavors are present and together they constitute a harmonious whole. A particular flavor draws attention if it is absent; for instance, if the food does not contain enough salt. The attraction of a meal is determined in part also by the way in which it is served and particularly also by the company in which it is taken. Man is a manifold question, and the answer to our question which we experience as meaningful is always a many-sided whole. We experience the meaning but in semidarkness. The "lived" meaning is nearly always ambiguous, that is, the answer in which we live hardly ever fully replies to the manifold question which we are. For this reason, that meaning satisfies us but never completely. We experience a negation in every affirmation. This negation gives rise to a tendency in us to improve our situation. Sartre not incorrectly refers to this tendency, this "project," as a "negation of the negation."[12] We object to the absence of meaning, for we are meaning-giving existence and therefore want to promote meaning.

To promote meaning, we have to become more clearly aware of what is present in meaning and what is absent from it. We are forced to analyze it. The term "analysis" is derived from the Greek verb *analuein,* which means "to dissolve," to "detach." We have to detach from the whole of meaning the aspects which are present as well as those which are absent. As we have seen, "pointing" with the hand is a first step in this direction. It draws attention to an aspect that is strikingly present or strikingly absent. It brings to light a certain aspect of our field of presence. The best way of all to draw attention to an aspect of the whole of meaning is our speaking. We make a certain combination of sounds serve to point to, to express, a certain aspect of meaning. By doing this, we detach this aspect from the whole of meaning and place it in the focus of our field of attention. This aspect is then brought to light in a pregnant way.

---

[12] *Critique de la raison dialectique,* p. 64.

That to which attention is drawn in this way is, of course, at first not something separate, for it is and remains an aspect of the field of meaning. Yet it is an aspect which to a certain extent has been detached from that field. This separation demands a second step, by which the detached aspect is attached to something. This connecting step is called "attribution." Our speaking always has the character of being a combination of analysis and synthesis, of detaching and connecting, of abstracting and attributing, no matter in what grammatical form this character may manifest itself. In all our speaking there is always *something about which* we speak and *something which* we say. The "something about which" is that from which aspects are detached, and the "something which" is the aspects which we detach.

*Meaning and Signification.* These detached aspects are nothing else but the meaning itself existing for us in a new way. At first, the speaking man is not even aware of the fact that the meaning exists now in a new way, for he aims at this meaning itself. A profound reflection is required to realize that the meaning is now aimed at by way of a process of analysis and synthesis. For this reason there are many who know nothing about this process although they are quite familiar, of course, with speaking.

Let us investigate now what this new mode of being is which meaning acquires through speech. The detached aspect of meaning manifests peculiar characteristics. It is taken from the "lived" meaning presenting itself here and now, but it transcends this here and now. It can be connected not only with the meaning here and now presenting itself from which it has been taken but also with what is absent, past, and distant. It transcends that from which it has been taken. It possesses, to express it more technically, an almost unlimited attributability. It can be attributed not only to the meaning which really presents itself but also to a fictitious meaning, to the world of fancy. If someone says, for example, that a person whose presence at a meeting is doubted is "really" there, this term expresses the presence of the present. But this same term can be applied to all forms of presence, for what-

ever is, is really. Again, if we call food "salty," we are referring
to an aspect which is found in many realities presenting themselves to us. The same applies to all aspects which we detach
from "lived" meaning. We cannot discover any aspect which is
applicable only to that from which it is here and now taken.[13]

We call meaning in this new mode of being a "signification."
Our words have a signifying function. The term "signification"
can be used in two ways. It can refer to the signifying function
of a term but also to that which is signified. When someone asks
me to describe what a term signifies, he refers to the second sense,
to that which is signified. It is in this sense that we use the term
here.

*Reality, Meaning, and Signification.* There are many misunderstandings regarding signification. Some have thought that
significations exist in our interior as a kind of mirroring of that
which is present outside us. This idea is not entirely groundless.
As we have already said, the signification has another mode of
being than the "lived" meaning. The latter is concrete, it is here
and now present, while the former is general and abstracted from
the here and now. Thus one could easily think that the general
signification is a kind of interior mirroring of the "lived" meaning.
Nevertheless, that idea is not tenable. Our own experience bears
witness to the fact that our words do not indicate an internal
phenomenon present in ourselves, but meaning itself. That which
our signifying words indicate lies in the world. What we speak of
is that which appears to us, for our consciousness is intentional,
i.e., it is always consciousness of the "other." In our speaking also,
our consciousness is directed to the "other." The signification,

---

[13] Language is the principal means through which man is humanized.
The reason is that "as a product of the intellect, language has an intelligible
and fundamentally general character. Through the intellect language ultimately obtains also that external form of abstract generality which the
communicable character of that which man conceives and thinks makes
appear to be something that is taken for granted." Wilhelm Seeberger,
*Hegel oder die Entwicklung des Geistes zur Freiheit,* Stuttgart, 1961, p.
335.

therefore, is not an interior image but the correlate of our conscious act.

The conception of knowledge which we oppose here presupposes that that which we know primarily is simply reality itself, something that is given in complete independence from us. The correlate of our knowledge is supposed to be reality itself. If this is true, the signification obviously cannot exist in this correlate. For it would be unthinkable that reality itself would be general and stripped of its here and now. Thus it would follow that significations have to exist in ourselves.

However, as we have seen in the preceding chapters, although reality presents itself to us, it appears precisely as meaning-for-us, and this meaning-for-us originates not in reality alone but in reality *and* us. The correlate of our knowledge is already permeated with our existence as giver of meaning. This compenetration makes this correlate be the correlate. But in that case, this correlate can exist for us in various ways according as we intend it in different ways. There is room in that case within the correlate for significations. The latter do not exist in us but in the world appearing to us, in the world-for-us, for we do not know any other world. A signification is the meaning itself, the meaning of the world which we make be for us in a new way. By our speaking the meaning appearing to us itself comes to be a signification. Or, differently expressed, reality itself begins to be for us in a different way. This statement is, of course, wholly unintelligible if one conceives reality as something that is entirely independent of us. It becomes intelligible only if one regards reality correctly, viz., as reality-for-us.

*Field of Significations.* There exist many significations, for we detach many aspects from our "lived" meaning. For this reason we may speak of a "field of significations." In ordinary conversation no distinction is made, of course, between the "lived" world and the world as field of significations, or rather, people have no awareness at all of this distinction. Nevertheless, this distinction exists even with respect to ordinary speech, as appears from the fact that a divergence may arise between the "lived" world and the "spoken" world or the "universe of discourse." Speech, as we have explained above, always implies that we detach an aspect from the world of meaning. The one who speaks naturally intends to give expression to the "lived" meaning. However, he may be unfaithful to this meaning. If that happens, he moves in a field of significations which deviates from the "lived" world. The correlate of his speech is then an imaginary kind of field which he thinks of as the real field of meaning. Once again, however, in ordinary speech people are not aware of the distinction between the "lived" world and the spoken world and, consequently, we do not realize that there is danger that the latter may deviate from the former.

As soon, however, as man begins to reflect in a scientific way, he will develop the field of significations in a more conscious and critical way. He carefully selects significations which are suitable for his scientific inquiry and rejects others. When that happens, he becomes aware of the distinction between the "lived" world and the world of significations, as well as of the danger that the two will no longer be in harmony. We will revert later to the field of scientific thought, that is, the field of scientific significations.

*A Twofold Mystery.* In all these considerations we have not yet paid attention to a rather obvious question. By speaking, we have said, we make a meaning become a signification. Why is it that we are capable of doing this? We make the concrete meaning come to be a general signification; we abstract the meaning from the here and now. How do we accomplish that modification? This question has frequently occupied the attention of philosophers in the past, and it continues to be a problem even today. However, we should realize that this question is not something special arising only in connection with speech. The very same question must be asked in reference to all modes of giving meaning. Undoubtedly, it is full of wonder that a meaning comes to be for us a signification. But it is not less wonderful that the world becomes for me a field of light and color, a sonorous field full of meaningful sounds, that food is tasty for me, that flowers present themselves to me as fragrant, or that the world is for me full of beauty. The question of how it is possible arises in connection with all forms of giving and accepting meaning. Within man's contact with the world things become meaningful to me in many ways.

There are two mysteries here which, strictly speaking, are nonetheless one—I am such that I can make reality become meaning for me, and reality is such that it lets itself be made to be meaning for me. Far too frequently matters are presented as if the metamorphosis of meaning into signification is a very exceptional event.[14] While it is true that this event has a character of its own, it raises a fundamental problem which presents itself wherever any form of meaning arises. There is no one who fully understands how the world becomes for us a field of light and color, how it becomes that wondrous world in which our gaze can dwell. Is it surprising, then, that no one has ever fully explained how for us and through us meaning comes to be signification? We experience our existence as a gift, for we find ourselves to be such that we are able to make reality be meaning in many ways.

The same applies with respect to signification. I find myself to be such that I can make meaning be a general signification. Kant placed here one of the main problems of his philosophy. He was right in seeing a problem here and in raising it, but he was too eager to find its solution. The phenomenologist does not deny Kant's problem, but makes it more universal and more radical. He realizes that the same kind of problem arises with respect to any form of meaning.

---

[14] The reason is that the distance between matter and mind is wholly placed between the perceived meaning and the abstract concept. For perception was ascribed to the senses, the body, and the concept to the mind. As soon, however, as one accepts that the mind is present also in perception, it is no longer necessary to posit such a distance between perception and concept, between meaning and signification.

*Reason and Meaning.* We are confronted here with a strange fact in the history of human reflection. It happens sometimes that the most stringent demands of rationality are made with respect to the forms of meaning which are most difficult to approach, while the same demands are not made with respect to other forms of meaning which are more readily accessible. From experience we know that by speaking we make a meaning become a signification, that the meaning begins to appear in a general way, stripped from the here and now. We are surprised and ask ourselves how this is possible. Some, however, when they do not succeed in finding a rational explanation, go so far as to deny the genuine signification, the meaning in its generalized form of being. They deny that whose possibility they cannot explain.[15] Those people seem to forget that we are unable to offer any complete rational explanation for any form of meaning and disregard the fact that we cannot fathom the conditions which make any form of meaning possible. Merleau-Ponty is quite right when he speaks about the *mystery* which the appearance of meaning is on any level in the whole we call "world."[16] If we were to make our acceptance of meaning depend upon our complete understanding of the conditions which make meaning possible, we would have to doubt not only general significations but also all other forms of meaning.

The same has to be said with respect to metaphysics and religion. Sometimes people require that the metaphysician demonstrate *a priori* the possibility of his approach. This demand is surprising and strange, for no science is able to offer such a demonstration for its own possibility. While we are certainly en-

---

[15] Let us keep in mind, however, that the denial of certain values is sometimes provoked by the way in which others affirm them. Some thinkers have denied the general concept because others had detached it from perception and thereby gave rise to a conceptless, despiritualized perception and an uprooted concept. In a similar way the denial of God is sometimes provoked by the way in which others affirm God. Likewise, moral principles are sometimes denied because others misuse these principles to preserve a petrified system.

[16] *Eloge de la philosophie*, Paris, 1953, p. 62.

titled to reflect upon the possibility of something that is *de facto* given, we can never make our acceptance of this factual datum depend on our complete understanding of its possibility.

Reason, then, may certainly occupy itself with meaning. As a matter of fact, we are at present reflecting upon meaning in a rational way and we have done it also in the preceding chapters. However, in its reflection upon meaning, reason must admit and respect our experience of meaning. Reason has to place itself in the light of our experience of meaning and must let itself be guided by this light. Reason may and even must try to understand what we experience. Merleau-Ponty and other phenomenologists sometimes plead for an "enlarged reason."[17] By using this term, they oppose a narrow view of rationality. This view exists in those who want to admit only that which reason can justify and explain. Such an attitude is entirely unreasonable and even untenable. One who assumes it will ultimately have to doubt also the meaningfulness of rational understanding itself, for reason cannot fully explain why such a rational understanding satisfies man, why he experiences it as meaningful.

We have considered the question how meaning obtains a new mode of being through our speaking. Our reply was that speaking makes meaning become signification. The meaning begins to exist in the form of universality, it is stripped of its here and now. A signification is not an interior picture but a correlate of our consciousness. There are many significations and together they constitute a field of significations. This field belongs to the world, that is, the world-for-us, the only world about which we are able to speak.

---

[17] Concerning this matter see Albert Dondeyne, *Contemporary European Thought and Christian Faith,* 2nd impr., Pittsburgh, 1963. Dondeyne discusses the accusation of irrationalism which is sometimes levelled against certain forms of contemporary philosophy. He considers this accusation not entirely justified. Contemporary philosophy does not go against reason as such but against the narrow views of reason which make themselves felt in certain types of sciences and in the way of thinking proper to some philosophers and theologians.

# CHAPTER FOUR

# The Field of Significations

As we have seen in the preceding chapter, by speaking we make meaning become signification. There are many significations, which together constitute a "field," for these significations show themselves connected and thus form a whole. This whole can be indicated in many different ways. With Merleau-Ponty we could speak of a "universe of discourse," the universe in which we place ourselves when we speak, or rather, the universe which we constitute by speaking. The term "spoken world" would also be suitable. Both these terms indicate the same thing which we refer to as "the field of significations." We must now consider this field more in detail.

## 1. THE FIELD OF SIGNIFICATIONS IS NOT THE MOST ORIGINAL FIELD OF MEANING

The truth of the assertion expressed in this title follows from what we have seen in the preceding pages. Our speaking gives a new mode of being to meaning; hence meaning has a mode of being which precedes our speech. A few examples may serve to illustrate this point.

*Examples.* When we speak about a landscape, we presuppose the existence for us of this landscape as a whole of meaning before our speech. If we consider our speech, we note that we give expression to something that was pre-given to us in a different way. Our speaking serves to make us conscious in a new way of what we already possessed. This example is particularly apt because the most proper knowledge of a landscape is found precisely in seeing it. One who genuinely and really sees a beautiful landscape usually lapses into silence. At such a moment speech can even become a hindrance because it prevents us from seeing. On the other hand, it is also possible that speech will be of service. For, as we have seen, we must learn to see. Speech can help us to learn in the sense that, by listening to someone who really sees the landscape in question, we learn to pay attention to the things that are important for seeing it.

A second example may be taken from space. Space with its dimensions exists for us before we begin to speak of it. A little child who climbs the stairs has to adapt his movements to the height of the steps. When we stretch out our arms to seize something, we have to adjust their motion to the distance at which the object is with respect to us. In making his clothes, man, even primitive man, has to adapt the materials to the dimensions of his body. Merleau-Ponty has made a profound study of so-called "lived space" and he has shown that this space is essentially connected with man's bodily being. We dwell in space precisely as embodied beings. On the basis of our bodily being we give orientation to space, make things be nearby or faraway, right or left, high or low. Man cannot live without measuring, but our most primordial measuring is present even in our existence itself. It is inconceivable to exist in space without measuring. It stands to reason, therefore, that when man began to devise units of measurement, he used his body as a norm. He measured land by the number of paces and materials by the length of his arm. Only in a much more advanced stage could man begin to use the dimensions of the earth as the fundamental principle of his measuring system, as he has done in the metric system. Thus we could say that life itself is a "science of measurements," or mathematics.

Life as mathematics also has developed through the intermediary of speech. When at a given moment ordinary language was no longer sufficient for this development, man created a special kind of language, which at first was merely a prolongation or extension of ordinary speech. This mathematical language is the system of mathematical symbols. Life as mathematics could make solid progress only by means of speech, especially scientific speech. The aid of speech is less important for the seeing of a landscape than for the development of life as mathematics.

*Dependence of the Spoken Meaning on Pre-Given Meaning.* These two examples contain certain common elements, but there are also important differences. In both cases the meaning existed already on a previous level and was brought to development through speech. In both cases also the spoken meaning depends on a pre-given meaning. In the second example, however, speech plays a much more important role and offers many more possibilities than in the first. As soon as man made the transition from "lived" mathematics to "spoken" mathematics and especially to scientific mathematics, his ability to measure began to increase greatly. The basis in "lived" mathematics on which the mathematical system is built is exceedingly small in comparison with the superstructure. We may even say that this basis has become practically invisible in the modern mathematical edifice. Those who describe mathematics as it has developed through speech usually do not even refer any longer to the measuring that is present in man's life. Scientific mathematics is generally described as a whole which can be understood in itself, as a whole built on the starting point of certain axiomatic insights. One would be inclined to think that our speaking in these matters is wholly independent, that the spoken meaning is not dependent upon a "lived" meaning. I would not want to go that far. If man's existence did not include the ability to measure distances, he would never have been able to develop a mathematics. The spoken meaning is always dependent upon a meaning which precedes speech, although the dependence in question is not always of the same nature.

It is, of course, impossible to describe the meaning which precedes speech. As soon as we describe that meaning, we make it a spoken meaning. However, if we carefully watch our speaking, we notice its dependence in many ways. Sometimes this dependence is indicated in a wrong way or at least one-sidedly. Some, for example, say that our speech is bound to the things of which we speak, and intend to express in this way that speech depends upon a reality which is given independently of man. This view is not entirely wrong, for our giving of meaning is always also an accepting of meaning. As a dialogue with the world, we are dependent upon this world. Yet this view disregards all kinds of intermediary links. For, our speech is not immediately dependent upon a world which is simply real and absolutely objective, but upon a world which has already become meaning-for-us on another level. Let us illustrate this assertion with a few examples.

One who philosophizes about space has to be guided by space as it is given to him, which is the space he wants to express in philosophical speech. This given space, however, upon which philosophical speaking depends, is the "lived" space that is already meaning-for-us. One who wants to speak about colors has to respect the objective reality of these phenomena; but these phenomena are already meaning-for-us. One who has to write a report about a particular person wants, of course, to express in what way that person is. The person in question, however, has become a fellow-man for him within a certain attitude which he himself has taken. Long before we speak with and about one another, we experience one another as human beings.[1] We ourselves are intentional beings, we are orientated existences. We

---

[1] Sartre points out that the human sciences presuppose that we know what being-man is. But how do we know this? We are unable, says Sartre, to indicate a complex of characteristics which together constitute a "human nature." Being-man is not a complex of fixed characteristics but rather a mode of having characteristics—namely, the mode of being in such a way that one always transcends what one is. This being-man is known to us in an experience which is explicitated by the philosophy of existence. Cf., e.g., *Critique de la raison dialectique*, pp. 95–103.

recognize the other man as the fulfillment, the actualization of orientations which live also in ourselves.

*Speech and Expression.* Accordingly, the field of significations refers everywhere to previous fields of meaning upon which it depends. For this reason we are not entirely free in developing our field of significations. Our entire mode of existence finds, and has to find, expression in that field. One would be guilty of a deceptive illusion of objectivity if one were to understand our speaking as an immediate grasping of things in which other modalities of our existence would not play any role. People sometimes think that only in speech, and especially in scientific speech, man penetrates into the real world, as if all the forms of giving meaning which precede speaking are not characterized by contact with the real world. This, too, is an illusion. For, if the forms of giving meaning which precede speech and upon which speech depends are not an unveiling of the world, then our speaking itself could not possibly be such an unveiling.

It should be clear now in what sense phenomenology considers speaking to be "expression." This term does not mean that speaking is the expression of a thought which precedes speech. As we will see in one of the following chapters, speaking and thinking cannot be fully separated. Likewise, the phenomenologist does not mean that our speaking gives expression to reality "itself," conceived in opposition to "appearing" reality. He calls speech "expression" because it makes a meaning which precedes speech exist in a new way. The spoken meaning is the expression of a meaning which existed already on another level. Our speaking of colors is the expression of seeing colors; our speaking of space is the expressed of "lived" space; the sexuality of which we speak is the expression of "lived" sexuality. Speaking is a very special level of giving meaning, one which gives expression to meaning which has arisen on other levels of giving meaning. The field of significations is the expression of fields of meaning preceding it. We speak about the world, the real world, but we cannot do that without speaking at the same time about the way in which we, on all kinds of levels, make the world be for us. It is true, of course, that as a rule we do not speak thematically about the way in which we make the world be for us on other levels. Nonetheless, we speak about the world from these levels.

## 2. OUR FREEDOM OF MOVEMENT IN THE FIELD OF SIGNIFICATIONS

*Freedom in Other Fields of Meaning.* The preceding section has emphasized the bond which connects the field of significations with preceding fields of meaning. We must now complement that section by pointing to the freedom which man enjoys in that field. We do not want to say that freedom is present only in the field of significations, for the preceding fields of meaning also reveal man's freedom. For example, work, the "grasping" of the world, is unthinkable without freedom. True, the man who makes a statue from a piece of stone is restricted by the possibilities offered by this material. Nevertheless, the stone does not, and cannot, determine what kind of form will originate from it. Work is unthinkable without freedom to give form.

Freedom reveals itself also in the world of play and games. In their play children give things a meaning which is not laid down in these things themselves and even less dictated by them. When, for example, they play "Run sheep, run," a small area is made a safe place and the surroundings are unsafe and full of danger. Nothing forces them to give these meanings to parts of their playground. When they play "Hide and seek," the child who is "it" has to discover the others and reach before them a previously selected spot. This spot is given a meaning which reality does not prescribe in any way.

That man is not restricted by forms imposed upon him by the world manifests itself also in the capriciousness of our dreams, in the wondrous play of man's phantasy. Moreover, seeing and other forms of perception likewise reveal something of man's freedom of movement. In the process of seeing, a certain object functions as a figure while the rest recedes as the field within which this figure appears. Seeing would be unthinkable without freedom to let now "this" and then "that" appear as a figure within a field. Only people who are physically abnormal lack this freedom.

*A New Mode of Freedom in Speech.* Freedom, therefore, does not begin only in the field of significations, but man's freedom of movement manifests itself already in many fields of meaning which precede speech. On the other hand, it is true that man becomes free in a new way in the field of significations.[2] For in this field the meaning is to some extent detached from the "lived" meaning, from the concrete, from what appears here and now. The significations arise, as we have said, through an analysis of the concrete meaning which appears here and now. These many significations together begin to constitute a new field. They lend themselves easily to being manipulated by man and can be combined in the most divergent ways. These significations greatly foster man's freedom of movement, for man is no longer bound to the here and now of the concrete. He is able to use them in a wonderful way as building blocks. He is able to plan new worlds, but all these worlds lie, of course, in the field of significations. These worlds are not interior worlds, for they are always correlates of man's conscious acts. We regard these worlds as something placed opposite us, but we ourselves can plan them in the most wonderful ways.

When man had learned to speak and begun to cultivate language for its own sake, he created, for example, the story. Even in the oldest known civilizations we find popular stories, in which man describes the origin of his people and his world. Such stories are usually called "myths." Man's marvellous freedom of move-

---

[2] In his previously mentioned book, *Hegel oder die Entwicklung des Geistes zur Freiheit,* Wilhelm Seeberger tries to show that Hegel's philosophy tends to bring man to freedom through spiritual consciousness. The author's intention is not so much to present a historical explanation of Hegel's philosophy as to situate Hegel's perspective—which he fully accepts —in the philosophical problematics of our time.

ment in the world of significations manifests itself already in the oldest of these popular stories. The same freedom reveals itself in a different way in novels and poetry, in the whole of literature. The world of writing shows the freedom possessed by man in his "universe of discourse." In the world of significations man is able to produce thrilling stories, humorous tales, he can paint in words the life of man. The ingenious creative power of the human mind manifests itself in this world of significations.

Man projects his own world. He does this, for example, by means of his work. Living in what is given, he is not bound to it. He takes it up with himself in the self-transcending movement of his existence. Man projects his own world also in his play and games, for here, too, he takes what is given to project into it a new complex of meanings. Through his speech man becomes the projector of a world in a new fashion. Because of the very special character of speech, man enjoys more freedom to project a world for himself in speech than in any other realm. He enjoys in it a certain freedom to connect past, present and future. He is able to create figures, bring human beings to life. The persons who figure in the world of the popular story and literature sometimes assume great importance for an entire people. In this world the author or story teller uses existing significations, for otherwise he would not be understood by others. However, these available significations are for him, as it were, the raw material which he transforms through his creative work.

*Bonds of Freedom.* One could perhaps ask whether all this does not eliminate the bonds of which we spoke in the preceding section. The answer is in the negative. First of all, man has to be creative by means of the available significations. A writer is free, of course, to create new significations, but the latter must be sufficiently connected with the available significations to be intelligible to others. These available significations have originated in the course of history. They themselves bear witness to man's creative power. Nevertheless, ultimately these significations must connect with the world of meanings in which man lives and which precedes speech. This world is recognizable even in man's most refined creations. If this were not true, then man's creation would become unintelligible. For this reason real life can be found in all human creations. We do not mean that real life and the real world is mirrored in everything, for such a crude realism would disregard man's creative power. What is true is that the world of meaning which precedes speech continues to make its influence felt in all human creations and can always be recognized in it. Man is a single meaning-giving existence; there is no mode of giving meaning which can detach itself completely from life.

Moreover, the worlds projected by man's speech always remain destined for man himself. Stories, novels, poems and humorous tales project worlds, but these worlds are projected as invitations to man to enter into these worlds. Man must be able to dwell in them, feel at home in them. Just as the world projected by man's work must be a world in which he can live, so the worlds that are created in the field of significations must be accessible to man. Sometimes a human creation in this field goes beyond the limit. There are stories so wild that one no longer can feel at home in them. They do not succeed and disappear as attempts which have proved to be meaningless. On the other hand, there are also writers who manage to create worlds so great and so universal that they are accessible to human beings of the most diverse countries and times. The works which built such worlds belong to the universal literature of man. A writer has to be an outstanding and universal mind in order to succeed in the creation of such worlds.

We say "worlds" in the plural, but one could also say that ultimately we may speak only of a single world. Both assertions are true. All the worlds projected by man in his work, his play, his plastic arts and his literature are extensions of his one "lived" world. The latter continues to make itself felt in all the worlds created by man. The reason is not that this one world is, as it were, faithfully copied and expressed in all the other worlds, but that man always projects and creates on the basis of the one world in which he lives. Complete discontinuity between the real world of life and the world projected by creative freedom is unthinkable. The one world of life is not a closed whole, but remains always open. Even in this world man is active as a meaning-giving existence. There is no world which is not meaning for man and through man. The world is always a field of meaning. This field is open, just as man himself always remains open to the future. For this reason new worlds can be added as extensions of the world of life and can be integrated into this world of meaning as new zones. All creations that are authentic, i.e., that can be "lived" by man, somehow fit into his world of life.

*Lack of Freedom in Scientific Speech.* In the preceding paragraphs we have spoken especially about those modes of speech in which man manifests himself mainly in his creative freedom. One could object, however, that there is another and more important way of speaking, namely, that in which man endeavors to give expression to the given world of meaning. While the litterateur may enjoy great freedom, the same cannot be said of the scholar and the scientist. The litterateur creates his characters in freedom, but the man of science intends to express the way in which reality is. The physical sciences, for example, bring nature to light, as appears from the fact that technology is an extension of these sciences. Precisely because man becomes more familiar with nature itself through the physical sciences, he is able to do more with nature. The same applies to psychology, the social sciences, philosophy and theology.

This book wants to speak about the phenomenon called "language." But language itself is a real and most important phenomenon in human life. If, then, this book is concerned with this real phenomenon itself, it becomes meaningless as soon as it disregards the reality of speech. For this reason, the objection concludes, we must make a distinction between scientific speech (including here also philosophy and theology) and literary speech. The former is not free, but the latter is.

This distinction manifests itself very clearly on the level of cultivated speech, i.e., the level on which the various types of speech are pursued in deliberate and advanced fashion. But even in ordinary speaking the distinction can be discerned. For instance, if a number of neighboring farmers get together to discuss the condition of a dirt road connecting their farms, they want to speak about a real situation. If, after solving that question, they continue to talk together while drinking a bottle of beer in the local barroom, their conversation may assume a quite different turn. One of them may be a man who is a real story teller or full of wit. During the earnest discussion of the dirt road, the others would not have tolerated the yarns he now spins; but during the happy friendly gathering in the barroom it would be absurd to assume that the truth of the various tall tales has to be checked. People rightly consider someone dull-witted if in ordinary conversation he shows himself unable to distinguish the various categories of speech, if he confuses tall tales with serious discussions. Sometimes a comical situation can arise when someone enters during a conversation, at first does not realize what category of speech is being used, and therefore reacts in the wrong fashion.

Accordingly, there is one kind of speech that wants to bring reality to light and is bound to this reality; there is also another kind which moves, as it were, in a vacuum and is creative. The first type is developed in science, the second in literature, humorous stories and modern shows. Thus our freedom of movement appears not to be always the same.

For the topic which we are considering here, further reflection on this matter is very important. By speaking, we have said, man constitutes a field of significations. We want to know more about this field. We must, therefore, investigate whether and to what extent this field is developed by man in freedom, as well as to what extent man is restricted in the development of that field.

## 3. FREEDOM AND BONDS IN THE FIELD OF SIGNIFICATIONS

*A Relative Or an Absolute Distinction?* The man of science is sometimes inclined to attribute a rather absolute value to the above-mentioned distinction. He often rejects certain books alleging that they are literature and not science. This rejection proceeds from a hidden intellectual attitude toward the world. A distinction is made between free speech in a kind of vacuum and speech that is bound. The latter brings reality to light and is valid for everyone, the former moves in the realm of fancy and has value only as "art." Speech in that realm may cause our admiration, but whether we admire it or not depends upon our taste. Some will like a certain creation of free speech, such as a novel or a poem, others will not like it. There are no objective criteria in this matter; at most, one could speak of criteria of good taste. If this position is true, "bound" speech, i.e., science, would have essential privileges over the other forms of speaking. Free speech and "bound" speech would be separated by an unbridgeable abyss.

Thus we would have to draw a dividing line through the field of significations. Sometimes significations would give expression to reality—we abstract here from the question of what is meant by the term "reality," i.e., whether it has to be understood in a realistic, idealistic, phenomenological or possibly some other sense. Sometimes, on the other hand, significations would be mere fictions of a freely moving spirit. Now they would be earnest endeavors to express existing meanings, and then they would be products of a fanciful mind. Although in both cases the same words and the same concepts could be used, they would function in entirely different ways.

We do not want to deny, of course, that there is a distinction between these two modes of speaking. However, that distinction should not be made too absolute. It has only a relative importance. In the following pages we will see that freedom is relative in so-called "free speech" and that in the realm of the "bound speech" of science there exists also freedom.

*Relative Freedom in "Free Speech."* Let us begin by paying attention to the novel. Free play of fancy has an important role in this kind of speech. The characters of the novel usually are not historical and, even if they are historical, they are not treated historically in the novel. Yet, strange as it may seem, a particular historical period can be made familiar to us just as well by the great novels of that period as by the serious efforts of self-analysis which it has produced. It is even possible that the novels will be more effective than the descriptive self-analysis.

For example, Dostoevski's novels paint Russia in the second half of the nineteenth century with unparalleled clarity. None of the characters in his novels is likely to be strictly historical, whether it be Raskolnikov, Sonja, the Idiot, Father Karamazov and his three sons, or the Grand Inquisitor. Dostoevski's creative imagination freely creates an imposing story. Yet this story presents a good picture of Russia as it was in his time.[3] Its social-economic problems as well as its human relationships appear in a strong light. The novels make us see the value and lack of value present in these problems and relationships. The objections of the Russian Christian against Western Christianity and especially against the Catholic Church starkly reveal themselves in the fiction of the Grand Inquisitor. The reader of this novel is spell-bound by the greatness of the story. He knows that it is only a story, fiction, but at the same time he realizes that all this is concerned with reality, as is evident, moreover, from the context of the whole story.

A second example may be taken from an entirely different field of free writing. Certain comic strips appearing in the daily press continue to be successful for many years; for instance, "Blondie." The strip's characters are freely developed by its author. Yet these characters are not without connections with our concrete world of experience. They express certain aspects of

---

[3] Cf. F. J. J. Buytendijk, *De psychologie van de roman,* Utrecht, 1961.

real life. A sign of this is that readers of these strips will often spontaneously describe real-life people in terms borrowed from their favored strip.

A third fact has to be added. Some contemporary thinkers express the same ideas in two kinds of writings. The best known example is probably Jean-Paul Sartre, although others have done the same in the past. Sartre expresses the philosophical perspective of his book *Being and Nothingness* also in novels and theatre plays, some of which have been filmed. His philosophical thought itself is embodied and given form in two different ways. Sartre's philosophical strength as well as his weakness reveal themselves in both types of writings. One could even claim that certain unacceptable aspects of his philosophy which are difficult to discern in his rational theoretical work stand out very clearly in all their unacceptable one-sidedness in the characters of his novels and plays. The defects of his philosophical approach reveal themselves perhaps more clearly in his plays and novels than in his philosophical treatises.

*Restrictions of Freedom in Humor.* Even in humor and cartoons with all their freedom and flights of fancy man tries to say something about the world in which he lives. Not without reason do major dailies and weeklies try to secure the services of great cartoonists capable of expressing the situation of the country and the world in a new way. A good cartoon is neither a photograph nor a sketch faithfuly reproducing a person's looks, but it places emphasis on certain aspects of his physiognomy in a most striking way. The humorist likewise has his own very personal way of speaking about recent events.

In these free and fanciful expressions man is nonetheless not entirely without bonds. True, one would not say that there is question here of truth or falsity. Yet we will evaluate them as not genuine or misplaced. The humorist, for example, may ridicule something without reason. This "something" is a real person or a real situation. In everyday life this person and this situation do not appear ridiculous, but the humorist places them in such a light that the ridiculous aspect, as it were, stands out and draws attention. However, his humor is not genuine or is misplaced if that aspect cannot really stand out, for in that case his humor fails to find a basis in reality.

It remains true, of course, that the humorous expression is creative. The humorist constructs the situation in such a way that its laughter-provoking aspect is emphasized. Even a photographer can sometimes do this. His creative glance through his camera can record or rather construct the situation in such a way that his picture makes everybody smile. The humorist looks in a special way at reality but nonetheless he looks at reality. He has to seek for situations which lend themselves to a humorous look. Occasionally one sees examples of "humor" which do not appear to refer to anything in particular. That kind of humor is not likely to be successful, for it does not speak to us, it is meaningless. When the genuine humorist makes us look at life through his eyes, he says something which man needs to be more fully human. He makes us have contact with life and the world in the free flights of his spirit. The fact that every era and place has its own brand of humor is another indication of the bond which ties humor to a particular situation. In addition to that kind of humor, however, there exists also a classical sort of humor, one which goes beyond a particular place or a particular time and appeals to many in the most diverse places and eras. Such classical humor is able to last because it touches life and the world in a profound way.

*Necessity of Bond with Life in Free Speech.* Novels and poems likewise may bring us in contact with real life. We do not mean to say that they faithfully render reality. The so-called "realistic novel," which for many years was the only type tolerated in the U.S.S.R. and which even now continues to prevail there, is utterly boring.[4] A novel is not a pure portrait of reality, but creates its

---

[4] Hundreds of novels were published during those years to describe the glorious battle for collectivation. Each of these novels would paint a picture of a village in which there was a struggle between reactionary

own characters. Yet these characters must be alive. To be alive for us they must fit into the situation with which we are familiar or can become familiar. If a novel creates utterly strange characters living in a world that is wholly unfamiliar to us and with which we cannot even become familiar, then such a novel impresses us as unreal and inauthentic. It must be possible for us to "live" in the world depicted by the novel or the play, to identify ourselves with its characters. Because we who have to do this are permeated with our real situation, there must be a bond between our real situation and that of the novel or the play. If such a bond does not exist at all, it will not be possible for us to enter into the described situation.

Accordingly, in all forms of free expression there remains a bond with the real world in which we live. We are able to and, of course, have to distinguish between our real situation and the fictitious situations. Nevertheless, the real situation remains, as it were, a kind of absolute reference point from which we cannot abstract. This real situation exercises also a normative function. Although the fictitious situation is not a pure portrayal of the real situation, it is nonetheless an expression of it. After living briefly in the fictitious situation, we are sometimes able to return to our real situation with our vision sharpened. We learn something about reality from the fictitious, even though we ourselves do not know how this happens.

For this reason the artist and the humorist sometimes have great influence upon real life. In their own ways they bring to

---

peasants, unwilling to give up their farms, and poor progressive peasants, who had found their way to the Party and wanted collectivation. In each of these novels, once the collective farm had been created, there would occur some difficulties in the beginning. Rains, floods, or drought would threaten the harvest, hidden saboteurs would cause damage; but the struggle would always be won under the guidance of a "positive hero," who would be a poor farmer, the manager of the collective farm, or better still the Party Secretary. The collective farm would grow prosperous and happy. As a grande finale a handsome, manly N.K.V.D. officer would appear on the scene and arrest the treacherous saboteurs, the despicable enemies of the people. Cf. Paloczi-Harcath, *The Writer and the Commissar,* London, n.d.

light aspects of reality which otherwise would perhaps have remained hidden. Men in high positions of government have reason sometimes to be afraid of the humorist and the novelist. In totalitarian states they therefore often feel obliged to lay down a political line to be followed in cultural productions. They want to make sure that the writer and the humorist are on their side.

It is possible for the philosopher to indicate that there exists a bond between the real situation and those which are created by the humorist and writer. This point is important for the topic which we are considering here. The word makes meaning become signification. In making meaning become signification, man sometimes enjoys a large amount of freedom. However, the fictitious signification remains connected with the meaning of life, and for this reason, in spite of all diversity, there is unity and interdependence in the field of significations. In this field there are no zones which are not related to one another either directly or indirectly. There is one absolute point of reference to which everything refers and upon which everything depends. On the other hand, the philosopher should beware of trying to indicate exactly in what way the fictitious situation is connected with reality. If he attempts to do so anyhow, there is great danger that he will fail to do justice to the creative power of man's free spirit.

At the beginning of this section we contrasted the freedom of the humorist and the litterateur with the restricting bonds imposed upon the man of science. We then noted that the freedom of the humorist and the litterateur does not mean that they are altogether without bonds, their freedom is not absolute. We must now see whether the restrictions imposed on the man of science imply that the latter has no freedom at all.

*Little Freedom in Systematized Science.* With respect to systematized science one is indeed struck by the fact that the human mind finds but little freedom of movement. One of the characteristics of science is precisely that it rigorously selects its terms and concepts. Its various statements, moreover, are interconnected in a strictly logical fashion. Any statement has to be justified either on the basis of previous statements or on that of rigidly controlled facts. This systematized science may be found in good textbooks, dissertations and scientific articles.

However, it would be wrong to pay attention only to the systematized form of science. For, the latter is constructed and written down only when the scientific research has been brought to a conclusion. The systematization no longer makes us witness how science grows and develops but rather confronts us with a picture of established science. It is, strictly speaking, a kind of succinct summary produced when a phase of development has reached a term. This summary proceeds in a strictly logical fashion and, as a rule, avoids all flights of creative imagination. Thus it seems that there is no freedom of movement but only necessity. The summary makes one think that man's thinking spirit can move only in one direction.

The history of the various sciences is often also presented in such a fashion. The growth and development of science are pictured as a rigidly logical pathway along which mankind's common thinking pursues its course. It is unfortunate that the acquaintance with science of students at our universities and other institutes of higher learning is largely limited to its systematized form.

*Freedom in the Scientific Search for New Understanding.* In real life, however, science does not grow and develop in that way. Logic with its rigid laws does not apply to science in the making but only to its subsequent systematized form. A new scientific insight does not arise by following the laws of logic. Its origin is not guided by the rigid coherence of terms and concepts. The importance of logic is often exaggerated in these matters. What happens then is that science is equated with its subsequent systematization: one observes there the presence of rigorous logicality and therefore claims that the life of science is dominated by this rigorous logic.

In reality, however, science grows only where the questioning mind enters a given field. The fundamental lines of this field are not yet clearly drawn, for otherwise scientific insight into the field would already exist and would not have to be sought. It is true, of course, that the questioning mind has already at its disposal a number of terms, concepts, and forms of thinking, or whatever other names one wants to give to the instruments used by the inquiring mind. However, in man's efforts to arrive at a new understanding even these terms and concepts often acquire new significations. When the human spirit really searches for a new insight, everything lies in a sphere of openness. The field of thought is open because the fundamental lines have still to be drawn. The available terms demand to be used in new shades of signification. Everything can get a new meaning, which, of course, is connected with the previously known meaning. The inquiring mind is often led here by intuition, although the latter usually arises from profound research and much reflection. In this intuition a certain fundamental line becomes visible. The thinker, however, does not yet know whether or not his intuition contains the solution of his problem. Wherever science is in the making, the human mind enjoys a real freedom of movement.

There is more than that, however. In his scientific inquiry the man of research bases himself, of course, on existing science. But when he raises questions that are really new and proceeds to draw new lines, that existing science loses its rigorous character and absolute necessity. The absolutely established character of that science reveals itself then to a certain extent to be merely appearance. Everything becomes open again for a new interpretation. It is an illusion to think that the achievements of science are firmly established in the sense that they are absolutely immutable and that new achievements will simply be added to the old ones. When a genuinely new insight is born, the so-called established ideas also acquire a new meaning. For this reason we must draw more attention to science in the making than to its established systems. The genuine content of the existing achievements manifest themselves in a new way in science in the making.

In these matters the layman often fosters illusions which are not shared by the men of scientific research themselves. The outsider often thinks that scientific concepts are immutably established and that scientific statements cannot be made in any other way than the way in which they are made. He believes that reality absolutely compels the man of science to say things as he actually says them. The man of science himself is aware of the fact that scientific statements are provisional and always open to amendment. He knows that the ultimate meaning of a statement is never fully established and that everything remains always open to a new interpretation. True, it happens occasionally that the man of science lapses into a false sense of self-assurance, but even then a genuine understanding of the character possessed by his statements ultimately regains the upper hand. Even in science there are creative geniuses, who not only discover something new but also give a new meaning to the previous achievements of science.

It is wrong, therefore, to think that the man of science is restricted in his speech in such a way that he enjoys no freedom whatsoever. If the man of science wants to think scientifically in the full sense of the term, he even has to proceed with a certain freedom. For he has to adopt a critical attitude toward what is handed on to him by the past. Without the help of the past he is unable to pursue any science, for no one of us can start wholly afresh in any field whatsoever. We always built on the past. However, what comes to us from the past is not all light but also darkness. Our task is to liberate this light from the elements of darkness, and this task demands a critical attitude. A great and creative mind will be critical of the thinkers who have preceded him. One cannot light a candle without removing the darkness that prevailed.

*The Necessitating Character of Science.* The objection could be raised that the man of science always feels himself forced to speak as he does by the object of his inquiry. Otherwise there would be no necessity in science; yet necessity seems to be a

97

fundamental characteristic of man's scientific pursuits. Kant has made this idea one of the starting points of his philosophical system.

It must be admitted that as soon as we transform meanings into significations through our speaking, these significations show themselves endowed with an inner logic. Once certain significations are given, we are no longer able to speak in all possible ways. It appears that once a field of significations is given, we simply are compelled to observe that a certain way of speaking is correct and another is false. There is truth and falsity in speech.

All this, however, is valid only once certain significations are given. The man of science is then compelled to speak in a certain way. However, he retains his freedom with respect to the factor which compels him, i.e., with respect to these significations themselves. In other words, he experiences necessity, but he enjoys a certain freedom with respect to that which imposes the necessity. History shows us many examples in which a complex of scientific judgments, judged to be necessary, later appeared to be not necessary because a certain contingency was discovered in the starting points of that complex. For instance, one who accepts certain mathematical axioms is compelled to speak in a certain way. For centuries everyone thought that certain mathematical axioms were to be accepted of necessity, or rather, no one could envision any other possible starting points. Later, however, the contingent character of these starting points was recognized. Euclidean geometry, which formerly was always held to be an absolute necessity, is now no longer regarded in the same way. To give another example, one who accepts the fundamental principles of Thomistic philosophy or of Kantian philosophy, is compelled to speak in a certain way. These fundamental principles themselves, however, can be subjected to a critical inquiry. Finally, anyone of the many psychological schools of thought that existed in the past took its starting point in certain fundamental ideas and from there arrived at a number of necessary statements. New schools which went into a different direction of inquiry did not deny that one who accepts the fundamental principles of the old schools would be compelled to arrive at certain judgments, but they attributed only a relative value to those fundamental principles.

*Meaning and Significations.* By speaking we make a meaning become a signification. This is the case also in science. Experience has shown that one and the same meaning can be made a signification in many different ways. Every scientific approach begins by establishing certain fundamental principles, whether the man of science is very much aware of it or not. A meaning does not absolutely compel us to form these particular fundamental principles, but allows a measure of freedom, of choice. Once, however, our choice is made, necessity reveals itself. Yet this necessity is always of a hypothetical character, i.e., once we have chosen certain fundamental principles, once we have drawn certain lines in the field of significations, then we are compelled to speak in a certain way. But one could also have drawn different fundamental lines. If we think that the object of our inquiry compels us to speak in a certain way, we forget that we ourselves have chosen to be compelled to speak in that way. The man of science himself also is active in the necessity he experiences in speaking in a certain way. He himself is partially responsible for that necessity.

All this does not at all imply a denial that there is truth. Once our project of certain significations is given, we have to speak in a certain way, some statements are then true while others are false. True is that which discloses meaning to us. True is that signification which really brings meaning to light for us. A false statement professes to bring meaning to light, but does not really do so. Truth, however, always comes into existence in a particular system of significations, and we are never compelled to project a particular system. This assertion does not mean that a system of significations is an arbitrary fiction. On the contrary, by letting the meaning become a signification, we bring it to light. The signification would not be a genuine signification if it did not bring a meaning to light. The same meaning, however, can become a signification in more than one way. A plurality of "truths," therefore, is possible.

*A Plurality of Fields of Truths.* This last statement should not be misunderstood. It does not mean that one could contradict oneself within the same system of significations, so that one statement could be both true and false within that system. Contradictory statements cannot be true at the same time. For example, it is not conceivable that the theologian would justly affirm the exisitence of God while the philosopher would be justified in rejecting that existence. But it is possible that there are different ways of throwing light on something which neither contradict nor affirm one another. It is possible for man to create two different systems of significations which, as it were, do not touch each other. In such a case both may be true, even though it may not be easy to find points of contact. Truth is the unveiling of meaning, or differently expressed, truth is the unveiling of being. Meaning lets itself be brought to light in different ways, and being allows itself to be unveiled in divergent fashions. It is an illusion to think that all the significations which man projects in his speaking have to belong to a single homogeneous field. All meaningful significations do not together constitute a single rational whole.[5]

Man is, as we have repeatedly said, meaning-giving existence. In his dealing with reality he makes reality be meaning, but in such a way that all giving of meaning is at the same time also an accepting of meaning. Our speaking is a mode of giving and accepting meaning. Through our speaking, meaning becomes

---

[5] According as we live in different circumstances and find ourselves in different fields, we assume a different attitude and speak a different language. If the President spends a quiet evening with a few intimate friends and is suddenly called upon by a government official to discuss an urgent question for a few minutes, he is compelled to assume an attitude in a different field. There is no question of contradiction but of a radically different perspective. Each perspective has its own significations, its own words, its own tone of voice. All of these together constitute a unity, just as our life is marked by unity. But the unity of our life is certainly not the unity of a rational synthesis.

signification. Meaning occurs in very many forms and this "pluri-formity" is present also in meaning as signified or signification. All meanings are connected, for every meaning is a meaning for the one human existence and belongs to one and the same world. This connectedness, however, does not imply that there is only one homogeneous field of meaning. In the same way there is not only one homogeneous field of significations. Consequently, there is not only one homogeneous field of truth.

Experience itself confirms this statement. If one would ask a number of prominent philosophers to write a book about the same topic, one would almost certainly receive a collection of the most divergent treatises. Yet we are dealing here with men who are all philosophers and all write the same language. However, each of them selects a different approach, because in his philo-sophical life each has developed his own field of significations. It could very well happen that all of them would speak the truth about the same subject matter, even though these various studies could not be united into a single whole. In the hypothesis of a single homogeneous field of truth, however, it should be possible to unite the truths contained in their studies into a single whole—more or less like the various parts of one jig-saw puzzle. But in practice that cannot be done. When a large congress is organized around a central topic, care is taken to divide this topic in such a way that the various introductions given by the many speakers illustrate different aspects of the same central topic and in this way present a unified whole. The organizers seem to be afraid that otherwise those introductions would repeat one another, so that there would be no variety in the unity. However, sufficient variation would certainly result if one and the same topic were simply assigned to a number of thinkers belonging to different trends of thought.

This very variety is what makes contact between human beings so interesting. If each one of us would simply possess little pieces of one and the same homogeneous field of truth, all of us together

101

would undoubtedly fit neatly together, but our encounter would not be very interesting.[6] We would simply find in the other something of ourselves. As it is, however, each one brings reality to light in his own way. Every man is a special way of throwing light upon the world. All of us are rooted in the same past, we live in a common tradition and for this reason we are able to understand one another. Nevertheless, when the other speaks, we encounter another way of throwing light upon reality. The other man is for us a revelation of the one-sidedness which characterizes our own existence.

*Truth, Freedom, and Tolerance.* Accordingly, there is much freedom even in the pursuit of science. Truth and freedom are not mutually exclusive.[7] They would exclude each other if truth were a purely objective datum, existing in a world that is independent of us, and if our knowledge would merely mirror this truth existing outside us. In that case truth would be imposed upon us from without and we would have no freedom whatsoever with respect to truth. Truth, however, comes into existence in part through us because we bring reality to light. Truth is one of the forms of meaning which we make be for us as giver and accepter of meaning. We are to a certain extent free with respect to the way in which we make being be truth, for we can bring being to light in many different ways. Truth is and remains truth, nonetheless, for what we bring to light is reality itself. Insofar as there is really question of genuine light, there is simply truth. This truth, however, is not a thing-in-itself, something that can be detached from the way in which we bring it

---

[6] "We find here a last and paradoxical definition of the condition which makes discourse with others possible. The condition of any discourse is that the other be concealed, that *the participants in the discourse be 'asymmetric.'*" J. H. van den Berg, "Het Gesprek," *Persoon en wereld,* 1953, p. 154.

[7] The compenetration of truth and freedom is emphasized by Martin Heidegger in his little work *On the Essence of Truth,* ed. in *Existence and Being,* intr. by Werner Brock, London, 1959, pp. 317–351. See also Albert Dondeyne, "Truth and Freedom," *Faith and the World,* Pittsburgh, 1963, pp. 168–194.

102

to light. As soon as this mode of bringing to light disappears, the truth in question disappears also.

All this is very important from the standpoint of tolerance.[8] The intolerant man is one who regards as good and true only his own way of existing, his own way of giving and taking meaning, his own way of drawing being from concealment. Because human beings live in groups, this absolutizing of the self usually assumes the form of an absolutizing of one's own group. This group is then made the possessor of absolute truth. The group is right and all other groups are absolutely wrong. The other groups have the truth insofar as they agree with one's own group and live in falsehood insofar as they disagree with this one group. Such a view thinks only in terms of truth and falsity, conceived in a fully homogeneous fashion. It disregards the "pluriform" character of truth, the difference in the way of throwing light on meaning.[9]

In spite of all differences, however, we are able to understand and enrich one another. This mutual enrichment does not mean that, as it were, pieces of ourselves and of the others are joined into a whole. Mutual enrichment means that all those involved become different. Rather than exchanging little fragments of truth, we exchange ways of looking at the truth. In this way we can develop and arrive at a single common way of looking at the truth. Yet, strange as it may seem, even then each one continues to have this common outlook in his own way. There is a common seeing of the truth, but in such a way that each of us possesses this view in his own fashion.

There is intolerance when one does not want to allow the others to be different, when one makes one's own way of existing

---

[8] Cf. Dondeyne, "The Positive Meaning of Tolerance," *op. cit.*, pp. 266–289.

[9] This point is important also for the ecumenical movement. Past ages regarded the difference between Christian denominations too much in terms of homogeneous truth and falsity. Our era begins to realize that the fundamental message of Christ can be regarded in different perspectives which do not always necessarily exclude one another.

or that of one's own group the absolute norm for all others. There are intolerant people in any society. The situation becomes dangerous when such people become the leaders of movements or political parties. The intolerant man is potentially a dictator. Sometimes the man who manages to impose his own way of being or his views on others is called a "strong personality." He is someone who does not want to let others enrich him but succeeds in imprinting his own stamp on them. If through the group of his adherents he is given a chance, he will compel the whole of a society to follow him. The intolerant man usually has a homogeneous concept of truth, and this concept is, strictly speaking, an expression of his tendency to absolutize himself. The intolerant man regards himself as truth personified in society.

Intolerance can be overcome only if individuals and groups learn to recognize the relativity of their own approach to truth. If intolerance is the absolutizing of the self, one becomes tolerant by relativizing the self. Tolerance does not mean that one wants to acknowledge as true everything which is put forward from every possible standpoint. It still recognizes the difference between truth and falsity; it does not demand that one always doubt the value of one's own insights and views. The tolerant man and the tolerant group, however, realize that they see things from a certain standpoint and approach them in a certain fashion, and they admit that other approaches are possible. Human truth is of such a nature that, on the one hand, it radically excludes its contradictory, but on the other, leaves room for an approach of a different kind. Once a particular approach is given, we sometimes have to speak in a particular way; but our approach remains one of many possible approaches.

In this section we have considered freedom and bonds in the field of significations. We concluded that there is always a bond but also always freedom, although the mutual relation of freedom and bond is not always the same. The presence of a bond is apparent from the fact that we can always exercise critique upon the way in which a man proceeds in the field of significations. In this respect it makes no difference whether this man speaks as a man of science, a poet, a novelist, or a humorist. Such a possibility of critique would be inconceivable if that man were entirely free, entirely without restraining bonds. Critique is possible only if man is at the same time both free and bound. In criticizing him we always ask whether he has spoken as he should have. Therefore, he must be free to speak in either this way or that way. At the same time, however, he must be bound by norms. How exactly freedom and bonds are related has not fully been answered in this section, which, we may add, did not intend to supply a complete study of that difficult question.

# CHAPTER FIVE

# The Power and Powerlessness of Speech

IT is difficult sometimes to know whether or not speaking is an important phenomenon. As we have seen in the preceding chapter, the freedom of movement which we have acquired in speech is sometimes exceedingly large. There is always much talk and sometimes we have the impression that most of it is rather meaningless. Modern technical inventions could help us to show how aimless and meaningless human speech often seems to be. If one were to place a hidden tape recorder underneath the counter of a barroom and later play it back before an audience consisting of the unsuspecting barroom guests, the latter would undoubtedly shake their heads in wonder over their own meaningless chatter. In a more serious vein, one who has to attend many meetings knows how much needless talk is produced at such gatherings. How many, even of the numerous lectures that college and university students have to follow, are really important? Briefly, one gets the impression that we live in a world of ceaseless chatter, in which only from time to time one can listen to a meaningful use of man's power of speech. Must we say, therefore, that speech is merely an unimportant accessory phenomenon in the margin of life? Is the "universe of discourse" an ethereal world bereft of solidity? Or is speech really a decisive aspect of life? In the following pages we will try to give a reply to these few questions.

## 1. THE SEEMING UNIMPORTANCE OF SPEECH

Let us begin by indicating the reasons why speech allegedly is merely an unimportant epiphenomenon of life. Our language contains many words connoting the unimportance of speech. We say that people chatter, prate and prattle, they gossip, gush and tattle, and when we proclaim that "silence is golden," we are not exactly underscoring the importance of speech. The motto of the State of Maryland, "Fatti maschii, parole femine," proclaiming that "deeds are masculine, words feminine," assigns the primacy to action rather than to speech. All this and many other similar examples would seem to indicate that speech is not as important as we have claimed it to be.

*Playful Misuse of Speech.* The preceding chapters contain points that can be used to confirm this seeming unimportance of speech. Speaking, we have said, transforms meaning into signification. While speaking, we no longer move simply in the real "lived" world of meaning but in the field of significations. This field is intended to be an expression of the real world of meaning, but there is no guarantee whatsoever that this intention will be realized. Our speech can fail to express the real world of meaning, and often we do not really worry very much whether or not the real meaning is done justice by our speaking. We often talk in a light vein and do not care about the real meaning. Sometimes we are inclined to joke about matters which deep down in our heart we nonetheless find important. We sometimes playfully misuse the broad margin of freedom which we have in the field of significations to represent important matters as unimportant and to make jokes about values which give fullness to our lives. It seems as if we try to find compensation in speech for the seriousness of real life. Examples are easy to find. Married men, wholly devoted to their wives and children, often talk banteringly about family life. They seem to seek a compensation for their serious devotion in light-hearted talk. Jokes about religious matters are most frequently heard among priests and ministers, who are *ex professo* deeply concerned with religion.

Moreover, it is very difficult to discover someone's real attitude in the course of a light-hearted conversation. The most astonishing standpoints are sometimes put forward in it. If people really thought what they say in such talks, if they really were what they seem to be during such conversations, the world would be one giant psychiatric institution. In other words, it seems that we should make a distinction between real life and our "talking life." In our talks we leave behind the world of reality and live for a brief moment playfully in an imaginary world. In that world of fancy we take liberties which we would indignantly reject in real life. For this reason we also laugh at someone who takes seriously whatever is said in a light-hearted conversation. There is a way of being serious which provokes laughter, for anyone is supposed to know the light-hearted banter which handles things, men and values in a joking fashion.

An objection that easily arises against the preceding paragraphs is that, although man delights in light-hearted conversation and wants to dwell playfully in its gay atmosphere, he also often speaks in a quite different way. In this different way of speaking, his speech is really important. However, even this objection is open to rebuttal. Meetings, for example, are usually conducted in great seriousness. Yet it is difficult to find elsewhere as much idle and empty talk as one can hear at certain meetings. In an appropriate lecture I have personally demonstrated once how a speaker can talk for fifteen minutes, using customary sentences of addressing a meeting, without really saying anything. When I ceased talking, the imaginary meeting had only started. Meetings can be utterly boring because they sometimes are entirely devoid of content. Doesn't this fact indicate that the world of speech is an empty world? Our newspapers appear daily and fill, day after day, many pages. It is hardly conceivable that they would be filled with really important matters. If one learns how to read a newspaper, he can really read it in about ten minutes. The world of speech appears to be almost empty.

*Ideological Hypocrisy of Speech.* According to Karl Marx, man is not what he claims to be. Marx, then, distinguishes between man's real being and its expression in words. He applies the same distinction to the life of the whole of society. One who wants to know what a society is should not listen to what that society says about itself. For there is no guarantee at all that its self-expression will coincide with its real being. The bourgeois society of the West in the second half of the nineteenth century regarded itself as very ethical,[1] but at the same time oppressed innumerable human beings by means of the structure of its process of production without suffering the slightest pangs of conscience. The bourgeois state claimed that it pursued the ideal of liberty, equality and fraternity, but in reality maintained and safeguarded through the use of force a social order in which harsh reality constituted precisely the opposite of that ideal. Such a way of speaking, which conceals rather than unveils reality, is sometimes called an "ideological" manner of speaking. Ideological speech calls a non-value a value and the ignoble noble. It conceals the true character of human beings and their actions under high-sounding names.

Speech, therefore, can be not only meaningless and empty but also deceptive. In politics one can observe its hypocritical character almost every day. A state which wants to violate its neighbor's boundaries begins by claiming that the enemy himself committed the first violations. Through such hypocritical claims the attacker hopes to succeed in making others accept that his action is pure self-defense. In such a case speech is even dangerous rather than unimportant. Respect for speech as the unconcealing of being seems to have disappeared in an alarming way.

*Deceptive Concealment of Truth.* Whether man's speaking is empty or dangerous, in either case we have to record that it is a deceptive screen concealing the truth of things from us. Speech

[1] Cf. Sartre, *Critique de la raison dialectique,* pp. 717 f.

109

allows man a margin of free movement, but this freedom seems to serve as a means to conceal reality. How then can one be expected to show respect for the world of speech? One could perhaps propose that a distinction be made between authentic, true speech and inauthentic, false speech. Although such a distinction may be acceptable in itself, it does not remove the great difficulty which we experience in discovering the few authentic true words among the many inauthentic and false or meaningless words. No matter how interesting man's speaking may be, it is usually empty, unimportant and deceptive. Even where people speak with the utmost seriousness, as in the lecture halls of a great university, their discourse is very often far from important. Students often complain that they are overloaded with intellectual ballast devoid of importance. It would be unreasonable simply to reject that complaint on the ground that they lack the power of discernment.

All these reasons, then, seem to militate against the alleged importance of speech.


## 2. Seriousness in Man's Playing with Words

*Playfulness and Seriousness.* It would hardly be possible to deny the facts recorded in the preceding section. However, these facts do not justify the conclusion that man's speaking is an unimportant or even dangerous playing with words.

We may begin by pointing out that man plays with everything, even with matters which he considers most serious, and that he becomes bored when he is denied the possibility to play. One can certainly not justify the claim that man does not take himself, his own body, seriously. Yet the body is man's instrument of play *par excellence.* Even the little child begins to play with its body, although it shows its uneasiness when this same body is in any way threatened by any danger. The adult also regularly plays with his body in many different ways. It suffices here to point to something which is a most serious affair for man

—his form of worship or liturgy, which contains numerous elements of play. Liturgy and folklore are closely connected.[2] One who regards life from a purely rational and utilitarian standpoint will be constantly annoyed by the fact that man is forever breaking through his rational and utilitarian frameworks.

Accordingly, the fact that man plays with speech is not at all an indication that speech is an unimportant epiphenomenon of real life with all its seriousness. People like to joke and to speak light-heartedly about many things. Yet one cannot fail to observe that precisely the persons and matters which are generally judged to be important are approached in such a fashion. Something which a group holds to be altogether unimportant does not offer enough interest to arouse its attention. Cartoons, for example, are made only of people who are regarded as important. Jokes center around topics of real interest. Many of them refer in one way or another to sexuality, its norms, and the relationship between man and wife. No one would claim that these matters are viewed as devoid of importance. It is also striking that jokes about norms of sexual behavior frequently originate in circles which are most concerned with the preservation of these norms. By listening to humorists and night club entertainers, one can deduce the matters judged to be really important in the lives of their audience.

The world of speech is full of exuberance. Man speaks far more than is really necessary. In his speaking he goes beyond the framework of the strictly rational, the sphere of the useful. Man's speech is playfully abundant. We may add that without that superfluity speech would be indigestible. If a speaker, introducing his audience to a certain topic, would say only the strictly necessary, if he would not repeat again in a different way something which he had already said, it would not be possible to listen to

---

[2] The renewal of the liturgy must be on guard against exaggerated rationalization. The celebration of the liturgy wants to place us in the presence of the mystery *par excellence,* and this intention can certainly not be realized in a rigidly rational fashion.

111

him. Precisely its playful abundance makes an address hold our attention and enables us to digest it.

*Group Conformity and Speech.* This playful abundance of speech should not induce us to think that man's speaking is nothing else but playfulness and superfluity. On the contrary, if we listen to the way in which a particular group speaks, we can clearly see certain fundamental lines in it. Certain things have to be said and others may not be said. To be acceptable to the group, one must stay within certain limits. Let us clarify this statement by indicating certain rules which have to be followed within the speaking community of the United States. With respect to Marxism, which is now a world-wide problem, one can now say that the Marxist viewpoint contains important perspectives, that no one can justify the complete rejection of everything Marxism stands for, and that Marxism deserves a serious study. Yet no one can say that Marxism is unqualifiedly a truth demonstrated by history and destined to be the ideology of the future. One who does it anyhow puts himself outside the American community. To give another example, anyone is permitted to make all kinds of jokes about democracy, yet no one may say that democracy is in principle a wrong form of government which should be replaced by a dictatorship. One who claims that Mussolini and Hitler embodied the ideal form of government puts himself outside the American community. Likewise, the spirit of rapprochement between the Christian Churches is commonly recognized as a valuable element; it is not fashionable to go against that spirit—to such an extent that even the P.O.A.U. organization has started to tone down its anti-Catholic utterances. It is acceptable now to be in favor of tolerance, and anyone who still defends the old forms of intolerance is considered to be out of harmony with our present society. Any plea in favor of South Africa's policy of *"apartheid"* is regarded as out of keeping with our common principles.

Within the American community there are, of course, many different groups. Each of these groups permits its members to

112

say certain things, but is adamantly opposed to others. One who addresses a campus fraternity and pleads for the restriction of its liberties will meet with a hostile reception; and one who tells the faculty that the independence of the individual professors goes beyond all bonds can hardly expect enthusiastic applause. Any religious group likewise sets limits to the freedom of speech of its members. One who wants to be accepted as a good Protestant or a good Catholic is expected to say certain things and to deny others.

On the other hand, any group allows its members to speak jokingly about all these matters. It permits humor, as long as this humor respects certain limits. Any community is at least obscurely aware of the fact that certain matters are of serious concern to it. By way of compensation, it allows this seriousness to be offset by humor as long as this humor does not deny the commonly accepted values. The members of a group do not mind it at all if their group is occasionally in a fitting way the object of a joke. They like to laugh from time to time even about themselves; they do not consider it inappropriate to take such a detached look at themselves from time to time. However, such humor may never go so far that it denies the essential values of the group.

In spite of all exuberance of speech, of all playfulness and humor, of the wide margin of freedom given to speech, there are always clearly discernible limits. The members of a community or group know these limits very well. We do not mean that they are always capable of indicating these limits in a theoretical fashion, but that they know them at least in practice. They have a feeling for what can or cannot be said. The more liberal members of the group will sometimes try to edge close to the border line. Yet they feel at once when they have gone too far and will then tactfully try to see to it that their remarks are not taken too seriously. One who goes beyond the limits is branded as dangerous or stupid. The others will avoid him, or at least see to it that he does not assume any responsible position within the group. Even if such people are not officially expelled from the group, there are all kinds of practical ways to isolate them in the group and thereby virtually expel them.

*Unofficial and Official Censorship.* Censorship is a well-known phenomenon. Some institutions control speech, especially in the form of the written word. Under a dictatorship censorship is a normal phenomenon, but it also occurs everywhere else in times of danger, for instance, during a war. In the Catholic Church censorship is a permanent institution with respect to certain types of publication. In addition to this official and institutionalized censorship, any society has a kind of unofficial censorship. It does not tolerate the expression of certain views. This unofficial censorship is not laid down in any law or formulated in any norms. Yet it exists and is very effective. One who violates the unofficial rules of this censorship places himself outside the community. If the community in question officially allows freedom of the press, there will always be some papers which disregard those rules. In that case the community will look upon those papers with suspicion and extend the same suspicion to anyone who subscribes to those papers. In some societies freedom of speech and of the press is officially formulated in their constitution, but in practice that freedom is nowhere without certain limitations.

Official censorship may be described as an institutionalization of unofficial censorship. It forbids what the large majority of the group regards as unacceptable. One may legitimately question, however, whether such an institutionalization is desirable. First of all, the idea of institutionalizing the previously existing unofficial censorship usually arises only when the latter proves to be no longer wholly effective, for one does not issue prohibitions in matters which hardly ever occur. However, when the rules of a group begin to be trespassed more or less frequently, this phenomenon generally indicates that the group has started to doubt its own self-imposed limits. The existing framework appears to be too restrictive and efforts are made to break this framework. At that junction censorship is sometimes institutionalized in order to protect the previously accepted limits, i.e., to safeguard the accepted way of speaking and to counteract changes in it. In other words, official censorship is usually conservative.

It is very much subject to doubt whether official censorship succeeds in its efforts. Sometimes it will produce just the opposite of what it intends. For it makes people more aware of the limits imposed on their speech and acts as a provocation upon their will to freedom, so that they will be more easily inclined to go beyond these limits. The result, therefore, will sometimes be that official censorship actually promotes what it intends to counteract. Institutionalized censorship may seem to be effective when it is supported by force and imposes heavy penalties on transgressors. Yet even this effectiveness is usually mere appearance, because it can touch only open speech and not "underground" ways of speaking. The result, therefore, is that there is considerable ferment below the placid surface of open and controlled speech. An example to the point is the rigid censorship which for many years prevailed in Russia under Stalin. When after his death this censorship was somewhat relaxed, pent-up forces broke loose in such an explosive fashion that Khrushchev himself became disturbed. This shows sufficiently that even a censorship which disposes of all possible means of control remained ineffective.

*The Origin of Unofficial Censorship.* However, we are not so much concerned with official censorship as with the unofficial, non-institutionalized form of censorship existing in every group or society. The latter appears to us to be a much more important phenomenon. How, we may ask, does such an unofficial censorship originate?

Man is an "ec-sistence"; his being is tied up with the world. We can live only in a humanized world, i.e., in a world adapted to ourselves. We develop ourselves by making the world our field of existence; our self-development is always a giving of meaning to the world. This giving of meaning takes place, as we have seen in the preceding chapter, on two levels, viz., by a real transformation of the world called "culture of work," and an intentional transformation called "culture of speech." The former

115

needs the latter, for we can work only in a world in which things are bearers of certain significations for us. We work in a world in which things are called by names. This statement applies not only to work itself but also to our ways of celebrating a feast and playing; in other words, it applies to activity in general. We live and work in a field of meaning, that is, in a field in which things have been given certain significations. They receive these significations when we assign a name to them. As we have said before, our reworking and naming of things exercise interaction. There is no need to develop this point here again.

Our life runs its course in a field of significations. In many respects, therefore, this field is important for us. We are able to work, play, celebrate and act only in a world that is full of significations. Such a world is familiar to us. If the field of significations were lost, we would be deprived of our familiar world.

As we have pointed out repeatedly in the preceding chapters, meaning and signification do not coincide. In many cases a meaning exists already for us before being spoken, before becoming a signification. While this is true, it is true also that by becoming a signification, by being given a name, a meaning becomes more familiar to us. Materially speaking, meaning and signification are not different, for the signification is the meaning as it begins to exist for us in a new way. The signification, as it were, fixes the meaning for us and makes it accessible to us in a new way. In this sense we may say that our life and our work run their course in a "universe of discourse," in a "spoken world," in a world in which things have names. The meaning does not originate solely through speech; yet it is true that speaking gives a meaning a clarity and accessibility which previously it did not have. The "spoken world" is the world that has reached clarity and has become accessible. By speaking, we are able to exchange ideas about meaning[3] and arrive at mutual collaboration. We assign names

---

[3] "By speaking we change the empirical being into an ideal being and consequently into a general being." Jean Wahl, *Traité de la métaphysique*, Paris, 1953, p. 510.

to the possibilities which the world offers us and to the dangers threatening us from that world. In this way we are better able to utilize these possibilities and to overcome these dangers. Dangers that cannot yet be named seem more fearful to us. Assigning a name to them is the first step toward overcoming them. In a word, our speaking gives rise to a familiar world, a world in which we feel at home.

We must add that our speaking about the world goes far beyond the radius of our action. By speaking about the world, we form a comprehensive image of our entire field of existence. It would be wrong to think that such a comprehensive picture arises only in philosophy, for man began to philosophize only at a late stage in his development, but long before that stage was reached he was already in possession of such a comprehensive view. Even the most primitive myths show traces of it. Although it is difficult to penetrate into the views held by primitive peoples, in one way or another a comprehensive view always appears to be present. This view seeks to provide a reply to the fundamental problems of life, especially the mysteries of birth, illness and death. Primitive tribes often have the strangest customs, yet most of the time these customs appear to have a meaning within the world view of such tribes. In more developed nations the comprehensive picture assumes a more developed form, such as that of a philosophy or of a more advanced religion. Man needs a humanized world, not only because he has to adapt the world to his material necessities, but also because he needs a familiar whole. He makes the whole familiar by giving it a name. In this sense naming the world is mastering the world, not as if the world becomes wholly a part of the field controlled by man's power but because it becomes at least a familiar whole for man.

The term "familiar world" is extremely ambiguous but it has a very pregnant signification. We become familiar *par excellence* with the world by knowing how to name that which it contains, its powers and secrets. Looking for clarity about ourselves, we can attain that goal only by becoming familiar with our world. For

117

this reason we give names to things. The life of a group or community is wholly permeated with the names which it has given to things. The "spoken world" is our field of existence. By losing this world, we lose our field of existence.

Any community or group wants to safeguard its familiar world and for this reason is attached to the way in which it speaks about its world. It feels ill at ease when the trusted names disappear because their disappearance is experienced as the loss of its familiar world itself. Man's tendency to self-preservation protects the group's common way of speaking. It is not difficult to find examples confirming these assertions.

When, for example, Christianity penetrated into the Roman Empire, it was regarded as a threat to the familiar way of speaking, to the names which the Romans had assigned to the forces and secrets of the world. Roman thought had shown itself capable of integrating many different ways of speaking, for it was characterized by great openness. However, the new Christian way of speaking did not harmonize with the Romans' "spoken world." Christianity attacked the fundamental features of the Roman world view. It refused to be integrated in the accepted way of speaking about the world. As soon as this feature of the Christian image of the world became known, persecutions began. The latter did not arise from a tendency to be cruel toward a certain group, at least not in the beginning. They originated in the instinct of self-preservation. The Romans experienced Christianity as a threat to the familiar world with which the very existence of the Roman Empire was intimately connected. Those persecutions constituted a desperate battle for the preservation of that trusted old world and, therefore, so it seemed to the Romans, for the safety of Rome itself.[4]

Most other persecutions must be explained in a similar way.

---

[4] In the first books of his *de Civitate Dei*, St. Augustine defends Christianity against the accusation of having caused the decline of Rome. These accusations clearly show that in the eyes of many the former views of life and the world, inclusive of religion, constituted an integral part of the Roman Empire.

They are a battle for the familiar world, the familiar field of meaning, with which the existence of a group is connected. To quote an example from our own time, the communist state does not permit any way of speaking which attacks the fundamental lines of the communist world picture. In this picture also things are given a name and with these names the whole mode of existence in the communist world is interwoven. The names assigned to things are stubbornly defended simply because the communists want to defend their own way of existence. The "American way of life," likewise is interwoven with a "universe of discourse," a way of speaking about life and the world. Unsurprisingly, therefore, Americans also tenaciously defend their way of speaking.

*The Conservative Power of Common Speech.* The field of meaning proper to a group or community is constituted by the group's common way of speaking. Most people do not realize this, at least not clearly. They consider the field of meaning in which their life runs its course so obvious and natural that they are inclined to regard speech as a simple accessory reference to that field. They think that they speak as they do because the field of meaning is what it is, i.e., the objective reality of the field compels them to speak in this or that way. They project the common field of meaning as an objective datum, as reality without any qualifications. One who deviates from the common way of speaking is regarded not so much as unfaithful to the accepted way of speaking than as a fool who is blind to reality. Man is inclined to take the result of common speech for granted and to forget that it is a result of speech.

In this way common speech becomes a conservative power. It creates many means to protect itself. A group or society does not permit anyone to go beyond the fundamental lines laid down by common speech. If the group in question is a religious society, it has a very special way of fixing its common way of speaking. For such a group will very easily regard its way of speaking as a divine revelation. As a consequence, deviations are

119

no longer merely stupid because they are out of harmony with so-called objective reality, but they are also illicit because they do violence to the divinity. If the way of speaking accepted in a society receives such a religious sanction, it becomes even more consistent and firm, so that it is very difficult to break its bonds.

Common speech is a power over the world of meaning, the field of significations, in which a society dwells. We do not want to say, of course, that the common way of speaking is wholly arbitrary. As we have repeatedly emphasized, our existence is both a giving of meaning and a taking of meaning. The common way of speaking is both constitutive and unveiling with respect to meaning and signification. It makes them be and it makes them appear. It is founded in that which is made a topic of speech and at the same time gives it consistency. As Heidegger correctly says, speech is the "dwelling of being," by which he means that the being of reality shines through our speech. Man constantly endeavors to correct his own speaking. These very efforts reveal his desire to make his speech be an authentic unveiling of being. Man wants to remove the subjective elements from his speech to make it bring reality more and more to light. Anyone who would deny that our speaking accepts meaning would do violence to its inmost nature, its most profound intention. Yet this aspect of accepting meaning can never be separated from that of giving meaning. We want to emphasize the latter here because it is most easily forgotten. Man is very much inclined to disregard the fact that common speech is also constituent of meaning.

*Common Speech and Human Values.* In this connection it is important to draw attention to the values accepted in a particular group or community. Any group believes in certain values. A life without values is meaningless. Our life is an endeavor to realize our values. A society considers persons prominent if they personify its recognized values. Sometimes such a personification is authentic, sometimes it is inauthentic, for there always are people who pretend to personify common values while they merely impersonate them. Here lies the core of pharisaism, which is a permanent phenomenon in society. A pharisaical person is one who acts as if he is the very embodiment of the values recognized by a society without, however, really making them his own. In his external conduct he is what society would want him to be, but his innermost being does not harmonize with his external behavior. He merely pretends to be what he is not. There are pharisees in religious communities but also in political groups. Communist lands have them also, and there they pretend to be perfect examples of the party line.

Values also acquire their consistency through the common way of speaking of a group. If all members of a group say that something is a value, it becomes a value. Reversely, something becomes a non-value if all of us in our speaking present it as lacking value. Common speech is a power over values. One becomes aware of this by paying attention to closed groups, such as religious orders. Among the older orders, such as the Benedictines, the Carthusians and the Trappists to name only a few, there exists a very striking affirmation of values. Certain things are most emphatically called values and others are rejected as non-values with equal emphasis. A complex of customs and regulations is connected with this affirmation and negation of values in such a way that they become a way of life. This way of life produces a distinct type of human being. Their way of life is inseparably connected with a common way of speaking—even if the group rejects certain forms of speaking because they regard silence as a value.

We do not want to claim that such an affirmation of values is without foundation, for here also man's giving of meaning is at the same time an accepting of meaning. However, we want to observe that these remarkable worlds of values have their source also in a common way of speaking and that they are preserved through this common speech. As soon as this way of speaking suffers damage, the world of values is affected. In such groups every effort will be made to safeguard the common way of speaking. Anyone who deviates from it is easily regarded as a

121

dangerous man and faces ostracism. Because every man wants to be accepted by his group, he is afraid to go against it, and for this reason finds it difficult to deviate from the common way of speaking.

*There is No Escape from the Power of Common Speech.* In the first section of this chapter we have pointed to the freedom, the playful character of speech. When we observe speech, we sometimes have the impression that man's talking is idle and harmless. There is so much talk that we do not have to take it seriously. Man is able to laugh at himself, to make himself the butt of his humor. It would be wrong, however, to exaggerate this aspect of speech. Our freedom of speech has certain limits, limits that are even rigidly fixed. Not even playful humor has an unlimited margin of freedom. Any genuine group or community is characterized by a common way of speaking, and in this way of speaking sketches a common field of meanings, a common world of values. The group does not permit its members to disregard this common world of values in their speech. Anyone who violates this norm places himself outside the group. The common way of speaking is power over meaning, power over values. Every man is subject to this power.

No one can ever liberate himself from the power of common speech. One may, of course, reject a certain form of speaking, but in that case, one will replace that form by a new form. The nineteenth century saw the rise of a group which in a very striking way broke away from the accepted form of common speech. This group is called the Marxists. It broke with the current philosophical way of speaking, with the religious way of speaking, with everything which Marx referred to as the bourgeois ideology. The Marxist way of speaking was so radically new that for a long time it remained unintelligible to many. Marxism was a real break-away from the accepted common way of speaking. However, this same group gave rise to a new common way of speaking, more striking perhaps than the common speech from which it broke away but at the same time also more tyrannically enforced than the tyranny of speech against which it revolted.

To give another example, any renewal in science always implies that one goes counter to the previously accepted way of speaking scientifically. At the same time, however, this renewal leads to a new school of thought which is characterized by a common way of speaking. Man is inevitably a member of a group, a member of a society, and the latter cannot exist without a common form of speech, a common affirmation of values. No one of us is able to develop a field of meaning entirely on his own, yet we experience a need for a world of meaning. We cannot escape from living in the world of meaning pertaining to the society to which we belong.

Modern thinkers often exhort us to think for ourselves, to exist in our own personal way, to affirm our own personal values. One could hardly object to such an exhortation. Personal thinking, however, cannot imply that we have to live as a kind of Robinson Crusoe in the world of meaning, the world of values. The individual cannot begin afresh to construct a world of meanings for himself in an entirely autonomous way. He is destined to live in a common inherited world. Common speech is contingent in many ways. It is at the same time a giving of meaning and an accepting of meaning, and there is no guarantee that these two aspects will be present in a healthy proportion. Any common way of speaking is always such that it contains unwarranted affirmations. By dwelling in commonly accepted speech, we run the risk of accepting these unwarranted affirmations. If we critically examine each of the "obviously evident" positions which we hold, we will realize how often we affirm them as members of a group and not solely on the basis of our own insights. We always affirm more than we really see. However, it is impossible for us to live in any other way. Life is risky in this respect also.

Let us repeat, however, that life without this risk is altogether impossible for us. One who wants to avoid this risk would have to return to an impossible level of primitiveness and would not be able to attain to anything in the sphere of a genuinely human existence.

## 3. Our Realization of Contingency

Contemporary man lives in a very paradoxical situation. It is typical of our era that formerly closed groups are broken open because we are living in a time possessing entirely new forms of communication. We are beginning to live and partially even think in terms of the whole world. Printing presses make it possible for us to become acquainted with all possible points of view expressed in books, which are produced so inexpensively that they are within the economic reach of the masses. Through radio and television we learn what is happening in the world and we become acquainted with groups and societies which formerly were unknown to us. We continue to live in our own group, our own community, but we are in it now in a new way because we now look also beyond its boundaries. We still accept what is "obviously evident" in our group, but its evidences have become less obvious to us now. We live in our group in such a way that we know at the same time its contingency.[5]

*The Relationship Between the Closed Character of the Group and the Firmness of Group Opinion.* To understand this contemporary phenomenon properly, we must make a distinction between the firmness of the group opinion as such and the firmness with which individual persons posit their viewpoint (which is nearly always a group viewpoint). The psychological dispositions of certain persons sometimes leads them to posit their views most apodictically. It is quite possible that they will frequently change their views in the course of their life; nevertheless, whatever viewpoint they hold, they will always put it forward in the most decisive fashion. One is occasionally surprised by the self-assurance of such people, the unwavering certainty with which they

---

[5] Man's awareness of this contingency is the fundamental idea pursued in the works of Merleau-Ponty.

defend doubtful standpoints. This kind of people has always existed and, no doubt, will be with us forever. Their existence and the way in which they speak does not determine the firmness of the group opinion, but should be explained on the basis of their individual psychological dispositions. The firmness of the group opinion belongs to a different category and points to the existence of a number of commonly accepted "obviously evident" positions which together are understood as a kind of "natural" world. The members of the group think that the things themselves are as they think. As we have indicated, this phenomenon should be explained in part on the basis of the group's common way of speaking.

The firmness of the group opinion which knows no doubt presupposes the closed character of this group. As soon as different groups come into intense contact, become acquainted with one another's opinions, and study the other's publications, the firmness of the group opinion becomes generally less. In our contemporary world with its wide range and intensity of communication, group opinions clearly show the expected tendency to become less firm.

A clear example to the point is provided by the various religious denominations. In former times religious groups were largely closed off from contact with outsiders. The little contact that existed was mostly a matter of mutual antagonism. These groups, even if they existed within the same general social framework or state, did not really share a common life. Before the rise of large cities, most people lived in villages and small towns; and even in the cities, sections existed which were almost exclusively populated by people of the same ethnic and religious background. According as they were settled by immigrants from Protestant or Catholic countries, these rural towns retained to a large extent the configuration which prevailed in the immigrants' homeland. They had little contact with outsiders, whom they referred to as "foreigners." Even in the cities, the immigrant groups would cling together as little "Italies," "Warsaws," "Germantowns," or "Dublins," and make little contact with others. The leaders of the various groups had, of course, often more contacts with others, but they came from these groups and largely shared their mentality. Each of these closed groups had its own complex of certainties and things that were self-evident and interwoven with the practical life of the group.

All this is greatly changed now. Urbanization and increased "Americanization" of the city groups has made social contact with others a normal phenomenon. Catholics, Protestants and Jews, regardless of their ethnic origins, work together at the development of a common way of life. Radio and television bring Catholic religious services into the homes of non-Catholics, and vice versa. Formerly closed groups have become aware of the world at large; antagonistic religious groups are discovering the growing menace of atheism and realize to what extent their members are really fighting for the same values. Their mutual antagonism is slowly disappearing. People, moreover, read more than formerly and find it impossible to limit themselves to books produced by members of their own group. At the same time leaders in the various denominational groups are making contact with one another on the level of theology as well as that of other realms. One could raise the question of what came first: contact on the theological level or contact in practical matters? I would not dare to give an apodictic reply to that question, but suspect that practical contacts have preceded the present theological rapprochement.[6]

*The Resulting Loss of Group Certainties.* The result of these increased contacts is that the group's own unquestionably accepted positions have been undermined. For one can accept such positions of one's own group with full conviction only if one rejects the unquestionably accepted positions of the other groups

---

[6] This suspicion is confirmed by the fact that the younger generation is not inclined to accept the existing division as permanent and finds it difficult to understand why that division is supposed to be justified. This new generation is certainly not so much motivated by theoretical considerations as by a more or less conscious feeling that the old division does not harmonize with the new situation.

in an equally absolute fashion. Contemporary man is no longer able to do that. He does not cease to belong to his own group and, generally speaking, remains faithful to the practices of this group. However, he is no longer ready to swear by those unquestionable positions. He attributes a more relative value to the differences between groups, and this relativation implies a diminution of his certainty with respect to his own standpoint.

This process has probably gone much farther than is currently realized. In countries where Protestants and Catholics have frequent contacts one can often hear "ordinary" people ask themselves whether there really is so much difference between the two groups. The same phenomenon occurs where two different Protestant groups have been in mutual contact for some time. As we have mentioned above, the rapprochement on the practical level probably precedes the theological exchange of ideas. Pursuing the same line, we may now add that the desired unity will probably likewise be born on the practical level. If we have to wait until the theologians have finished their discussions, we would probably still have to wait a very long time.

What, then, one may ask, do the theologians do in this matter? The reply is that they interpret the standpoint of the group on a scholarly level. They determine what this standpoint is, they embody the firmness with which the group adheres to its position and opposition. In this task the theologians depend on the certainty with which the group holds on to its convictions. The theoretical certainty of the theologians is rooted in the group's security of existence. If this security diminishes, the theologians will begin to speak with less theoretical apodicticity. In a certain sense they feel that their foundation is sinking away. When the practical rapprochement of different groups makes progress, the theoretical oppositions are no longer taken as seriously as before or they are even no longer tolerated. In other words, the practical rapprochement forces the theorists to find a similar rapprochement on the theoretical level. A very remarkable process is taking place in this matter. Oppositions which in the course of

127

centuries had become very sharp are now becoming much less on the practical level, and the theoretical level is beginning to take steps toward the removal of these oppositions from the world of thought.

All this can easily be understood in the light of the preceding considerations. The common field of meaning, the common world of significations, originates, as we have said, in part from the group's common way of speaking. The isolation of groups presupposes the isolation of speaking communities. But this latter isolation is beginning to disappear. We are becoming familiar with the way of speaking proper to the other groups and through many encounters build and develop a common language. The result is that the separate group convictions begin to weaken. Their members realize that the former oppositions were merely something contingent to which people incorrectly attributed a necessary character.

Quite a few people are terrified by this phenomenon. They have a feeling that the solid rock on which they thought they had laid the foundations of their beliefs is sinking away. That which they always regarded as part and parcel of their faith now becomes subject to doubt. The realization that the world of meaning with which their existence is interwoven has a contingent character affects them painfully. They feel more or less lost.

We have stated above that the opposition between the various views of life and the world begins to become less strong. This weakening process is possible only because the rigid lines of these world views are becoming more or less vague. This process is undoubtedly connected also with the contemporary dialogue between science and man's view of life. For the world of meaning arises in part from our common way of speaking, and at present, speech from the view point of science and speech from the standpoint of world view increasingly permeate each other. In this connection it will be useful to devote a few words to a remarkable development which has taken place during the past centuries.

128

*Phases in the Relationship Between World View and Science.*
Roughly speaking, we can distinguish three phases in this relationship. In the first phase man's scientific speaking about reality
was controlled by his world view. During the Middle Ages, the
sciences, to the extent that there was question of them, were integrated into, and controlled by philosophy. Metaphysics was
"the queen of the sciences." The same idea can be clearly seen
even in Descartes' *Discourse on Method.* He says that philosophy
is in a state of confusion and that the sciences, since they borrow
their principles from philosophy, are therefore also in the same
state of confusion. Philosophy itself was controlled by theology.
In this way speech inspired by world views exercised control over
scientific speech. Those who pursued science could count on
being taken to task if in the opinion of the theologians they
went too far.

In the second phase the sciences gained their independence and
escaped from the control exercised by the world view personified
in the theologian. The latter found it difficult to resign himself
to this fate. This phase therefore is marked by opposition and
conflict between science and world view. We must add that the
sciences themselves sometimes added fuel to the fire by presenting themselves as a new world view; in other words, they went
beyond the limits of their own competency. During this phase
suspect scientific statements were usually countered by theological arguments. It is sufficient to refer here to the reactions against
Darwin's theory of evolution. This period ended only in recent
times, and many of us have received part of our education under
the ideas prevalent in that stage.

In the third phase, the one we are living in now, the sciences
have given up their claim to be a new world view. They have discovered their own limitations and come to realize that they cannot give answers to the most fundamenal questions regarding
life and the world. The world views, on the other hand, have
given up their antagonism against science and realize that they
have to revise their standpoint with respect to many issues in the

light of scientific discoveries. They are aware now that a world view is in some respects a remarkable mixture of profound visions and primitive views. As we have stated before, man always wants to form a total picture of reality. Such a picture was presented by the various world views. But many primitive ideas played a role in that comprehensive view of reality. Today's world views are willing to revise themselves in a living dialogue with science.

*The Contemporary Dialogue Between World View and Science.* It is not difficult to present examples of the dialogue which is now going on between world view and science. The Old Testament gives us a description of the creation of the world. Its creation is situated in time and described in a rather concrete way. In the past, Christians regarded the way in which creation was described there as part of God's revelation and, therefore, sometimes protested against the findings of science as contrary to revelation. At present, if we abstract from the so-called "fundamentalists," Christians no longer have any difficulty if creation is pushed back several hundred million years, and they are ready to go even further if scientific discoveries would demand it.

In the name of the Bible's story of creation Christians used to oppose the theory of evolution. Now, however, they are ready to accept that theory. Theologians thought and often continue to think that theological truth forces them to admit the descent of all human beings from a single couple. At present, however, there are clear signs of hesitations in this affirmation.

The theologian likewise used to make a sharp distinction between body and soul and often thought in a strongly dualistic way. Modern science does not deny man's "spirit," but it has discovered that the whole of the "life of the spirit" is rooted in man's bodily being.

Our world view no longer opposes such scientific findings, but is willing to revise itself in the light of these discoveries. We now witness the fact that the various world views are undergoing an imposing self-revision. Their adherents claim that these corrections are not concerned with the essence of the religious truths in question. While we do not want to dispute that claim, we wish to observe that the corrections nonetheless are important—so important even that some people become disturbed and anxiously ask themselves what still remains standing of all their previous certainties. This question is often raised today. All we want to say about it here is that the world views are liberating themselves of primitive elements.[7]

*Awareness of Contingency.* All this implies that our way of speaking from the standpoint of our world view has discovered its own contingency in many points. So many changes happen in rapid succession that one cannot escape noticing this contingency. Moreover, the limited horizons of the vision contained in the comprehensive picture of man and the world are disrupted in many points. The creation of the world is pushed back from a few thousand years ago to an unimaginably distant past. God's providence is now conceived in such a way that it leaves room for the immanent laws of history, and these laws are many and far-reaching. God, who has also created man, be it by way of evolution, has made him in such a way that within his being-man there is room for an imposing process of humanization. We now know a little about the distance separating our existence from that of the primitive and we know also how much we owe to the common development of mankind. We find it increasingly difficult to speak of a human "nature" and of a "natural law." Although the religious man does not give up religious truths, the latter no longer constitute a closed and easily grasped total picture of the world and of life. The small and familiar universe is definitely past. We now know that our existence extends to distant dimensions with which we are not familiar at all. We

---

[7] Many appear to be afraid that absolute truth is rendered relative in this process of relativation. Undoubtedly, there is a danger that the absolute itself would be made relative. However, in the past the relative has often been absolutized with frightening recklessness. The present anxiety is in part the result of past mistakes. In the past we have often created false certainties, so that now we have to resign ourselves to see these certainties disappear. This disappearance may even be regarded as a liberation.

know better than ever before how fundamentally contingent man is.

In former ages the accepted common way of speaking offered a field of meaning which man could easily understand. This is no longer the case now. Common speech has ceased to offer us a little world with which we are well acquainted.[8] It now opens a perspective upon awe-inspiring distances. We know less about God, the soul and heaven, the origin of man and his destiny. Many people continue to believe, but the faith of these believers has undergone a change. This change contributed to the disappearance of the former sharp differences between world views. For all of us are now convinced that we know far less than our ancestors thought they knew. The latter often opposed one another on the basis of their supposed knowledge, they relied too much on an overestimation of their knowledge.

We experience the powerlessness of our speech. In former times the common way of speaking offered man a familiar field of meaning, but our speech is no longer able to do so. We discover the powerlessness of speech, precisely at a time when our speech is more powerful than ever. We discover what the real possibilities are which our speaking contains and find that these possibilities are limited. This discovery has caused great anxiety to many because they cannot bear to look at their own contingency.

## 4. THE PARADOXES OF MAN'S SPEECH

*Importance and Unimportance.* The paradoxical character of speech should be evident from the preceding sections of this chapter. It would be difficult to indicate anything in man's exist-

---

[8] Because our horizons have expanded, we must now live in greater dimensions. There is a form of security which is being lost and has to be lost. Many people are scared by the dimensions which unfold themselves for their existence. This anxiety, however, is one of the phenomena accompanying the birth of a new kind of man.

ence that is as unsubstantial, as volatile, as the speaking of man. Nothing else is handled as playfully by man as his words. Nevertheless, the common way of speaking really establishes the common world of meaning; it gives rise to the common values, and draws the fundamental lines in the field of existence. No matter how volatile and playful speech may appear to be, it is power over meaning. One who would control man's speech would have control also over the human world of meaning. For this reason dictators try to exercise control over man's speech.

The name given to things seems to be devoid of importance, for, after all, "what is in a name?" Nevertheless, the name given to things fixes their meaning and their signification. By having a name, a thing has a place in the human field of significations, it occupies a position in the human world of meaning. As soon as man assigns a name to something, he has situated it. To name things is to control them.

Man experiences the importance of naming when he becomes its object in a disagreeable fashion. When he is generally spoken of as unreliable or despicable, he really becomes unreliable or despicable within the community of speech which designates him in this way. Once a community's speaking turns against someone, his life can become very difficult and even impossible. For this reason those who want to get rid of certain elements in a society will first try to make this society look down upon them and speak about them as unworthy and despicable. Once this purpose is accomplished, they will be able to do with those people whatever they want. Our own time has given numerous examples of such procedures.

*Activity and Passivity.* As in many other aspects of life, we are both active and passive in this matter. We are active because we take part in common speech and therefore co-determine the common field of meaning. Not all of us are equally active; a famous writer, for example, is more active than an unknown member of society. Yet everyone is active to a certain extent, for he contributes to the way in which people speak about things in his area of contact with others. At the same time, however, we are also passive, for we find and take over the language which we speak as well as a world in which things are already called and spoken about in a certain way.

*The Power of Language over Man and Man's Control over Language.* To a large extent man is made by the language which he speaks. Our existence is interwoven with the field of meaning in which we dwell, and this field is connected with the language we speak. Although we make this language our own, we have not created it.

We often speak of someone's mastery of a language. The expression is correct, for language is an instrument serving us. We master a language. Nevertheless, one could and even should also say that language has power over us. In our infancy we enter, as it were, into the language spoken by those around us; we find and take over this language together with its structure. Language, as we have said repeatedly, brings reality to light, so that any given language is connected with a given world of significations. By taking over a pre-given language, we accept also its world of significations. It is simply impossible for us to master a language without being at the same time controlled by it.[9] We give form to our language, but at the same time this language forms us.

One could raise the objection that we seem to give language an autonomous existence and present it as if it were a reality capable of acting in its own right. But language does not exist and act in that way; it exists only in the speaking of man. In reply, we admit, of course, that language does not exist as an autonomous thing or person. Nonetheless, it exists in reality, in such a way even that it transcends us in all directions. It exists as the common treasure of a speaking community. We take over this treasure and make it our own, but in such a way that at the same time the wealth of language exercises its formative power over us. The riches of a language greatly transcend us. Not even the greatest genius would be able to seize all the wealth hidden in

---

[9] Cf. Sartre, *Critique de la raison dialectique,* pp. 75 f.

134

the English language. In the course of his life man constantly discovers new aspects of the treasures contained in his language.

Frequently efforts are made to arrive at complete control over the wealth of language. These efforts want to make it possible to speak in a wholly critical fashion and not to say anything which is not understood in all its fullness. This attempted critique is not at all a senseless undertaking, for without critique no science is possible. On the other hand, however, total critique is altogether impossible. For in the very act of criticizing we have to make use of our language itself and this language contains all kinds of unquestionably accepted aspects which have not originated in us. A total reflection upon language is excluded because in our act of reflection we have to make use of language itself. For this reason we can never make language wholly an object because in its objectification we have to make use of it. Language always appears to stand on the side of the subject. No matter how much we try to master language actively, we never escape from being dominated by it. We live in a world in which things are known by names and terms which we ourselves have not chosen. If we had to begin afresh with the naming of everything, we would have to travel the entire long road from a state of utter primitiveness to civilized existence.

*Our Power and Powerlessness over Speech.* Common speech, we have said, is great wealth. It is a precious possession, for by means of it we possess a field of meaning, a world of significations, a field of existence with which we are familiar and in which we can live. Nothing, however, is entirely meaningful in our human world. In everything presenting itself as meaningful to us we also find meaninglessness.

In our speaking with one another, we give names not only to things but also to one another. Our common way of speaking sometimes puts groups of people in a difficult position or even in a situation unworthy of man. Entire nations or ethnic groups are sometimes called inferior and, by the very fact that everyone calls them inferior, they are made to be inferior. Our speaking, as we have said repeatedly, gives meaning; within our human world it gives shape and form to reality. If we officially brand human beings criminals, they bear this mark forever. Sometimes, when a person has been caught a single time in an act of dishonesty, we call him untrustworthy and, because we continue to call him untrustworthy, society continues to regard him as such. Once people living in certain parts of a city have been called asocial, they continue to be regarded as asocial. It is quite possible that they will adapt themselves to the name given to them, to what we expect of them. Common speech can be very cruel and unjust.

The common way of speaking constitutes our human world. It appears very difficult to escape from its influence, especially when the official policy of a country sanctions that way of speaking. In Nazi Germany, for instance, it required heroic courage to call the Jews human beings of equal value as Arians. In the States one cannot call any individual communist a trustworthy human being. It would be considered out of tone to say anything in favor of Castro. Shortly after World War II, public opinion would not have tolerated anyone pleading for leniency for war criminals. Life is difficult for anyone who has the misfortune of being a born homosexual and who is known as such.

All these examples show how we give names to one another through our common way of speaking. These names are often as difficult to remove as the brand marks which in former ages were burnt into the living flesh. Sartre's statement that it is not possible to keep our hands clean in a dirty world applies also to the realm of our speech. Our speaking cannot be lily white in a world whose speech is tainted. This, too, shows how powerless we are with all our power over speech. Man's speaking is indeed a paradoxical reality.

# CHAPTER SIX

# The Speaking Person

IN the preceding chapter we have seen that the person depends upon the common speech of his group and that, in general, he moves within the limits laid down by this way of speaking. His community exercises a kind of censorship over his speech. We have seen also that the speaking man is both the master of his language and controlled by it. Thus the question arises whether and to what extent man's speaking has a personal character. Our era emphasizes the personal character of man's existence and demands that he assume an attitude based upon personal thinking. Now, it would seem that if anything at all is personal in our life, it is speech. Yet several points raised in the preceding chapter point in a different direction. For this reason it is necessary for us to consider here the problem of the personal character of man's speaking.

## 1. THE DEMAND OF AUTHENTIC, PERSONAL SPEECH

*Inauthentic Being.* Heidegger's book, *Being and Time,* contains a passage which has made a profound impression and is often quoted. It refers to authentic and inauthentic being.[1] Inauthentic being is the being of the "they" (*das Man*), the impersonal and anonymous being. In inauthentic being man does not live in person but dwells in the anonymity of the impersonal "they." Heidegger

---

[1] Heidegger, *Being and Time,* New York, 1962, pp. 210–224.

indicates several symptoms of this inauthenticity. The first is "idle talk" (*Gerede*).[2] The individual does not speak out what he himself sees but repeats what everyone says. Another symptom is curiosity. One is interested in matters in which everyone is interested without asking oneself whether these matters deserve our interest.[3] Desires expressed in common talk are put forward: if everyone says that this or that should be done, one likewise affirms its desirability. However, one does not really pay attention to what is desired in such a way, so that it can even happen that, when the desire is brought to realization, one's mind has long ago ceased to worry about it. Heidegger speaks in this connection of "ambiguity": one is present with one's desires in such a way that one is not really present with them. The same ambiguity, Heidegger says, occurs also in the sphere of intersubjective relations: people are present to each other without really being together.[4] He refers to this inauthentic mode of being as "falling" (*Verfallen*).[5]

It is not our intention to present here a commentary upon this passage of *Being and Time*. What Heidegger really means can be explained only within the context of his whole philosophy. All we want to do here is draw attention to a demand made by many of our contemporaries. Our speaking, they say, must be personal and should not be a mere repetition of what others say.

*Public Opinion and Personal Opinion.* It is undeniably true that there exists something which is the generally accepted way of speaking about things. Although statements are always made by human persons, many of them should be prefaced by, "It is said that." Many statements are made by persons who do not realize the scope of what they are saying. In many countries there exist powerful means to form public opinion, such as press, radio and television. If these three systematically and continually push in the same direction and repeat the same opinion, it does not

---

[2] *Op. cit.,* pp. 211–214.　　[3] *Op. cit.,* pp. 214–217.
[4] *Op. cit.,* pp. 217–219.　　[5] *Op. cit.,* p. 219.

take long before almost everyone makes that opinion his own. However, can we really say that the opinion in question has become "his own?" Certainly not. To have a personal opinion regarding a question, one must have a profound knowledge of the issue involved and of everything that is in any way connected with it.

An example may serve to illustrate the point. The question of Vietnam is very acute at the moment. To be able to form a personal opinion about that issue, one would have to be familiar with the country and its people, with its history of the past few centuries, with the motives underlying the opposing factions and all the international ramifications of the issue. One would have to be able also to estimate the future possibilities and dangers of any proposed "solution." It is evident that very very few people in the States possess the necessary qualifications to advance a personal opinion in the matter. Nevertheless, almost everyone defended a standpoint for or against the regime of Diem.

The same phenomenon occurs, of course, anywhere else in the world. In the U.S.S.R. capitalism is regarded by most people as the great curse of modern time, communism is the savior of mankind and the system of the future. In the U.S.A., on the other hand, communism is almost synonymous with evil itself, as may appear from the fact that anyone who opposes a cherished prejudice or a privileged position in the name of human dignity is likely to be suspected of communist sympathies. How often doesn't it happen that Negro leaders in the South, fighting for equality, are branded as communists!

Few people think, yet nearly all have a definite opinion. The result is often that large groups of people find each other in massive opposition.

*"Speaking" and "Talking."* It does not seem difficult to indicate the root of this evil and to point to the remedy. We must not let ourselves be guided by the way "everybody" talks. Our speaking should come forth from our own "seeing." The evil consists precisely in the fact that one makes unwarranted affirmations.

139

One affirms what one hears others around him affirm. Our talking is a repeating of what the others say. Yet such a procedure goes against the very nature of speech. For when one puts forward his meaning, he presents himself as intending to give expression to things themselves, to reality as it discloses itself. He desires that those who listen to him follow his opinon. This desire is not motivated by the intention to impose that opinion forcefully upon others. No one will say to the others: "You must think as I do because I think as I do." The desire to have the others accept one's own opinion is motivated by the way reality presents itself, by the evidence of the matters themselves. If the listener does not agree with the opinion of the speaker, the latter will think that he does not really see things as they are. Speaking presents itself as the expression of understanding, of a genuine realization that things are as the speaker says.

Anyone will sooner or later discover that on this or that occasion he spoke in an unwarranted fashion. He will find that he based himself on incomplete or uncontrolled information. When that happens, we are dismayed, we feel that we have not spoken as we should have done. Our words were unjustified. If we examine speech, we find that its inmost and essential intention is to give expression to things. One who lies deliberately feels that he is doing violence to speech.

*Faithfulness to Reality.* We are not concerned here with subjective intentions, which contemporary science justly abhors, but with the inner intentionality of speech. Speech is essentially meant to draw attention to the reality which appears, discloses itself. The speaker wants the listener to adhere to him, not for his own sake but for the sake of the reality which becomes apparent in his speech. The speaker knows that it is possible for him to be unfaithful to this reality. Such unfaithfulness can be the result of a deliberate attitude, as is the case in a lie. But it may also flow from mental blindness, from the lack of critical sense. In either case our speaking is not what it ought to be according to its own inner intention. It is unfaithful to its own reality. Our speaking must be an embodiment of real "seeing," it must be faithful to the reality which it wants to discuss. Blindly repeating what others says does not fulfill these requirements. It is inauthentic. Inauthentic speaking which presents itself as authentic speech is a degenerative symptom of society.

Education, especially on the university level, must promote authentic speech. It must endeavor to bring speech to its true reality. It should teach us to say only that which we really see. This ideal manifests itself even in ordinary life, for there also our speaking should be critical. The desire to be critical is what has given rise to science in the broad sense of the term. Science is a new form of self-criticism, of self-justification on the part of speech. It appears to be difficult for man to arrive at a warranted way of speaking. Yet, in spite of all difficulties, we may not give up the ideal. To the extent that we do not succeed in attaining this ideal, we speak inauthentically and live in a "fallen" state.

## 2. WE SAY MORE THAN WE REALLY SEE

We do not want to deny the ideal expressed in the preceding section. This ideal is at work in man and, at least in part, has given birth to science. Nevertheless, we think that this ideal must be situated in the reality of our life and that in consequence it will also be made more relative. For, if the ideal in question is posited in an absolute fashion, one fails to take the reality of man into consideration and becomes guilty of an exaggerated spiritualism.[6] Man is a person, endowed with a spirit. Even in the most materialistic philosophies there is a constant reference to the human spirit. Marxist writings likewise speak of man's spirit. Man is spiritual because he himself thinks, because he himself determines his own standpoints in both the theoretical and the practical orders. This self-thinking, however, is only one of the aspects of our being-man. If one approaches man only from this

---

[6] Such an exaggerated spiritualism is certainly present in Hegel's philosophy, for Hegel attributed too much to becoming-conscious.

standpoint, and if one wants to formulate what a justified way of speaking is solely on this basis, then one uses a very one-sided approach. While it is true that man himself thinks, it is true also that in his thinking man is dependent upon society. This dependence is not merely an unfortunate accident or an initial situation that can be overcome, but a permanent phenomenon.

*The "Speaking Word" and the "Spoken Word."* Merleau-Ponty makes an important distinction between *"parole parlée"* and *"parole parlante,"*[7] which we may translate as the *"speaking word"* and the *"spoken word."* Whether in French or in English, at first these expressions are not very eloquent. They become meaningful only when they are viewed within the context of the perspective opened by Merleau-Ponty's philosophy. Their sense will become clear, we hope, in the course of the following paragraphs.

During our childhood we are taken into a speaking society in which the things of the world and man's situations already have been given names. There is an accepted way of speaking as there is an accepted whole of human behavior. Speech is a part of a whole which we could call "praxis." Our speaking is not the more or less accessory expression of a world of meaning which fully precedes this speaking. As we have seen in the preceding chapters, speaking itself is a mode of giving meaning. Speech develops the world of meaning, makes it become a field of available significations. Merleau-Ponty calls the accepted way of speaking the "spoken word." For speech possesses the remarkable characteristic that, once something has been said, it can be repeated both by the original speaker and by others. What has been said can be said again. In this way arises what Merleau-Ponty calls the "spoken word."

The "spoken word" finds its origin in the "speaking word." What is generally said now must once have been said for the first time. Proverbs are striking ways of saying something and everyone makes use of them. Yet there must have been someone

---

[7] *Phénoménologie de la perception,* Paris, 1945, p. 229.

who spoke them for the first time. The "speaking word" is creative; it gives rise to meaning and signification. It makes use, of course, of available words, but it makes them say something which they had never said before. In the "speaking word," says Merleau-Ponty, our existence reveals its function as giver of meaning. The same function is at work in artistic expression, in the projection of new ways of acting, in a word, in every creative development of our existence. The "speaking word" lies at the source of the "spoken word" and, moreover, sees to it that the latter never becomes a closed whole. There always are people who make available words say something which they had never said before. These people are the creative masters of the word and creative thinkers.

*The "Spoken Word" as an Essential Aspect of Our Human Situation.* It would be a serious mistake to identify Merleau-Ponty's "spoken word" with Heidegger's "talk." Merleau-Ponty does not at all want to say that the "spoken word" is a phenomenon of degeneration, something which makes human existence fall into inauthenticity. Likewise, he does not intend to say that the "spoken word" is merely an initial situation and that only in the "speaking word" man attains to speech in the authentic sense. The "spoken word" belongs just as essentially to our human situation as the "speaking word." Let us see why this is so.

It is characteristic of man to integrate himself into the world of speech in its accepted and current form. One has only to observe a child to see the truth of this statement. Children imitate grown-ups. They take over their way of conducting themselves, they repeat their words. At first, of course, they do not understand the full meaning of these words, they do not situate themselves among men in the same way as adults situate themselves. For this reason children sometimes say things that are entirely inappropriate, as is exemplified by the numerous jokes about this matter. Man, then, at first enters the world of speech without knowing its real meaning and certainly without being aware of its full scope. It would be wrong to think that, unlike children,

143

we adults know the meaning of speech in all its fullness, make this meaning entirely our own, and transform its darkness into perfect light. To a certain extent we also remain in the situation of not knowing fully what we say.

This ignorance is not a provisional imperfection which in principle can and should be overcome, but belongs essentially to man's speaking. Let us turn our attention to the way in which we speak when we really intend to bring something to light, for there are also many forms of speech in which the speaker does not have this intention. When we want to bring something to light, we are aware of a kind of darkness and search to dispel it through light. We want to arrive at clarity with respect to a certain problem. In our attempt we use words, whether we make the latter resound externally in a dialogue with others or use them only internally. No matter how much we search for light, the words arise in our mind from a certain darkness; we do not know why these words come forward and not others; in different thinkers different words come forward. These words combine, as it were, spontaneously into sentences, and we do not know how this combination takes place.

Primitive people use the structure of their language without having any explicit knowledge of this structure. If we have been scientifically trained, we may know something about the structure of the language we speak. However, when we reflect upon a particular problem, we do not make use of the theoretical knowledge we possess of the language structure, at least not to a significant extent. If we had to pay attention to this structure, we would no longer be able to concentrate on the problem which we want to investigate. Language functions in us without demanding our attention. We use it as a means to bring light but leave, and have to leave, this means itself in darkness. We do not offer a justification for the fact that these particular things are known and indicated by these particular words, but simply take that for granted. We do not offer a justification for the way in which the

144

words combine into sentences, but are ourselves greatly surprised sometimes by their way of combining.

*Speaking and Understanding.* It is correct to say that we speak from our "seeing." One who speaks or writes undoubtedly has a certain outlook on reality. Later we will revert to this question of the relationship between thinking and speaking. Right now we want to complement that assertion by adding that language makes us see. Our speaking is born from our understanding in such a way that at the same time it leads us to understanding. This statement does not apply, of course, to a speaker who has written down what he will say and then simply delivers his text verbally. In his case understanding was arrived at when he wrote down his address. Let us add, however, that frequently a speaker suddenly begins to see things more clearly while he is delivering a lecture which he had previously written down. He will then often deviate from his written text in order to give this living vision a chance to embody itself in his words. In general, a speaker learns even while he is speaking, just as a writer learns while he is writing. The struggle to attain clarity does not precede his speaking or writing but takes place during it. We ourselves do not know how light arises in our speaking. The same is true also in other realms. The painter does not know how the meaning of his painting is born from lines and colors on his canvas, and the musical composer is ignorant of the way in which his melodies arise.

Language is one of the most mysterious realities. It seems to be a world full of clarity as long as one does not reflect upon it, for language is the means *par excellence* to bring light. Yet this light is born without our knowing exactly how it comes into being. The accompanying darkness belongs to the essence of "functioning" language. A distinction can be made between "functioning" language and "contemplated" or "studied" language. Contemplated language, language which is reflected upon, is poorer than functioning language. By reflecting upon language, we attempt to understand something of the mystery called "language." It is

145

possible to understand something of that mystery—otherwise this book would be attempting the impossible—but language as reflected upon is only a poor expression of real or functioning language.

In our speaking, light arises to some extent in a conscious way. I search for light, I combine words into sentences, and I am responsible for the way in which I do this. Nevertheless, what happens here is not something of which I am fully conscious in every respect. In a very striking and meaningful expression Merleau-Ponty says that thought, as it were, passes through us. It is as if a power is at work in us which seeks clarity.[8] This power is my consciously working ego, we agree, but it is also more than that. We can be so captivated by the search for light that this search continues in us even when we do not want it. It happens sometimes that people are tired and want to stop searching for clarity in their thinking. With respect to writing, one can easily make such a stop, for it is sufficient to lay down the pen or close the typewriter. But we do not always succeed when we want to stop thinking. Thought sometimes continues its course, even when we lay down to rest. We are, as it were, helplessly captivated by the course of our thinking, to such an extent that sometimes we continue to think without willing it and even when we deliberately desire not to think.

*Collective Enlightenment.* By thinking, by bringing to light through speech, we continue a growth of enlightenment which transcends us in every direction. It is as if everywhere around us in the human world this growth of light permeates the atmosphere. Certain things which used to be said are now no longer accepted, and other things have to be said. In a period of transition it can easily happen that one adheres to an outdated type of philosophical thinking, a system which is antiquated because it is no longer a real expression of the world in which we live, because it does not throw light on our real world but repeats what former ages have said. If that person is fortunate

---

8 Merleau-Ponty, *Signes,* Paris, 1960, p. 27.

enough to have a feeling for his situation, he mentally feels as if there is a catch in his voice. He continues to know what he knew before and even to say what he used to say. Yet it becomes more difficult for him to speak. There is a conflict between his philosophical way of speaking and his life. His life shares in the enlightenment which is taking place in the contemporary world of life. But there is a short circuit between his life as a participation in the common enlightenment and his philosophical way of speaking. If he is in a position where it is possible for him to come into contact with other ways of speaking philosophically, ways in which this short circuit does not exist, he feels at home. These other ways attract him. He finds it easy to breathe in them, he does not experience any discomfort. Yet he did not deliberately seek to be uncomfortable in his old way of thinking. He did not deliberately try to create in himself an affinity to the new mode of speaking, for he did not even know this new mode of philosophizing.

No thinker can claim that he has developed his way of thinking in a fully conscious and systematic fashion. Of course, that development did not take place without him. He has worked long and hard at it. Nowhere can anyone accomplish something without effort and perseverance. Nevertheless, it is true also that the growth of our speaking, of our bringing to light, runs its course without us. It is true also that we are carried along by something which runs its course in us without knowing how this happens. I have personally often experienced dissatisfaction with an article or a lecture after writing them down. I often tried then to rewrite such an article or lecture in part to make a number of corrections. Usually, however, the attempted partial rewriting failed and a different article resulted from my efforts. Once a different beginning has been made at a certain point, the resulting text is too divergent and contains the development of a new line of thinking. The effort sets into motion a process whose course one cannot foresee.

One who brings something to light by speaking uses, as we

have said, means which he finds available without having created them in person. He can dispose of the accepted ways of speaking that are used around him. If he is a creative thinker, if it is given to him to embody the "speaking word," he will make words say things which they have never said before. In that case he promotes the common search for light; in him his community moves forward in thinking in such a way that he himself cannot fully grasp it. What happens in him is of importance also for the others, for they are also involved in it. The thinker in question takes up the collective growth of light which many others had started and developed. The light that is at work in him is a light that belongs also to others. It works through him without his knowing how it happens. When he succeeds in increasing this light and expressing it in words, then it is as if the others were waiting for this increased enlightenment. They recognize themselves in his new way of speaking. It even happens that he gives expression to thoughts which had remained latent in them. They are surprised and wonder why they themselves did not say what this speaker or writer has put forward.

*Our Speaking Goes Beyond Our Knowing.* We know what we say, but it is also true that we always say more than we know. The words we use, the language we speak, and the structures we utilize contain latent forms of visions which do not entirely escape us but nonetheless are not wholly understood. We Westerners approach everything in the Western way, not only in philosophy and theology and our sciences, but also in our daily conversations and in our practical life. This Western approach permeates the very structure of the language we speak. We ourselves have created this approach—although this "we" is to be understood here in a very broad sense. We can hardly say that this approach is strange to us, for we have, as it were, merged with it. Nevertheless, we cannot say that we know this Western approach. "Ordinary" people know almost nothing about it, and probably even the theorist who consciously reflects upon it understands only a little of it. For, when we reflect upon the Western approach, we cannot avoid using it in our very effort to make our reflections. Yet it remains true that we bring things to light through this approach.

Thus it should not appear strange that later thinkers are able to know more about a particular philosopher than he knew about himself, that they can better situate his philosophy than he himself did, and that they understand its import more profoundly than he did. All this would be impossible if his bringing-to-light had been fully transparent to himself, but it makes sense if all our light is permeated by a measure of darkness. For this reason we must also say that no enlightenment is ever completely and in every respect mastered. Any form of intellectual light is always mastered in such a way that it also still remains a task, something that is not yet complete. The reason is not merely that complementary viewpoints can be added to what has been achieved, but also that the very meaning of the light is never wholly free from a kind of darkness.

We can ask, for example, what Karl Marx has really seen. Our question does not refer to a mysterious kind of seeing hidden behind his work and of which his work is supposed to be the expression. The question refers to the seeing which reveals itself in his work. Some may regard this question as absurd. A writer, they would argue, knows very well what he sees. Of course, we do not want to claim that he does not know at all what he is seeing. Nevertheless, it is certainly true that he does not know it completely. It is quite possible that, if he were asked to summarize the core of the vision embodied in his works, he would make important mistakes. Marx himself, for example, expresses the fundamental lines of his vision in two pages of the Preface to *Contribution to the Critique of Political Economy,* and he himself adds that these fundamental lines have always guided him.[9] It would be wrong, of course, if we were simply to disregard Marx' attempt to express his own fundamental vision, but on the other hand, we should beware of following it blindly. For it is not

---

[9] *Zur Kritik der politischen Ökonomie,* Dietz ed., Berlin, 1958, pp. 11–14.

impossible and even probable that Marx has expressed himself one-sidedly when he attempted to make a brief statement about his own vision. The question of what Marx has really seen remains still an open question. It is a typical mistake of any kind of orthodoxy to want to settle that question once and for all.

In a similar way the question regarding the fundamental meaning of Christianity still remains an open question, even after twenty centuries of Christian faith. It would be foolish, of course, to claim that we know nothing at all about that meaning. However, it would be just as foolish to say that we know everything about it. If Christianity could no longer unfold its own meaning and signification in a progressive fashion, it would be dead. This statement does not merely mean that the possibilities to apply Christianity can still become more evident. Undoubtedly, that also is true, but there is more. Even the inner meaning of Christianity and Christian existence is known only in such a way that they can and must be unveiled still further.

## 3. The Person and Collective Enlightenment

In the preceding pages we have used the expression "collective enlightenment." We must now develop this theme in greater detail and discuss how the person is related to this common origin and development of light.

*Examples of Collective Enlightenment.* It is a striking phenomenon that sometimes a particular period unquestionably accepts something which in a later period is just as generally denied. There was a time that nearly everyone in Europe thought that witches really existed. Most people agreed that witches deserved severe punishment and even that they should be burned at the stake as dangerous beings. Anyone who did not agree with that view ran the danger of becoming himself suspected. Today witches appear only in children's stories. No one in his senses suspects that among the people he meets in the street there are perhaps some witches.

150

Another example. Until recently all Catholics and many others did not have the slightest doubt that all human beings descended from a single couple, Adam and Eve, whom God had directly created. Many people still hold this view. It becomes more and more difficult, however, to maintain this standpoint unqualifiedly before a gathering of anthropological paleontologists. In a few decades it is not likely to be defended any longer.

Some centuries ago everyone considered it entirely normal that torture was used during judicial inquiries. Even today it unfortunately still happens occasionally in times of great stress, such as civil wars. However, it would be difficult still to find jurists who in principle are in favor of such procedures. No state any longer makes torture a part of its official legal system.

To give a last example, the West has undergone a change in the way in which it discusses Marxism. Until a few decades ago, many intellectual circles simply dismissed it as an absurdity undeserving of serious attention. Now many intellectuals make a serious study of Marxism.

*Collective Enlightenment.* These examples, which could be multiplied by many others, reveal a remarkable phenomenon. No one can claim that it is due to his personal genius that he no longer speaks as his forebears did; for instance, that he does not believe in witches because of his own matchless intelligence. Any one of us can point to geniuses of the past who were endowed with more intelligence than us and who did not see what we are seeing. Reading their works, one constantly discovers instances of one-sidedness and forms of blindness to which we are no longer subject. It would be foolish to ascribe my enlightenment to my own eminent degree of intelligence or my own unremitting work of research. In such matters there is not so much question of personal merit as of a collective growth of light, a development of collective vision.

The term "collective vision" may sound very strange. Mental vision or insight would appear to be a personal attribute *par excellence.* The more an action is material or external, the greater

151

also the possibility is to do it together. Together we can pull a single rope to move a heavy object, together we can serve a single machine, but how can there be question of seeing something together, collectively? One could appeal here to René Descartes and his sharply formulated emphasis on the personal character of insight and understanding.[10]

*Descartes' Stress on the Personal Character of Understanding.* Before formulating his most profound ideas, Descartes described how he arrived at his understanding. He studied literature, but found there only the most bewildering variety of opinions. Studying a large array of different sciences, he saw everywhere a lack of clarity. He then tried to find wisdom in man's practical conduct, but again failed to find a clear confirmation of values. On the contrary, what one accepted as a value, the other would reject as a non-value. Descartes could not find anything outside himself that could help him to arrive at clear and distinct ideas. He was therefore, he says, compelled to rely on his own resources. Moreover, he adds, work that is done by a single individual often shows more perfection than works carried out by many. Let us look, for example, at an old city in which many architects have planned and constructed numerous buildings in the course of centuries. All kinds of buildings are mixed in hopeless confusion and lack of harmony, streets are narrow and crooked, and going from one place to another often presents needless difficulties. How much more rational and orderly a city would be if it had been planned and constructed by a single architect! In other words, ultimately not much can be expected from the help of others for Descartes' effort to arrive at understanding. It is even a distinct advantage if one is forced to rely only upon oneself. Understanding and insight, therefore, are strongly marked by a personal character. Descartes even attributes a far-reaching degree of independence to the person.

However, Descartes' illustration is not at all convincing. Cities

---

[10] See the first chapters of his *Discourse on Method* for the following paragraph.

which have slowly grown over the centuries through the work of many architects draw our attention more than others and have become centers of tourist attraction. We zealously try to preserve the relics of the past and would abhor the idea of a Paris, Amsterdam, or Bruges planned and executed by a single architect. The reason why we like these cities is precisely that they offer such a variety of styles. Although we can discern unity in that variety —the fundamental unity of the style proper to the period in which the core of these cities came into existence—we rejoice that this fundamental unity displays itself in a variety of styles. The unity in the variety, the variety in the unity, are what gives these cities their wealth and harmony. Although there is sometimes a lack of rational coordination, resulting from the haphazard origin of their constituent parts, this very lack adds to the charm of the whole. We would not like to see in such cities only broad and straight avenues. We discover in them the individuality of the various architects and artists, even if we do not know their names. At the same time, as we have said, we are struck by the fundamental unity of style which reveals itself in everything, at least if the city's core or section has taken shape during a given period of culture. This unity permeates everything and at the same time transcends each particular building.

One can hardly claim that the artists and architects of that period were fully aware of that fundamental style. This style permeated everything and surrounded them as an atmosphere which was so much taken for granted that it did not draw attention. Sustained by this atmosphere or fundamental style, the artists managed to reach a high level of beauty, sometimes so striking that even the ordinary dwellings of the period continue to make us marvel. The creative man is sustained and raised to a high level by such an atmosphere.

This fundamental atmosphere made these creative people see. It opened their eyes for the possibilities offered by their bodily powers, their tools and materials. It opened their minds for the attractiveness of certain forms of expression. It outlined the basic

153

pattern for their expression of their artistic talents. These people, too, were free, they often made a choice, just as we do. Yet their freedom operated within a field that had not been laid down by their own individual freedom. This field should not be regarded merely as a limitation of their freedom. It was, of course, also a limitation, for this field made it impossible for them to express themselves in the way of, for instance, artists of the twentieth century. Despite this limiting character, this field was at the same time a realization of their freedom, for it opened their eyes to possibilities and offered them ways of self-expression. The existence of this field made it precisely possible for them to make, within the field, a free choice.

The preceding paragraphs refer to artistic vision and artistic creativity. Yet they disclose something which Descartes had disregarded—namely, that the individual seeing takes place within a kind of collective seeing, that the individual vision realizes itself within a field having a collective character.

*Collective Vision as a Common Field of Existence.* From the preceding remarks it should be more or less clear now what is meant by "collective vision." It obviously does not mean that, in addition to the seeing of the individuals, there exists also a separate and different type of seeing. The fundamental unity of style prevailing in a given period does not exist outside the various styles in which the individuals express themselves, but is the common fundamental sphere within which these individuals agree and differ. Collective vision exists within the individual's vision. The individual's seeing occurs within a field which does not originate in the individual, goes beyond him on all sides, and is found in numerous other individuals. All of these simply take that field for granted. Twentieth century Europeans and Americans likewise see, think and are creative within such a field. But we, too, hardly know that field and we have not consciously chosen it. There are people among us who want to be one hundred percent original in various realms. We may say that this

154

desire is probably characteristic of our field of existence. At least, it did not exist or existed only in a less striking way in other periods. Using a paradox, we could say that a person's desire to be original is not at all original, for this desire reveals precisely the common style of our period.

That common field of existence must, of course, be discernible somehow. One can find it, for example, in the means and techniques of expression which a given period places at the individual's disposal.[11] It exists in the currently accepted customs and ways of behaving, the accepted fashions of clothing and the accepted ways of eating, dwelling, meeting and having contact with others. It exists in the words which a particular language places at the disposal of those who speak it and in the combinations of words that are accepted. It exists in the way in which people relax and seek recreation, in the literature and art of the period. This field opens our eyes to certain possibilities, and it cannot do so without closing them at the same time to other possibilities. It opens ways for us to realize our lives in our dealing with the world, but in such a fashion that other ways of dealing with it are henceforth less obvious and less taken for granted. It makes certain forms of truth easily accessible to us, while others now become more difficult to understand. This field is a most profound reality, for all the realities of a given period of culture are rooted in it and exist within its fundamental lines.

*Scientific Reflection and the Common Field of Existence.* All this is known to sociologists and psychologists, to those who pursue the modern sciences of man. They realize that the individual man is profoundly influenced by his field of existence. Their eyes have been opened to the influence which history and society exercise on the lives and works of individual persons. The person is an exponent of the group. Strange as it may seem, however, those who pursue these human sciences do not always seem to be aware of the fact that their own way of pursuing science is influenced

---

11 Sartre, *Critique de la raison dialectique,* p. 75.

by this common field.[12] They speak and write sometimes as if they are able to describe the field, or rather the fields, of existence as objective outsiders capable of surveying these fields with a superior glance.

That idea is, of course, an illusion. One who pursues a science always first exists within a particular field and the way in which, next, he begins to pursue science is decisively influenced by the field in which he lives and even by the way in which he personally is situated in that field. The pursuit of science may be called a reflection, for he who devotes himself to the human sciences withdraws from the immediacy of life in order to reflect upon it. We must, therefore, make a distinction between this reflection and life in its immediacy. Yet it should be clear at once that the reflection is made on the basis of life in its immediacy. Moreover, to pursue a science we need all kinds of tools, such as a scientific terminology and method, as well as problems with which we can start our work. These, too, are found within the field of our existence. For these reasons the pursuit of a science is permeated with the spirit of a particular period.

If scientific objectivity had to be understood in the sense that we have to withdraw from our field of existence, the sphere of our life, the spirit of our period, and that we have to rise above that field, then scientific objectivity would be in principle impossible. What has been said here about the human sciences applies also to philosophy and theology. Once again, we assume that those who pursue these disciplines are familiar with this fact. Yet they sometimes write as if they know nothing about it.

*Limited Horizon and Human Creativity.* One could remark that we therefore appear to be encompassed by a limited, historically and socially fixed horizon and draw the conclusion that we are not able to reach the truth. That conclusion, however, does not follow. Although our field of existence has a limiting charac-

---

[12] Cf. Merleau-Ponty, "Le philosophe et la sociologie," *Signes,* pp. 123–142 (English tr. in *Philosophy of the Social Sciences: a Reader,* ed. by Maurice Natanson, New York, 1963, pp. 487–505).

ter, its most profound reality does not lie in this limiting aspect. The primary reality of the field is that it makes us be and makes us see. It opens our eyes. It is the only way in which man can be man and able to see. If such a field did not open possibilities to us, we would be less than the most primitive of all men. Man can exist as a man only if he is sustained by such a field. In other words, it would be wrong to consider that field solely as a limitation.

The fact that the individual is sustained by such a field and that this field is the horizon of his personal existence does not mean that he cannot be creative. It does mean, however, that his creative possibilities come to maturity within this field. It was impossible, for instance, for a Roman to invent a television apparatus or for a medieval man to create a phenomenological philosophy. Man's creative activity is never a making from nothing, but the discovery of new possibilities within a given field. For this reason a creative genius, no matter how original he may be, can always be understood in terms of his period. True, we cannot derive his creations in a categorical way from the constellation of factors and conditions in his time. For example, we cannot analyze a given period and derive from our analysis that it had to produce a Rembrandt or a Descartes in the same way as we can derive the correct solution from the data of a mathematical problem. The individual owes to his period his field of existence with all its possibilities; the period owes its own fruits to its individual creative geniuses. In the individuals and through the individuals a given period becomes fruitful. Their achievements can be understood within their field of existence and through this field, but the possibilities of this field reveal themselves in the achievements of individual geniuses.[13]

---

[13] For this reason it is important that in any group the safeguarding of its common values is accompanied by a maximum of freedom for the individual persons. If the group does not permit any freedom of movement to the persons, the common values will atrophy. The history of philosophical and theological thought in the Catholic Church during the past few centuries illustrates this assertion.

*Collective Enlightenment and Orthodoxy.* From these considerations it should be possible to deduce what is meant by collective enlightenment, the collective growth of light. The development of our field of existence makes certain things visible while others become invisible. In a given period it appears quite natural to say certain things and not to say others. To speak is to draw reality from concealment. The individual speaks but always within a field of existence, within a community. He draws reality from concealment, but it is the common field of existence which makes it possible for him to do so. We modern men are privileged to see certain truths which were hidden in former times, but we have no right to conclude that therefore we are greater geniuses than our forebears. We live in a period in which things, formerly invisible, have become visible, but we do not owe this light to ourselves.

Any orthodoxy which fixes its doctrine in a system will have difficulty assimilating the common enlightenment. For, as we have seen, the field of existence proper to the period in which the doctrine became fixed in a system plays a role in this fixation. As a consequence, its fixed form is in many respects tied to the phase of enlightenment prevailing during that period. As soon as a further development occurs in this collective growth of light, the fixed form of the doctrine becomes untenable in some respects. Any doctrine which is rigidly fixed will inevitably be overtaken in some respects as time goes on.

The experience of the Catholic Church serves to confirm this assertion. Its theologians wanted to fix its doctrine to the utmost. They developed a system of dogmatic statements, an imposing complex of theological and philosophical principles and conclusions, a moral system in which everything was fixed down to the smallest details. They thought it possible to create a theological system which could resist the ravages of time and would not be overtaken by the course of history. All that, however, has revealed itself to be an illusion. The collective growth of light has now forced them to recognize the relative character of their fixed system.

It stands to reason that such a recognition does not come about without shocks and painful incidents. The first, natural reaction of any orthodoxy is to defend itself against the new light. This reaction denies that the new light is really a light. It considers itself a light and calls the new enlightenment darkness. Gradually, however, it becomes so evident that a new light has really arisen that the orthodoxy is finally willing to recognize the relative character of its own fixed system. At first, this recognition appears as a loss, for it implies giving up the solidly organized system in which truth had been embodied. Yet this loss is only apparently a loss, for it does not force the orthodoxy to abandon a single genuine truth. Only pseudo-knowledge and self-proclaimed understanding have to be given up. Whatever was genuine knowledge is retained and known even better than before.

*Collective Enlightenment and the "Universe of Discourse."* The common growth of light occurs most of all in the world of speech, as should be evident from what we have seen in the preceding chapters. We live in a field of meaning. Our speaking makes meaning become signification. It encompasses all meaning. Every meaning can be made a theme of speech, albeit not always in an adequate way. In his speaking man attains a certain freedom with respect to meaning because speech always implies that one places oneself at a certain distance from that which is spoken about. For this reason one can readily see that the dynamic movement of our existence centers primarily in our speaking.

It is important to realize how much we owe to that common enlightenment, how much our vision depends upon that common growth of light. A few of us may have the privilege of contributing something to this growth, but even then we owe much more to this collective enlightenment than we creatively add to it. The pretence to originality, the claim of being entirely original, which is often heard in our time, has no justification. Far too often such so-called original ideas are bizarre assertions rather than embodiments of really new modes of understanding.

In the preceding section we have mentioned that we say more than we see. It should be clear now what this statement means. Our speaking takes place within the "universe of discourse" in which we live. We take over the accepted way of speaking proper to our period and thereby make its vision our own. For the accepted way of speaking embodies that vision. However, there is no guarantee whatsoever that we will authentically make our own that vision of which accepted speech is the embodiment. Anyone is likely to have experienced that for many years he had appropriated an accepted way of speaking before he suddenly began to suspect the wealth of insight and wisdom contained in it. While such an experience is a happy sign of growing wisdom, it also serves as a warning. It indicates that we often speak without authentically making the meaning of a statement our own.

Nevertheless, when we realize this, we should not think that we live in an inauthentic way, in a way that is unworthy of man. For it is proper to man to live in a field which is his own and nonetheless exceeds him on all sides. With Sartre, we could call the appropriation of the common field of existence an "interiorization." This term then indicates that we authentically make that field our own, we make its meaning ours in the full sense of this term. Interiorization takes place in such a way that it is never entirely complete. No one has ever interiorized all meanings of his field of existence. It is proper to man never fully to interiorize his field. In this respect also our future always remains open.

The incompleteness of our interiorization is an added reason why men differ from one another. One interiorizes this form of meaning, and another interiorizes that form. A meaning which is not interiorized by anyone no longer belongs to our field of existence. Precisely because as interiorizations of meaning we differ from one another, our encounter with our fellow-men can be fruitful. If someone had interiorized all meanings of his field of existence, it would be useless for him to encounter anyone. He would not need a dialogue, he would not need to listen, but could offer only a monologue. Fortunately, such people do not exist. The ideal of "authentic existence" can be exaggerated to such an extent that one who would attain that ideal would cease to be human. Heidegger himself did not propose such an ideal, but some writers who have taken over his terminology express themselves in that extravagant way. They do not seem to realize that they have failed to interiorize the meaning which they discuss, they do not really understand the scope of the terms which they use.

### 4. LIGHT AND DARKNESS IN SPEAKING

Speech has been repeatedly referred to as a bringing to light. It goes without saying that in our speaking we search for light. If discussions are organized about political or business matters, the reason is that there are unsolved problems to be dealt with and their discussion can lead to clarification of the issues involved. The clarity, however, that is sought does not always lie on a purely rational level. It sometimes happens that people who live together have become or remained emotionally and affectively strangers to one another; they find it difficult to converse and seem unable to approach one another on a personal level. In such a case it is not impossible that they will find one another in a conversation that has nothing to do with the difficulties between them. Suddenly confronted with a common problem, such as a disaster threatening them equally, they are forced to come into contact and may then "discover" one another. This mutual discovery or rediscovery is capable of removing their prejudices against one another. There are many ways in which we try to find clarity.

Speaking, then, may be considered to be the growth of light. Yet this light has many connections with darkness. Let us con-

161

sider a few of these bonds by which the light of speech remains tied to darkness.

*Darkness in the Starting Point of Speech.* First of all, there is darkness in the starting point of our speech. We would not begin to seek light in speaking if we were not conscious of a lack of light. Darkness can be a beginning of light only if we are aware of it as darkness. In other words, a fruitful dialogue does not arise from an existence that knows no problems. The fruitfulness of our speaking is tied to our human restlessness.

A distinction, however, has to be made here, namely, between "lived" problems and "raised" problems. A "lived" problem is one which occurs in the concrete course of man's life. It occurs, for example, when man lives with unsatisfied needs, when a hungry man finds no food, when a man lives in a situation which prevents him from being at ease with himself. Before such a "lived" problem puts man into action, it has to be "raised," that is, man must become conscious of the "lived" problem and must cease to experience it as an inescapable fate. It often happens that people experience a situation unworthy of man as an inescapable necessity. They do not feel at ease in the situation but see no possibility to change it. In the nineteenth century, for example, innumerable laborers lived in a most unpleasant situation, yet it did not move them to action because they did not "raise" their "lived" problems, they did not penetrate into the foundation of their situation, and did not see any possibility to arrive at a change. Once, however, a "lived" problem is "raised" and faced as a problem, it becomes capable of making man move to action.

It is possible, of course, that a "raised" problem fails to embody a "lived" problem. Or it may happen that at one time it expressed a "lived" problem, but it no longer does so now, even though some people continue to raise it. By speaking man wants to bring reality to light, but it can happen that his speech no longer touches reality. If a "raised" problem has no connection with real life, it will reveal itself as unfruitful. Unfortunately it is true that very often people raise problems which are unreal.

162

These will fail to move man. If, however, the "raised" problem is really the expression of a "lived" problem, man becomes aware of the darkness surrounding it, he begins to search for light, he is put into action and begins to speak in a way which will really result in light.

One could think that the more man speaks, the more light he will bring and that therefore his search will become proportionately less. Yet that is not at all the case. Speech, genuine speech, brings real light and we rejoice over this light. But it seems as if the light that is thus born is at the same time a revelation of its own limits. The more man knows, the better also he understands the limits of his knowledge and the more he becomes a questioning man. Our time has at its disposal an untold wealth of scientific data in every conceivable field. We possess the literature of many countries and many periods. We are acquainted with many views of life and many forms of philosophical thought. We have more information than ever before. At the same time, however, it is true that modern man is more than ever a questioning man, a seeker.

Part of the reason must be sought in the fact that there are questions which transcend all our answers. There are questions which become greater in proportion to the light that our speaking about them throws on them. Speech has not only the character of an answer but also serves to expose the scope of the question to light. Certain fundamental questions may be compared with the dimensions of the material universe. In former times, when little was known about these dimensions, theories were proposed which claimed to offer a complete picture of them. At present we know far more about the dimensions of the universe, but the more we make progress in our knowledge, the greater also the difficulties become to offer a complete picture. We may even say that such a picture is no longer possible now. Every time we learn something new about the universe we also become more aware of our inability to fathom it completely.

A similar situation exists with respect to the fundamental questions regarding man himself. We arrive at new understandings and insights, but every new understanding reveals new dimensions in the question itself. We find more light, but this light also reveals darkness. This happens, for example, with respect to questions about the meaning of life, about the origin of life and of the universe, about God and religion. Our speaking concerning such matters resembles a beam of light shining into an abyss of darkness. We make progress in our knowledge, but every new form of knowledge is a revelation of our lack of knowledge.

Accordingly, there is darkness at the starting point of our speaking. Our speech does not remove this darkness but rather makes us aware of it. We become conscious of the impenetrable dimensions of the fundamental questions. We continue to ask questions which have been asked over and over again for thousands of years. We realize that man will always continue to occupy himself with these questions.

*Darkness in Speech Itself.* Secondly, there is darkness also in our speaking itself. Speech brings to light, but we do not know how. If we take speech for granted and simply accept it as something given, if we start with recognition of the fact that things have names, that words have significations, and that there is a whole field of significations, then we can make use of speech to bring light. As soon, however, as we want to reflect on all this, the light submerges in a mysterious darkness. Why do things have names? What is a name? Why do things have these names and not others? How do I find words? How do I live in the world of speech? In what way are these words at my disposal? How am I able to use speech in order to bring things to light? Man has no adequate reply to these and other questions about speech. Of course, he can say something in reply to them, but the answer does not solve the whole question. Speech is one of those mysteries which become more and more mysterious in proportion to our increase of knowledge about them.

For the "ordinary" man who exists in the immediacy of life, speech is no problem at all. The linguist raises all kinds of problems about the genesis and structure of language, but for him also speech itself is something which he unquestionably takes for granted. The philosopher in his reflections raises the fundamental questions of language itself. He knows that in its physical reality to speak is to expel air with the organs of speech in certain positions, so that articulated sounds result. The mysterious aspect of speech, however, is that these sounds are filled with meaning and construct a field of significations. When one watches a painter, one is confronted with the mystery that beneath the painter's moving hand meaning begins to exist on the canvas. In a similar way there is a mystery in the transformation of sounds into significations. The philosopher's words draw attention to this mystery, but all he can do is point to it. The more he penetrates into it, the clearer it becomes to him that an adequate explanation is not possible. Man has to accept speech as a gift, just as he has to accept his entire existence as such a gift.

He finds himself, for example, as a sexual being, as a being who together with one of the other sex can give rise to a new man. Much reflection has been devoted to this mystery, but it has never been explained and will never be fully explained. We simply have to accept this aspect of our existence as a mysterious gift. In the same way we find ourselves as beings able to bring things to light through speaking. Neither science nor philosophy can explain this mystery. Philosophy simply draws our attention to it and makes us aware of its mysterious character.

*Darkness Arising from the Body's Role in Speech.* The third reason why there is darkness lies in the fact that in our reflections upon speech we become aware of the important role played by the body.[14] Man likes to speak of the lucid character of thought. Unquestionably, there is light in our thinking. Yet this light reveals itself tied to our speaking, our words; and speaking is a bodily phenomenon, something that is tied up with our body. The light of our thinking therefore is rooted in our body. Man is so convinced of this tie that, if there is doubt about the human

---

[14] This role is one of the major topics investigated by Merleau-Ponty.

nature of excavated skulls, he examines them to see whether they are formed in such a way that speech is possible. If the reply is in the negative, he concludes that the remains are not human. We do not want to consider whether such a line of reasoning is correct, but merely report it here to indicate that there is a clear connection between thinking and speaking, between speaking and the body. Our speaking, therefore, shares not only in the light which thinking is but also in the darkness which characterizes the body.

*Darkness Arising from the Past.* Finally, there is darkness in our speaking because we are rooted in a past which we do not know at all or of which we know only a little. Unconsciously we often live by tradition or from an unknown past. This past is still active in our speech, in the words and structures which we use. We are rooted in a community of speech which we ourselves have not chosen.

Although speech may be referred to as a growth of light, this light itself reveals many aspects of darkness. The philosophy of language is very suitable to make us wonder about ourselves. We must now reflect upon the relationship between speaking and thinking. An awarenes of the intimate bond between these two will make us realize even more how mysterious speech really is.

# CHAPTER SEVEN

# Thought and Speech

WE must now devote our attention to the fascinating but difficult problem of the relationship between thinking and speaking. Obviously these two are intimately connected. Greek philosophers even used the same term, *logos,* to indicate both "word" and "world soul" or "world reason." The development of thought is inseparably united to that of speech, for every new development in the realm of thought reveals itself in the realm of speech. One who wants to exercise thought control must control its embodiment in speech. The Holy Office, for example, which wants to safeguard Catholic orthodoxy, is inevitably compelled to pay attention to the religious speaking and writing of Catholics. Because of the intimate connection between thinking and speaking, it stands to reason that this relationship is a topic of great interest to philosophers.

*Sense of the Term "Language."* Before we consider this problem, it will be necessary to indicate more exactly what we mean here by the term "language." We want to study the relationship between thinking and the use of language in general. Man uses language in many ways. Its most primordial use consists in man's conversation. A conversation is often referred to as an "exchange of ideas," which again indicates the intimate bond between thinking and speaking. However, we make use of language also when we reflect in silence. This "internal reflection" generally makes use of words. We use language also, of course, when we

167

write. Because we are concerned here with the use of language in general, it is immaterial for us in what way language is used.

Moreover, we are concerned here not only with ordinary language but also with the technical languages which have been created as extensions of ordinary language to make certain sciences possible. In other words, the system of mathematical symbols is also a language for us. Although the most elementary mathematical units can still be described in ordinary language, the latter appeared inadequate when mathematics developed and became more refined. The mathematicians then developed their own system of symbols, which is still continually undergoing further developments. The science of statistics likewise has its own system of symbols. All such systems are included here under the general term "language."

*Two Extreme Views.* We do not want to examine here all views which in the course of time have been put forward regarding the relationship of speaking and thinking, but will limit ourselves to two extreme positions. While recognizing the bond between thought and speech, some thinkers have greatly emphasized their distinction. Thinking, so they said, is an interior "event," something that takes place in man's mind, in his consciousness. Speaking, on the other hand, is a bodily phenomenon. We are able to form a concept of reality without expressing it in words. Speaking is an external indication of thinking. It is related to thinking as a sign is to the signified. Any sign is, of course, dependent upon that which is signified, for the sign is meaningless without the signified. Yet that which is signified can exist without the sign.

Others stress that our thinking is essentially bound up with our speaking. Thought and speech, they say, are, strictly speaking, identical. Thought comes into existence in speech. Our thinking spirit is essentially a speaking spirit.

Accordingly, the first view makes a sharp distinction, even a separation, between thinking and speaking; the second declares them identical. Between these two extremes there are all kind of intermediary views, which we will not analyze here.

## 1. THINKING AND SPEAKING ARE NOT SIMPLY IDENTICAL

*Practognosis.* From the preceding chapters it should be evident that we may not simply identify speech with thought. Our existence is a giving of meaning (as well as an accepting of meaning) and, as we have seen, there are many ways in which meaning can be given. Our speaking is only one of these many ways. Others undoubtedly also contain thinking.

For example, we think in our actions. Following Grünbaum, Merleau-Ponty speaks in this respect about "practognosis," by which he wants to indicate that our *praxis* or activity also is intrinsically a kind of *gnosis* or knowledge.[1] For, our *praxis* always takes place in the world; that is, in order to act we must transform the world into an action field and we must give things an "action meaning." We cannot do so unless we understand things. We always act with our body and therefore must understand the possibilities of our own body. For its action our body usually needs "extensions" in the form of tools or instruments, and we must understand the possibilities offered by these instruments. Wordless as it is, our *praxis,* our acting, is already a kind of knowledge.

*Examples of Practognosis.* The truth of this assertion manifests itself when, for example, we watch a nurse taking care of a helpless patient. She knows what he needs and understands his desires. She is aware of what causes him pain and tries to make his treatment cause as little discomfort as possible. She dextrously handles the instruments used in taking care of her patient. She understands the possibilities of motion which both she and her patient possess and adapts herself entirely to the patient's situation. She knows, moreover, albeit perhaps not in a theoretical way, that the sufferer needs human contact and gives it while she

---

[1] Merleau-Ponty, *Phénoménologie de la perception,* p. 164.

takes care of him. At the same time, however, she knows that this human contact must be accompanied by a certain respect and distance. It is not possible to be a good nurse without a broad understanding of the patient.

Nevertheless, there are many excellent nurses who would not be able to say much about the way they perform their task. They cannot put it into words, yet they know it. They have learned to understand their patients while practicing their profession. Their actions are guided by their perception, for they can see whether or not the patient is at ease. Much of their activity consists, of course, of routine treatment, but these routine actions are constantly modified somewhat according to their perception of, or feeling for, the patient's situation. It is beneficial to the patient to be treated by a nurse who understands her profession. While taking care of him, she talks with him, but this conversation generally avoids the topic of the treatment that is being given. It is quite possible that the nurse's talk is part of her professional activity; for instance, it may serve to take the patient's attention away from a painful treatment. Dentists often use similar tactics. Accordingly, there exists a real but wordless thinking in that action itself.

Another example of practognosis may be found in driving a car.[2] We move in a thinking way through traffic. We understand the possibilities of our car and know what this car demands of us; we know, for instance, if it wants us to shift to another gear. We feel that the curve ahead demands that we cut down our speed. We adapt our speed almost automatically to the view, to our possibility to see ahead in the traffic situation. No matter how much driving is a routine job, we are guided by our understanding of the car, the traffic situation, our own possibilities. When our understanding of these factors has reached the point that we can take it for granted, our mind is free again for reflection and able also to converse with others in the car. If, however, the

---

[2] Cf. D. J. van Lennep, "Psychologie van het chaufferen," *Persoon en Wereld,* pp. 155–167.

traffic situation suddenly becomes complex and demands concentration of attention, we stop the train of our reflection or our conversation with the others.

Other examples of practognosis are offered by sports and games. One who plays football or tennis must understand the situation of the game while he is playing. This understanding extends to many aspects.[3] He has to know the possibilities offered by his own body, the ball and other "tools" used in the game, and the area of play in which he moves. He has to understand also the movements and intentions of the other players. Because the game moves in a fast tempo, this understanding has to take place in a mere fraction of a second. There is no time at all to work everything out in a theoretical reflection.

Understanding-in-action belongs also to the essence of all forms of art that are exercised with the hands or other parts of the body. Because he understands, man is able to paint, sculpture, dance, play musical instruments and figure skate. An artist does not at all have to be a theorist.

*Practognosis and Theory.* As we have mentioned, the thinking-in-action which practognosis is does not require theoretical reflection, it is as a rule not the execution of a plan previously drawn up on the intellectual level. It may happen, of course, that we first reflect to lay down a carefully detailed work plan, but in ordinary life such a plan is rather exceptional. Even if we have a plan of action, we must remain ready to modify it at any moment in reference to the concrete situation facing us. In other words, thinking-in-action is not the application of a previous theoretical reflection. In our action we know many things which we do not know at all on the theoretical level. Yet there is clarity in this realm, but a special type of clarity. Like any other clarity, the clarity of practognosis results from man's thinking. Thinking-in-action, as all our thinking, is an unveiling of the world. It even happens very often that in our action we know much more about the world than in our theories. Through practognosis a football

---

[3] Cf. Remy C. Kwant, *Philosophy of Labor*, Pittsburgh, 1960, pp. 29–34.

player knows much more about ball control than he knows in theory. A successful businessman who has to deal with many people knows much more about interhuman relationship than he may be able to explain in theory. Many psychological theories of the past were extremely poor in content as compared to the inner wealth of understanding contained in our knowing-in-action.

*The Importance of Practognosis.* Understanding-in-action plays a very important role in our life. It enables us to conduct ourselves as human beings. Practognosis makes it possible for us to behave properly when we dine with others, when we visit strangers. It enables us to cross a street or to work. All our work is at the same time thinking-in-action. This is the reason why only man can work in the strict sense of the term. Man is able to work because he understands the working situation, the possibilities of his body and those of his tools.

The examples given above show that understanding-in-action can be marked by genius. We must avoid the idea that we have to do here with an inferior kind of thinking and that thinking-in-words is *per se* on a higher level. The terms "higher" and "lower" do not apply here. Rembrandt's thinking-in-action, for example, was simply the thinking of a genius. Man's activity manifests that man is someone who understands. For this reason the observation of someone's behavior can show whether or not he is intelligent. Intelligence, however, does not always reveal itself immediately, as is evident from the fact that we can be misled by routinely performed actions. If someone has been carefully drilled in routine, he may at first impress us as being fully in control of the situation and knowing very well what he is doing. The son of a wealthy businessman who is not very intelligent but has been patiently drilled in business administration may through family connections succeed in obtaining an executive position. He may manage to perform his duties rather well for a time, as long as only routine decisions are made by him. However, the moment will arrive when routine is no longer sufficient and his decisions have to be modified because of the concrete situation. At that moment his failure will become evident, for his action would now have to be inspired by a kind of genuine intelligence which he lacks. One who has known another person for a long time and possesses sound judgment will know also whether this person is intelligent or not. Parents, for example, who are able to evaluate their children objectively often know much about their intelligence even before they go to school. In the case of feeble-minded children, their lack of intelligence reveals itself very soon in their actions.

*Thinking and Speaking are Not Identical.* Accordingly, thinking and speaking are not identical, for, in addition to thinking-in-words, there are many other forms of thinking. The single term "thinking-in-action," as appears from the above-mentioned examples, applies to many different forms of thinking. There are people who, despite their intelligence, have great difficulty with thinking-in-words. Yet our educational system is almost entirely orientated to the latter form of thinking. One who does not do well in that system is often much too easily regarded as unintelligent. Of course, most of the children who fail really are unintelligent, but we may not automatically conclude from such a failure to a low degree of intelligence. It happens sometimes that such "failures" later become successful businessmen, even without much backing by their relatives. That success shows that they really are intelligent. Their intelligence, however, is of a different kind from that which is developed in our schools. One who is very good at sports likewise must be very intelligent in some way, although this assertion may not be valid for types of sport in which brute bodily strength alone suffices to reach the top.

As we will see more in detail later, our modern world is eminently a world of speech. The intermediacy of words assumes an ever increasing role in many realms of life. This development contains a certain danger. People who have trouble thinking-in-words but are able to arrive at clear understanding in other areas run the risk of being bypassed in our world. We should therefore be on our guard lest we base ourselves on the world of speech to impose unreasonable demands with respect to practical matters. Diplomas which guarantee—or pretend to guarantee—theoretical knowledge should not be required for practical functions that can be performed without theoretical training. Respect should be shown for the qualitative variations of intelligence. We may not make a single form of intelligence the norm of all others.

## 2. THE EXISTENTIAL CHARACTER OF THINKING

Thinking and speaking, we have said, are not identical. Two very different reasons, however, can be put forward to support that claim. First, one could claim that thinking is a very special and separate activity, raised above all forms of existence and having no need of bodily roots. Secondly, one can say that, although thinking is an existential activity, it exists also in other forms of existence than speech. From the preceding section it should be evident that this second view is defended here. We must now devote our attention to the existential character of thinking, for this point is of decisive importance from the relationship between thinking and speaking.

*The Platonic View of Man's Knowledge.* In the history of philosophy we often encounter a spiritualistic view of human knowledge. Man's knowledge is described as something which in its inmost nature transcends the body and the world. No one, of course, has ever claimed that the world is not the source on which man's thinking nourishes itself, for experience shows with all desirable evidence that the opposite is true. The world supplies us, as it were, with the material for our thinking. This statement, however, does not necessarily imply that our thinking is intrinsically, in its structure and its innermost nature, tied to the body and the world. For, no matter how much our thinking is nour-

174

ished by the body and the world, it still remains possible that in its innermost reality it is a supra-corporeal and supra-worldly activity.

The idea expressed in the preceding sentence contains the view taken by Platonic philosophy. Although Plato died several thousand years ago, one cannot at all claim that the fundamental idea of his philosophy has been overtaken by history and should be discarded. Many philosophers continue to think in Platonic fashion. Plato belongs to the group of so-called "classical" philosophers, which means that he has put forward a view destined to play a perpetual role in the philosophical approach to reality.[4] According to Plato, our thinking, despite its dependence upon the body and the world, has a supra-worldly origin. The human mind possesses a light of its own and this light arises from a supra-worldly sphere. Plato speaks of a kind of world of ideas of which our material world would be a mirror-like reflexion. It is difficult to determine exactly what he meant by this world of ideas. He probably had an intuitive inkling of a higher, supra-worldly reality with which our mind is connected, but did not succeed in expressing it in a clear fashion.

Accordingly, in the Platonic view our mind is related to a higher, supra-material world. From this world it has received a "light," but this light alone is not sufficient to give us actual knowledge. It has first to be, as it were, activated in our contact with the material world. In this sense we need this world to arrive at knowledge; nevertheless, the material world is not really the source of our knowledge. This world awakens something in us which we possess from within through our relationship with the higher world. The material world is the occasion rather than the cause of our knowledge.

*Supra-Worldly Origin of Ideas.* Plato uses the image of re-

---

[4] Gerhard Krüger's work, *Grundprobleme der gegenwartigen Philosophie*, Frankfurt a.M., 1958, clearly shows that the Platonic approach is not yet past. The book offers a historical perspective, but intends to show the fundamental truth of Platonism.

membrance to illustrate his idea.[5] If later in life we pay a visit to the paternal home in which we spent our youth, all kinds of memories awaken in us. Events which we had thought forgotten suddenly come again to our mind when we see an old tree, a water well, or a staircase. The house itself is not the source of these images coming to our mind. It is merely the occasion which makes that which is hiddenly present in us reveal itself clearly. Plato refers to our knowledge as a kind of remembrance. Because of our relationship with the higher world, we carry in our bosom a hidden treasure, but our own power does not suffice to make us conscious of this treasure. We need to come into contact with the world to become aware of it.

Let us illustrate the matter by means of an example. In our world we meet good things and good people. The goodness of things and men is concrete and passing. Yet our contact with them makes arise in our mind the idea of goodness as such. This idea cannot be explained on the basis of the good which we encounter in the world, for it is richer and fuller than the world's concrete good. We realize that the good in the world is not goodness itself, but only a deficient embodiment of the absolute good, in which it participates. In the light of the idea of the good we know the deficient character of the good found in our concrete world. Our idea, therefore, functions as a norm. This is a clear indication that this idea does not have its origin in the world itself. For otherwise our idea of the good could never transcend the good which we encounter in the world.

Our ideas, therefore, transcend the body and the world. They are supra-worldly. Accordingly, we must make a distinction in ourselves between a part which belongs to the world and a supra-worldly part. In man there is a supra-worldly part, which is called man's "soul" or "spirit." Plato sometimes refers to man's body as a kind of prison of his supra-worldly part. In this way he is led to demand of man a kind of asceticism: in order to do

---

[5] Concerning Plato's theory of remembrance and its importance see W. N. Klever, *Anamnēsis en Anagogē*, Assen, 1962.

justice to his supra-worldly part, the most important dimension of his being, man must detach himself from the bonds tying him to the world. One who cultivates these bonds disregards his own supra-worldly dimension.

*Platonism and Christianism.* Platonism naturally appealed to Christianity. Plato affirmed our relationship to a higher reality, and Christianity affirms man's relationship to God, for he is made to the image of God. Christ made us look forward to a new mode of existence, destined to replace our present way of existing. Christianity therefore attributes only a relative value to our present mode of existence. Plato did likewise although in a different way. Both Platonism and Christianity demand detachment. For these reasons Plato's dualistic view was able to penetrate into the world of Christian thought. By "dualistic view" we mean the sharp distinction between a worldly and a supra-worldly dimension in man, between body and spirit. This distinction finds expression in the generally accepted Christian statement that in man we must distinguish between a mortal body and an immortal soul. When the body dies the supra-worldly part of man continues to exist.

It is entirely in line with this vision to conceive thinking as an activity of man's supra-worldly part. Although man's thinking is nourished by the world, it is a supra-worldly event occurring in the spiritual part of man. Even after death man continues to think, although then his thinking is no longer nourished by the world. For this reason medieval philosophy indulged in all kinds of speculations regarding the way in which man's separated spirit would know after death.

Thomism affirms a stronger bond between spirit and body than is affirmed by Platonism. For it conceives the human spirit as the substantial form of the body and consequently as intrinsically connected with the body. However, Thomism also asserts that the human spirit can exist without the body, even though such an existence is not normal for it. Thomism likewise holds that thinking is an activity which is intrinsically incor-

177

poreal, raised above the body.[6] In this view man's thinking depends upon the world as its nourishing source, but is not existent in man's bodily being in the full sense of this expression.

These and other similar views regard knowing as an activity of what may be called "the mind's eye."[7] This "eye" is nourished by the body and therefore indirectly dependent upon the body and the world, but itself is not of a bodily nature. In this view man's knowledge contains aspects derived from the character of this "eye" itself. Knowledge, for example, has a universality that cannot be explained on the basis of its worldly source. The world is contingent and transitory, and everything in this world is concrete and passing. Our knowledge transcends this concrete and passing sphere because of the nature of the "mind's eye." Many efforts have been made to explain the universal and absolute character of our knowledge on the basis of its worldly sources. The theory of induction, for example, tried to offer such an explanation. Although the perceived facts, it said, happen only once and are contingent, nevertheless the regular repetition of such facts justifies a universal and necessary conclusion. This claim, however, revealed itself unable to resist the objections made against it. Thus it seems that we have to arrive at the conclusion that we will never be able to reach universality, necessity and absoluteness unless they are present at the very start of our knowledge. In man, however, a Platonic philosopher will add, these features are present from the very beginning, not on the basis of the bodily source of his knowledge but because of his "mind's eye."

*Contemporary Difficulties Against the Dualistic View.* As we have mentioned already, this view cannot be said to have been overtaken by history and to be now antiquated. It is based on solid foundations and will find adherents in the future just as it

---

[6] Thomists sometimes speak about the dependence of the intellect upon the body as an extrinsic dependence which safeguards its intrinsic dependence.

[7] St. Augustine often speaks of the *oculus mentis,* the mind's eye. He raises this "eye" above all forms of bodily being.

178

has them in the present. Nevertheless, the contemporary climate of philosophical thought has many objections against that view. Surprisingly enough, these objections arise not only from philosophical circles but also from theology. Contemporary exegesis penetrates more profoundly into the Old Testament way of thinking, which has influenced, of course, also the writings of the New Testament. The comparison of Christian thought, as it has developed in the course of centuries, with the Scriptural way of thinking shows that Platonism is, strictly speaking, a foreign element that has penetrated into Christian thought. Theologians ask themselves whether the dualistic view can really be called a Christian view, whether Christian doctrine has not been too readily interpreted in a Platonic sense. The New Testament, at any rate, does not put the emphasis on a spiritual soul which continues to exist after death but on the resurrection, i.e., the restoration of the whole man.

However, it is not our task to examine the theological reasons which play a role in the present, widespread renewal of thinking. We are interested in the philosophical reasons. The latter are closely connected with the development of the empirical sciences. This connection should not surprise us. Man seeks light in many ways, in everyday practical life, in the arts and in the sciences. There is a common sphere of enlightenment covering many realms. The philosopher endeavors to give expression to the fundamental lines characterizing this growth of light and is, therefore, sensitive also to the light arising from the empirical sciences.[8] Among these sciences, psychology and psychiatry make it increasingly evident that all human activities, including man's thinking and willing, are conditioned by the body. The human psyche with its uniqueness permeates everything. Bodily disturbances affect all his activities. For a psychologist it is difficult to accept that there are activities in man which would be internally

---

[8] Merleau-Ponty often stresses that the light arising in the sciences has a philosophical significance. It is the task of the philosopher to pay attention to this light and to take it into account in his reflections. This, however, implies the duty of becoming familiar with the sciences.

179

independent of the body. Biology places an ever increasing emphasis on evolution. Although the theory of evolution has perhaps not yet been definitively proved and continues therefore to be an hypothesis, nevertheless, this hypothesis becomes constantly more probable. The number of its opponents decreases steadily and that of its adherents continues to grow. Evolution, so it seems, involves the whole man. This view does not harmonize with the thesis that man is man primarily not through his bodily being but through a supra-bodily part.

Moreover, through the development of the historical sciences, of archeology and of anthropology, we now know better to what extent man has come to be man. Former ages conceived man as a finished and fully developed being from his first beginning. When they thought of the first men, they pictured them as fully developed cultural beings. One has only to read the Genesis account of man's origin: it ascribes to the first human beings all essential forms of culture, such as language, agriculture, cattle breeding, the building of towns, arts and metal crafts. Today, however, we know how primitive the life of the first human beings must have been. We now prefer to speak about the development into man rather than an eternal and immutable human being. We hesitate more and more to speak of "human nature" and when we still do it, we know less and less what exactly the term means. In general one may say that all our contemporary discoveries and our scientific conclusions indicate how deeply our human existence is rooted in the body. We become constantly more aware of the darkness in which our existence is rooted.

*Antispiritualism.* Contemporary thought is characterized by a strongly antispiritualistic tendency. This expression, however, is easily misunderstood. Antispiritualistic thought does not deny the spiritual aspect of man. On the contrary, the thinking of existentialism and phenomenology precisely places great emphasis on the human spirit. They stress that man is man because he transcends the blind interplay of natural forces. They often repeat that the cultural order cannot be reduced to the natural order. Man is, they say, a subject. He makes the world meaning-for-himself, he is the center of a world of meaning. The antispiritualism, then, of contemporary thought is characterized not by the denial of man's spirit but by that of the separateness of that spirit. It rejects the distinction between a bodily and an unbodily dimension of man. It does not deny the irreducible and proper character of man's spirit, but only its separate entity. It affirms the spirit but denies that this affirmation must necessarily lead to dualism. It opposes the metaphysical dualism which makes the body and the spirit or soul, matter and mind, two separate entities and denies that man is a composite of these two entities.

The use of the term "antispiritualism" is not without danger. It easily creates the impression that antispiritualists are against the whole idea of a human spirit. While that may be true of some, many antispiritualists are only against the metaphysical and philosophical theories in which the affirmation of the human spirit found expression and gave form to the distinction between matter and spirit. It would be better to speak only of antidualism in reference to these thinkers. Nevertheless, there is a historical reason why the term "antispiritualism" is used: the old spiritualism and to some extent even that of today thought that it had to be dualistic. Many believed that the rejection of dualism would make the affirmation of the spirit impossible. They defended dualism in the name of spiritualism and in this way forced antidualism to present itself as an "antispiritualism." Even today one who denies dualism exposes himself to the reproach of denying the spiritual aspect of man.

*Dualism and Creation.* Strange as it may seem, dualism has sought support in the Judaeo-Christian idea of creation. Yet, strictly speaking, that idea is opposed to dualism. One who accepts the idea of creation regards God as the absolute origin of all beings. God Himself is conceived as a spirit. That means, therefore, that all beings are participations in God, in the Spirit. Thomas Aquinas says that all beings are something insofar as

181

they are a likeness of God.[9] If, then, God is Spirit, doesn't it follow that everything bears a likeness to this Spirit, so that one cannot posit absolute opposition between matter and spirit?

We must add that the Greek philosophers who adhered to dualism never came to the idea of creation. We may even go further and claim that it was impossible for them to formulate such an idea. Once an absolute opposition is admitted between matter and spirit, it is logically no longer possible to claim that both originate from one and the same source. Dualism is not supported by the idea of creation but rather in conflict with it. One cannot admit that everything has its origin in God, in the Spirit, without acknowledging at the same time that everything, matter included, is a participation in the Spirit, i.e., without denying dualism. As soon, however, as this participation is accepted, it is no longer strange that matter can develop into the human spirit. Viewed in this way, the idea of evolution is no longer unchristian but rather a continuation of a fundamental Christian view.

A "Monistic" Conception of Man. A new view is gradually taking shape, a view which refuses to place matter and spirit in opposition. This view permits us to say that man is material, as well as that matter has a spiritual character. According to this conception, all matter is potentially spiritual and this spiritual character manifests itself most strikingly in man. The wealth of being possible for matter reveals itself when man is reached. As Dr. van Melsen correctly points out, this view is misunderstood if one reproaches it for reducing man to the level of matter.[10] The reproach arises from a dualistic mentality: it first

---

9 *Summa contra Gentes,* lib. III, c. 19.

10 Andrew G. van Melsen, *Science and Technology,* Pittsburgh, 1961, p. 151. On pp. 146–170 the author discusses the dualistic and the monistic hypotheses. Although he does not make a definitive choice, his preference appears to go toward the monistic view. The monistic hypothesis, he says, does not have to be regarded as a degradation of man. One could just as well regard it as a raising of matter to a higher level. Cf. also van Melsen's forthcoming work, *Evolution and Philosophy,* to be published by Duquesne University Press.

distinguishes between unspiritual matter and immaterial spirit and then accuses the monistic conception of reducing man to unspiritual matter. If the reproach were valid, the monistic view would indeed fail to do justice to man's innermost essence. The new conception of man, however, does not regard man as matter in opposition to spirit, but as matter which is potentially spiritual.

If man is viewed in this way, he reveals, especially in the life of his spirit, the wealth of being that is possible for matter. Moreover, this view does not reduce everything to a common denominator. For, the potentialities of being contained in matter unfold themselves very gradually in the various types of material beings. In living bodies matter reveals itself as life, which is not yet the case in non-living matter. In animals it unfolds into a psyche. In man, finally, matter reveals itself as a self-conscious spirit. Matter, then, can exist on different levels of development, and the distinction between these levels must be maintained. On the other hand, this view leaves room for the idea of evolution, for the different levels can gradually evolve from matter.

At the beginning of this section we gave a brief description of Plato's ideas and pointed out that Platonism is not at all past as a philosophy. As we went on, however, we seem gradually to have reached a point where Platonism appears antiquated. Plato was a dualist, and the dualistic view becomes constantly less probable. In reply, we may say that the most valuable elements of Platonic thought are not lost in the new conception of man. Plato correctly saw that man's knowledge, the scope of human ideas, cannot be explained on the basis of the world around man. This Platonic insight remains valid also in the "monistic" view, for according to this view also we must maintain that the possibilities of being contained in matter become manifest in man himself. Man himself is the highest revelation, the highest realization of the potentialities which matter has for being. What being is, what matter is, becomes really evident only in man. One who leaves man out of consideration, would not even know what being-material ultimately means. Matter becomes conscious of itself in man.

One could call man the consciousness of the world, the being in which the world becomes conscious of itself. Man is, as Sartre expresses it, the interiorization of the world, the one in which the world arrives at self-consciousness, at a thinking-about-itself. In man the world attains to an interior life. For this reason we must not say that the human mind is a "sheet of paper on which nothing is written," a sheet which is inscribed from without, a darkness illuminated by an external light. In man matter becomes light. The way in which the world becomes light must always be understood also on the basis of man himself. The light of knowledge can never be understood exclusively on the basis of infrahuman reality. Man finds this light more in himself than outside himself. He belongs to the world and is therefore orientated outwardly. But he orientates himself outwardly precisely as the consciousness of the world. One could say that the world becomes self-conscious precisely insofar as it is the field of man's gaze. Man makes the world truth.

It would be meaningless to call infrahuman reality, as such, light or truth. The world becomes light or truth within man's gazing at the world and because of man's gaze. Plato considered it impossible to understand what we call truth on the basis of a man-less world, and he was right. Man's knowledge has a scope and width which can never be understood on the basis of infrahuman reality alone. Man's knowledge, the world become truth, must be understood on the basis of man. Plato realized this, and contemporary thinking does not want to argue against his position in this respect. However, it doubts that the dualistic conclusion which Plato drew from this insight is justified.

*Man's Tendency to a Total View.* After these reflections we must ask the question whether it will ever be possible to prove the metaphysical, monistic conception of man described above. In former ages dualism was widely accepted and its adherents thought that they could prove its validity. Their proofs, however,

184

have shown themselves to be ill-founded, thus making dualism more a hypothesis than an established truth. Must we not say that the new conception is likewise only a hypothesis? Can it ever be demonstrated? Is it possible definitively to refute dualism? In our reflections on these questions we should not forget that man always seeks to obtain a total view of reality, a world view.

Even at a time when he had only a few data at his disposal, man formed such a total view and expressed it in his myths. Such mythical total views can be found even among the most primitive tribes. As soon as he began to investigate reality in a more objective way, and could dispose of some data which we would now call "scientific," man tried to arrive at a philosophical total view. Now that the sciences have developed greatly and gathered an enormous wealth of data, man endeavors to arrive at a total view on the basis of these sciences. In this endeavor he sometimes fails to pay attention to the fact that such a total view always transcends the strictly scientific level.

With the followers of Marx one can claim that the old total views were manifestations of a morbid metaphysics, a kind of idealism, a complex of ideas cut loose from reality and running wild. Paradoxically as it may seem, however, Marxism reveals itself as a new total view, a view possessing its own dogmas and its own catechism. The tendency to form a total view is so inherent in man that it is dangerous to call it an expression of man's excessive self-esteem. On the contrary, we should say that this tendency manifests man's innermost essence. In his primitive stage man had to try to satisfy this tendency with the primitive means at his disposal. The resulting total views were, of course, primitive and are now antiquated.

Man is the consciousness of the world, in him reality attains self-knowledge. Should he, the world's self-consciousness, be reproached for trying to attain a world view? There is no justification for rejecting man's tendency to arrive at a total vision as a morbid symptom. Of course, man must continue to gather more data and to pursue his empirical research. At the same time, how-

185

ever, he must endeavor to use the available data to build up a total view. Those who profess to reject such attempts, nonetheless in one way or another unwittingly endeavor to arrive at a total view. Like people of former ages, we will not escape from the fact that our total view also will contain primitive elements. For this reason we must always be ready to correct our view. But we have the right and even the duty to search for such a view. If one wants to call that search a metaphysical pursuit, metaphysics will always continue to exist.

A contemporary total view which has made a profound impression is that of Teilhard de Chardin. He himself claims that his writings have the character of positive science. No matter, however, how many positive data he has gathered in them, ultimately his work is of a metaphysical character precisely because he builds up a total view which transcends his scientific data.

*The Importance of These Questions for the Philosophy of Language.* The title above this section indicated that it would deal with the existential character of thinking, but in the course of our considerations we seem to have deviated very much from the perspective of the philosophy of language. It was necessary, however, to do so, for in the philosophy of language questions about the background against which we philosophize play an important role. One who professes dualism, one who sees man in his ultimate reality as a spirit raised above the world and materiality, will have to ascribe man's thinking to this spirit. He will have to detach the inner core of thinking from language and from all other forms of existence, for language is evidently a bodily phenomenon. Although the dualist is able to regard language as a bodily support of thought, he cannot escape from claiming that in its innermost essence thinking transcends speaking.

From all this it should be evident that we are confronted here with a very difficult problem. We first discussed the dualist hypothesis, which forces its adherent to make a sharp distinction between thought and speech. We then considered a new metaphysical hypothesis, the monistic view, which is rapidly gaining more supporters but nonetheless lacks convincing proofs. In either case, therefore, all we have is a simple hypothesis. One may rightly ask whether it is justified to base a philosophical inquiry into language on anything that is a mere hypothesis.

Our reply is that there is no escape in philosophy from proceeding on such a hypothetical basis. Whoever philosophizes always somehow bases himself on a philosophical hypothesis. The inner core of genuine philosophy always is of a metaphysical nature. Implicitly or explicitly a total view is always present in man's philosophy. Whether one reads the works of Plato or Aristotle, St. Augustine or Plotinus, St. Anselm or Thomas Aquinas, Descartes or Locke, Comte or Marx, Jaspers or Sartre, Marcel or Merleau-Ponty, a total view always reveals itself in their philosophical writings. Such a view is present even, but only in a latent fashion, in analytic philosophy. Although the English empirical mind is very much averse to unjustified total views, analytic philosophy implies a fundamental theory concerning the possibilities and scope of human knowledge. No philosopher can escape from placing himself on the standpoint of a vision which he cannot justify down to its last details and its most obscure ramifications. The question whether or not thinking has an existential character is connected with the presence of a world view in all philosophical reflection.

*The Existential Character of Thinking.* After these long preliminaries we must now try to indicate what exactly is meant by the existential character of man's thinking. Experience teaches us that, while thinking, we make use of many auxiliary means, for instance, our eyes. We say that our eyes measure the distance and that they survey the traffic situation while we are driving. We use our tongue and taste food and drink with its tip. We think with our hands when, e.g., we touch cloth to judge its quality. We make use of words. In our internal reflection we try to attain clarity through the use of words. A chess player thinks, as it were, in chess-men; lying in bed at night, he can keep the chess-board before his mind and move the pieces to see the result of his imaginary moves. The question, now, is whether man's thinking takes place *in* all this or merely lies *behind* it. Some would be inclined to reply that, although our thinking makes use of seeing, hearing, touching, external and internal speech, ultimately all these things serve merely as external means. They regard thinking itself as raised above all such means, as not existing *in* them but lying *behind* them.

Strange as it may seem, if we want to raise that question, we have almost inevitably to make use of localizing terms. We ask whether thinking exists *in* the above-mentioned activities or lies *behind* them. Considered in itself, such a localizing terminology is, of course, wholly incorrect. We are not concerned with localizing man's thinking in any particular part of his body, although even that kind of localization constantly recurs in the way man speaks about thinking. For example, in the Old Testament people are presented as thinking with their hearts, while we use our brains for the same purpose. What we are concerned with here is the relationship between the so-called "auxiliary means" of thinking and thinking itself. Two possibilities present themselves here. Our thinking could be fused with these means in such a way that it becomes a manifold of distinct activities in the plurality of means. It could also be true that thinking as such must be distinguished from these means, that it is a single activity which in its uniqueness transcends the plurality of means.

Differently expressed, Is thinking essentially interwoven with the many bodily means of which it makes use or is it something apart from these means? We defend the position that thinking has an existential character, that is, we consider it essentially interwoven with the bodily means. We do so not without a certain hesitancy, for we realize that it is difficult to prove this position with absolute certainty. The reasons for this difficulty have been explained in the preceding pages where we spoke about the metaphysical background with which this problem is connected. In the following section we will formulate the reasons pointing toward the existential character of thinking.

## 3. REASONS POINTING TO THE EXISTENTIAL CHARACTER OF THINKING

*Obscure and Clear Forms of Knowing.* It is rather striking that often there appears to be no logical connection between the many forms of knowing which are latently present in us. Our knowing has very many forms, and it can even happen that there are contradictions between them, that we affirm in one form of knowing what we deny in another. For instance, it may happen that we are carried away by the general admiration people have for a particular person; we follow others in giving expression to this admiration and even enumerate reasons for it; at the same time, however, in our personal contact with him we feel that this admiration is greatly exaggerated. Our explicit and expressed admiration is accompanied by an obscure feeling that there is something wrong. In such a case it is not possible, of course, that both evaluations would occupy a focal position in our field of consciousness. If then at a later date the truth about that person becomes known to everyone, we could not incorrectly claim that we knew it all the time. To give another example, it happens also that the society in which we live makes us take over its affirmation of certain values and sanction certain institutions, although we obscurely feel deep down in our hearts that those values are not genuine and that those institutions are antiquated. People often feel not quite at ease with a mode of existence which, together with their society, they approve and confirm. In such undefined feelings of being ill at ease, a dark kind of knowing plays an essential role.

This distinction between clear knowing and obscure knowing is very important. Clear or supposedly clear knowledge is as a rule knowledge that has been put into words. It refers to our "universe of discourse," our "spoken" world. Obscure knowing, on the other hand, lies deeper in our existence itself; it is present in the concrete way in which we exist with people and things. In both cases there is question of genuine knowledge, although

189

we often do not realize what we know when our knowing remains obscure. The two forms of knowledge are not always in agreement. The contradiction between our "lived" world and our "spoken" world can sometimes be very painful and confront us with grave problems. The dark knowing we have in our "lived" world usually is the source from which we proceed to renew our "spoken" world.

*"Lived" Forms of Meaning and Value.* There are many forms of meaning and value for which we have a feeling, which we understand, because we "live them." A distinction should be made between "lived" meaning and a meaning that has been rationally formulated and motivated. In both cases there is question of knowing a meaning or a value, but the "lived" meaning and the "spoken" meaning obviously are not always in harmony. Some people are rigid and one-sided in their speaking, their "universe of discourse" impresses us at first as closed; yet in their "lived" dealings with others they reveal themselves endowed with much empathy and feeling for the other's situation. On the other hand, there are also people whose discourse appears broad and open to many values, yet their way of existing with others shows them to be narrow and closed. It would be wholly unjustified to call only rationally formulated knowledge of meaning or value genuine knowledge. Our "living" of meaning and value certainly also implies that we know and understand them. Yet, if we are permitted to play upon words, our "lived" understanding of meaning cannot be separated from our standing-in-meaning, but is wholly interwoven with our existing-in-meaning. Let us illustrate the matter by means of a few examples.

If we want to persuade someone to join a sports club, to take up a particular hobby or form of recreation, we try to convince him that he should do what we are proposing. All kinds of rational motives are put forward in our efforts to make the proposal meaningful to him. We are then dealing with him in the sphere of "spoken," formulated meaning. If he continues to hesitate, we are likely to say: "Why don't you come and try it?" We are then inviting him to "live" the meaning by trying to exist in it. In inviting him to try, we hope that he will then experience that meaning, so that further explanations become unnecessary.

On the other hand, it can also happen that a meaning which once was a real "lived" meaning perdures merely as a "spoken" meaning. A case in point is an organization or a society which has lost its meaningfulness but continues, nonetheless, to exist. It will go on affirming its meaning in words, and its words will even become louder according as this meaning itself diminishes in vitality.[11] It is always a bad sign when too much emphasis has to be placed upon the value of a way of life, of an organization or a society. The necessity to emphasize that value so much can easily arise from the fact that the experience of its meaningfulness is no longer sufficiently clear and that its relative emptiness forces people to seek another way of affirming value.

Accordingly, there is a knowledge of meaning or value which is inseparably united with man's existence in meaning or value. By "living" a value, our eyes are opened to it. For example, it happens occasionally that for a long time we have not occupied ourselves with a certain type of work, with attending the meetings of a certain society, or seeking the company of a certain group of people. During that time doubts may have arisen in us concerning the meaningfulness of that activity, those meetings or that companionship. If, next, we decide to try it once more, two possibilities present themselves. Either our doubt is confirmed and we conclude to the meaninglessness of that activity, or we experience again its meaning, so that our doubt vanishes. The kind of knowing involved in that last try has undoubtedly an existential character.

*The Manifold Forms of Existential Knowing.* Existence-in-

---

[11] Groups, whether religious or non-religious, will be inclined to affirm their value more emphatically when they find fewer followers. The usual alibi offered for this lack of interest is that people are becoming more wicked, more indifferent, less zealous. They are not good enough for the group. It would be useful if such groups considered also the opposite hypothesis—namely, that their particular group is no longer good enough for the people.

meaning is manifold and for this reason the knowledge which is inseparably connected with it is also manifold. These manifold forms of knowing, however, do not constitute a logical whole in the accepted sense of the term. In our work and study we are serious and experience the meaningfulness of being-serious. In a light-hearted conversation we exist in a different way and experience the meaningfulness of not-being-serious. Sometimes we occupy ourselves with necessary and useful things and we consider then that it is meaningful to spend our time usefully. Sometimes, however, we pursue things that are of no conceivable use to us and we then feel that usefulness should not be the norm of our life or at least not its exclusive norm. The various forms of meaning must somehow fit together, at least if we want to lead a harmonious life. Yet they do not at all constitute a logical whole,[12] they do not belong together as parts of a single rational system.

An example may serve to illustrate the point. I recall that one time someone spoke to me about a mutual friend. He had been shocked and dismayed by the fact that on a beautiful summer day he had found that friend flat on his back lying in the grass, doing absolutely nothing but watching the sky. Yet it can be very meaningful to spend some time in that way. If one insists on asking why, our discussion may be short or long but ultimately our rational motivation of that meaningfulness will fall short of the goal. Rational motivation neither teaches us meaning when we first become acquainted with it nor what its most profound essence is. It fails likewise in trying to make life a single meaningful whole. A rationalistic morality, which wants to assign a rational basis to every meaning, which wants to make life a single all-encompassing whole of meaning in a rational fashion, is a very dangerous kind of morality. Basing themselves on rational motives, adults often tell youth that certain forms of play, recrea-

---

[12] The various forms of meaning constitute, of course, a whole, a Gestalt. But the different aspects of that whole do not fit together in the way a rationally conceived complex constitutes a whole.

tion and dancing are meaningless. The young, however, experience them as meaningful and go on with them until finally, sometimes, adults want to try them also and share in their experience of meaningfulness. We do not want to argue, of course, against reason or against rational knowledge. All we want to say is that understanding meaning in an existential way, by "standing-in-meaning," is also a form of knowledge.

*The Existent Spirit.* From the preceding considerations it is evident that we may not attribute all knowledge to a single so-called "mind's eye." If one insists on using that term, he should say that we have many "eyes of the mind." Every form of man's existing is connected with such an "eye." While playing, we "have an eye" for the meaning of play; while joking, we "have an eye" for humor; while swimming or walking, we "have an eye" for the meaning of body movement; while studying, we "have an eye" for the meaning of insight and understanding; while speaking, we "have an eye" for the meaning of speech. We are knowing spirits, but the knowing spirit is not a single point from which we survey everything in the whole of our existence. The knowing spirit is, as it were, dispersed over the whole of our existence and shares in its manifold aspects. It exists in the eye that sees, in the tongue that tastes, in the hand which touches and works, in the ear that listens. Man is a knowing spirit in constantly different ways, so that it is difficult for our knowing spirit to give expression to its own unity. One who begins to exist in a new way becomes an existent spirit in a new way. Man is power to know. It would be dangerous, however, to conceive the possibility we have to know as a single power, a single faculty. As cognitive power we are present in our entire existence and become many in the plurality of aspects pertaining to this existence. We are one person but our unity is internally permeated with plurality. We are unity in plurality. The human spirit has too often been regarded as an absolute center of unity in our plurality. Man is a spirit, but an existing spirit, and for this reason the manifold character of our existing permeates also the spirit itself.

The illusion that the spirit has absolute unity is derived from man's speaking. Speech, as we have seen, is a new form of giving meaning. This form is characterized by the fact that it encompasses all other forms of giving meaning, for everything can be made the subject matter of speech. Any meaning can be made into a signification. By speaking, we can give a new mode of existence to any meaning, we can transpose any meaning into the field of significations. In this field all meanings acquire a certain kind of uniformity, for they become there rational significations; they are taken up into a single "universe of discourse." The speaking spirit prevails in the rationalistic Western world and increasingly also in the whole world. The reason is that by making it enter into our "universe of discourse" we foster the growth and development of meaning. Thus it is not surprising that we are inclined to absolutize the speaking spirit and simply to identify the human spirit with it. The speaking spirit is the reflecting spirit, the spirit which withdraws from the immediacy of life. If then the speaking spirit considers its own speaking as an external addition of merely secondary importance, if the speaking spirit divorces its thinking from its speaking, thought becomes an internal occupation surveying everything. In this way the spirit as the power to think is placed outside human existence.

It is against this tendency to compartmentalize that we are arguing here. Thinking, as understanding of meaning, must not be divorced from existing-in-meaning. As we have seen, the thinking spirit is an existent spirit. But the reflecting spirit also is an existent spirit, a spirit existing in speaking. We have rejected the identification of thinking and speaking, not because we want to divorce these two, but because the spirit which exists in speaking exists also in many other ways. We reject the identification of thinking and speaking, not because we deny that speaking is a form in which thinking exists, but because it is not the only form. As soon, however, as the spirit becomes a thinking spirit, thinking and speaking can no longer be separated.

*Inseparability of Thinking and Speaking in Reflection.* The arguments for the above-mentioned standpoint have been formulated in a masterful way by Merleau-Ponty.[13] We will follow them here, not because we want to render an account of his philosophy of language, but because we do not see any better arguments in favor of that standpoint.

If we carefully pay attention to ourselves, we realize that no finished thought precedes our speaking. We do not first arrive at clarity in our thinking and then only proceed to give expression to this clarity in words. Our thought does not reach maturity before we put it into words. On the contrary, in being worded our thinking becomes clear. We seek clarity and find it in our speaking. As should be evident, we are not referring here to the so-called "spoken word," the repetition of what has already been said. With respect to that "spoken word," clarity is present even before it is repeated, but that clarity had already been put into words previously. We are referring here to the "speaking word," in which we try to say what has never been said, in which we make words say something which they have not yet expressed. In this "speaking word" we find thought trying to find itself and this effort is inseparably connected with speaking. The author who writes a book develops his own thinking while he is writing. He himself is sometimes surprised by the thoughts born while he is writing. A chapter may develop quite differently from the way he had originally planned.

The word therefore is a source of meaning. By "word" we do not mean the lifeless entries made in a vocabulary but the living, functioning word. This word is the instrument, the vehicle, of the living and thinking spirit. By means of it the spirit gradually attains clarity. Learning to think is learning to use words. Our conversations sometimes show us how creative of meaning speaking is. In a conversation we sometimes hear a word which brings progress to our common situation, but we can also hear one which radically destroys it. Someone may pronounce the "liberating word," the word which solves an impasse. Searching for clarity

---

[13] *Phénoménologie de la perception*, pp. 206–221.

we may have the feeling that our speaking does not really come to the point, until we find the word which liberates us. This liberating expression gives peace to our mind, a peace that will last until we begin to search again.

The word is a source of light. Scripture ascribes creative power to the word of God: He spoke and things came into existence. Our word does not create, but it does bring light. As we have mentioned previously, man speaks and things become clear. Our speech is power over light, power over meaning. As soon as man has put a meaning in words, he can use it in his work, at least if the worded meaning lies within the manipulable world. According to Francis Bacon's famous statement, "science is power." He made this statement in a period when man's knowing began to withdraw from the realm of metaphysical speculations and became a clear knowing of the world. In other words, man's knowing withdrew to the realm of the manipulable. Knowledge of the manipulable certainly is power. It does not merely lead to power but is power. Man's word is a grasping of meaning. The ancients were not entirely wrong when they attributed a magic power to speech. By putting a meaning in words, we make it present and bring it within our reach. We strip it of its strangeness, we make it belong to our "universe of discourse" in which we move freely. Western man owes his power to his science, that is, to the fact that by speaking he brings things to light. Other peoples, who want to acquire Western man's power, have to become familiar first with the Western way of speaking, as they realize very well. If we were to forget the speech which brings to light, we would lose at the same time the world of light connected with this speech.

Because this connection exists, there exists also a very remarkable phenomenon: by reading a thinker's works, it is possible for us to make our own the world of light in which he lived. The thinker is dead, but his thinking, the light in which he lived, has not disappeared. It exists in his works, as is evident from the fact that we can find it there. If that light was not present in his works, we would never be able to find it there. The same applies also to living thinkers. We can make their light our own by listening to them. That means that their light exists in the words which we hear.

Accordingly, the meaning of speaking, the light of thinking, cannot be separated from the word in which this meaning, this light, exists. No one will try to separate the light present in other means of expression from these expressive means. For example, one does not attempt to separate the meaning of a painting from the canvas, lines and colors, the meaning of music from sounds, the meaning of a statue from its materials, or the meaning of a dance from the movements of the body. In the same way it is not possible to separate the meaning of speech from speech itself.

*The Manifold Existential Forms of Thinking.* Speaking, as we have said, is one of the forms in which thinking exists. It is a privileged form because it encompasses, as it were, all others. We think in many ways, our thinking has many existential forms, and therefore there are many forms of thought meaning. We can more or less successfully try to make every thought meaning a worded meaning, for we can try to put any meaning into words. No matter, however, how privileged speech is as a mode of existence of thinking, it is not the only mode. Yet people are sometimes inclined to forget or to disregard the other forms in which thinking can exist.

Merleau-Ponty himself seems to do this when he unqualifiedly refers to silence as the cradle of speech.[14] He is right if by "silence" he means solely not-yet-speaking, but in that case his statement is void of content. All it really means then is that speech puts into words that which had not yet been put into words.

In reality the negative term "silence" covers a very differentiated world, a world that can even contain a wealth of meaning. Man's thinking has many forms, and we understand a meaning

---

[14] *Phénoménologie de la perception,* p. 463.

within our existence before we put it into words. By thinking in words, we express what we had already understood in a different way, we transfer the meaning that is already for us to our "universe of discourse." In other words, Merleau-Ponty's silence is not at all a uniform silence. Sometimes it is poorer than speech, but sometimes also much richer, for there are forms of meaning which are easily understood but very difficult to put into words. We find it difficult to speak about music for which we have an intense feeling or about a painting which we admire greatly. We can only stammer a few words to express what the love and affection of a fellow-man mean for us, but nonetheless we know very well what they are from our experience of their love and affection. We know from experience how wholesome and invigorating it is to converse with friends, even if that conversation is apparently aimless. But we are lost for words if we had to express the wholesome character of that conversation. The same applies to religion. The religious man knows and feels what contact with God means for him, yet how could he put it into words for someone who is not a religious man?

There are realms of knowledge in which almost everything depends on putting it into words, realms of which we acquire genuine knowledge only in and through speech. However, there are also many other realms of which we have genuine knowledge, but with respect to which putting that knowledge into words does not help us very much. In our Western world we greatly overestimate, I fear, the importance of putting things into words. We are too much inclined to identify it with bringing things to light. We tend to be doubtful about any meaning that does not allow itself to be put into words. We sometimes unduly make the word be the norm of all meaning. A meaning which does not, or not adequately, lend itself to incorporation in our "universe of discourse" is often regarded as not a real meaning at all but only a subjective experience void of any value.

For example, religious meaning cannot be adequately put into words. It is very difficult if not impossible for us to express in the sphere of rational language why there is a God. We are unable to account for our contact with Him in the world of speech. Religious people have sometimes overdone it when they tried to put that contact into words. Their efforts have given rise to or increased doubt about religion. We do not mean, of course, that God and religion may not be the object of reflection. One who would draw that conclusion from our remarks would identify thinking with worded thinking, which is precisely what we are protesting against. Man simply has to recognize the fact that he knows also in other ways than in worded thinking and that these other ways sometimes possess greater clarity. Those who blindly follow the exaggerated esteem of the West for worded thinking can hardly avoid doubt concerning the value of any form of thinking that is not put into words.

Fortunately life is often wiser than the explicit theories of man. There are many forms of meaning which we cannot put into words but which nonetheless we undisturbedly continue to "live." Modern man is fascinated by science, by worded knowledge, yet life continues to exhibit many aspects which escape the grip of science and in which man feels entirely at home. I have the impression that the realm of these aspects is not diminishing but rather increasing. The reason for it probably is an existential protest against the overesteem of worded knowledge. We continue doing things which we are unable to understand or justify in the sphere of worded knowledge.

*The Relativity of Worded Knowledge.* Worded knowledge must make an effort to realize its own relative value within the whole of life. It must realize that sometimes it can only inadequately express what man knows in an entirely different way. It must recognize the reality, the value, the great importance of other forms of knowing. All this does not mean irrationalism, but merely is a recognition that man's thinking can assume many forms.

Worded knowledge brings things to light. It encompasses everything because everything can become a topic of speech. Yet

199

it is not the only way in which light arises, the only way in which we can bring things to light. It has the wondrous capacity of drawing everything into its own sphere of light, yet it is not the only sphere of light. It is not the norm of all light, although it can critically discuss all forms of light. Worded knowledge acts, and rightly so, as a judge. It calls all other forms of meaning and value before its judgment seat. In our worded knowing we consider whether something has meaning or value, we distinguish in every conceivable realm between value and non-value, meaning and meaninglessness.

Nevertheless, our worded knowing, which brings things to light in a very special way of its own, may not let itself be guided exclusively by its own way of giving light. It has to be sensitive to other forms of light arising in different ways. When worded knowing proceeds to judge meaning or value it often has to let itself be guided by a light which does not originate in itself. Let us illustrate the matter through an example. The staff of a school discusses whether the children receive sufficient physical training and have enough opportunity to let themselves "go" in their natural mobility. Their worded thinking evaluates the facts and proceeds to take the necessary steps. In doing so, the teachers must be guided by the living needs of the children, they must understand the child's typical condition and its bodily way of being. If they fail to do so, if they have no feeling for children, they will make the wrong decisions. To give another example, when we discuss whether a particular television comedy has been interesting, our worded reason speaks. But to be able to judge the matter, our reason must have a sense for humor, and this sense does not lie in worded reason itself but in a different sphere. Worded reason must be sensitive to the proper character of all forms of light if it wants to judge them properly. That is difficult, of course, but necessary.

The relationship between thinking and speaking is very complex. Thinking, as we have seen, has an existential character. When we are thinking in words, we cannot separate thinking and speaking, but our thinking is then existent in our speaking. Nevertheless, thinking and speaking are not identical, for thinking can assume many existential forms. On the other hand, thinking-in-words has a privileged position because it can encompass all other forms of thinking. In this chapter we have made a plea for the existential character of the human spirit: its thinking is not something separate but is present and multiplied in all forms of human existence.

# CHAPTER EIGHT

# The Manifold Forms of Speech

A MEASURE of one-sidedness has crept into the preceding chapter. It was inevitable that this would happen, for it is not possible to stress simultaneously all aspects. We spoke about language as a certain way of giving meaning, pointed out that thinking-in-words is not the only form of thinking, and stressed that the speaking intellect may not consider itself the absolute norm of all meaning. Yet the speaking intellect which proceeds to judge is reason as trying to reach objective statements. It endeavors to obtain objective clarity in its statements. The use, however, which is made of language in this way is not the only form of speech. Language can also function in an entirely different way. A mother, for example, who takes care of her infant, uses many words of endearment, without in any way trying to make statements. People in love have moments when they feel, as it were, entirely merged into one. They still speak words, but they have no intention whatsoever to formulate statements. A poet likewise speaks, but he seems more like one who paints with words than one who makes statements. In the preceding chapter we restricted ourselves to a single form of using language, but there are also others. That restriction was necessary for the purpose pursued in that chapter. We must now take care to correct the resulting one-sidedness, or rather to complement its considerations by paying attention to the many forms which our speaking can assume.

## 1. EXISTENCE AND EXPRESSION

In Merleau-Ponty's main work, *Phenomenology of Perception,* one of the chapters is entitled "The Body as Expression, and Speech." It is striking that he refers to the body itself as expression. His intention, however, would be misunderstood if one draws the conclusion that according to Merleau-Ponty there is something other than the body which expresses itself by means of the body, i.e., that the body is the means used by a bodiless spirit to express itself. Such an interpretation must be rejected, first, because Merleau-Ponty rejects the existence of a bodiless spirit; secondly, because he denies that man gives expression to a pre-existing meaning.

*An Erroneous View of Expression.* Expression[1] is often understood in the following sense. There are three phases in expression. First, there must be something that is given expression; for instance, a thought, an idea, an emotion or a feeling. This first element is understood as something that is real in itself prior to being expressed. Secondly, there must be a material of expression, that is, something in which the pre-existing thought or emotion can be expressed. Examples of such material are the canvas and paint of the artist, the stone of the sculptor, man's own body as a possibility to move, and the sounds which he can produce. Finally, that which is being given expression is "translated" into the material of the expression.

This idea of expression used to be rather general in the past and even today has its followers. We may say that one who begins to reflect upon expression will be inclined to look at the matter in that way. A student who is unable to answer a question may offer an excuse by saying that he knows the answer but is unable to express it properly. He thereby implies that knowing precedes expression.

---

[1] Merleau-Ponty has shown the close relationship existing between verbal expression and other forms of expression. A fundamental function, he says, is active in all forms of expression and this function gives rise to meaning in the body and in the world.

Yet that view is wrong. Expression does not simply make manifest something that is pregiven in fully finished form in man's interiority. Man is existent in his expression, he realizes himself in it. We have seen this in the preceding chapter, where we considered how thinking realizes itself in speech. The same is true also for the artist. The painter and the sculptor do not have a finished ideal image in their mind which, next, they express in the materials of their choice. Of course, they prepare their work, they have an image in mind representing what the painting or the statue will look like. This fancied image, however, is not an ideal to which the finished work is related as a copy, but rather has the nature of a preliminary and preparatory expression. It is more or less like the rough sketches which artists sometimes make. They begin by expressing themselves in an imagined material then proceed to draw a sketch on a piece of paper. These activities are incipient forms of expression preparing the way for the artist's proper work. Only in that proper work of expression does the artist fully realize himself.

*Inseparability of Existence and Expression.* Art is an explicitly willed and systematically pursued form of expression. Life itself, however, contains many modes of expression that are almost just as natural as our existence itself. When, for example, a mother looks at her child in the morning, she sees at once whether or not the little one is feeling all right. As soon as a member of the family enters the dining room, we see immediately in what mood he is. From experience we know the various types of behavior manifesting joy, sorrow, anger, annoyance, exuberance, etc. All of them are forms of expression. They are, of course, connected with a mood, but it would be entirely wrong to say that this mood is deliberately given expression in the body. Feeling joyful and acting joyfully merge, as it were, in a natural unity. A child is not even capable of making a distinction between them. One who would forbid a child to act joyfully would forbid it to be joyful.

Man expresses himself also in his surroundings. A look at the

204

way a house is furnished shows what kind of a woman takes care of it. A teenager who is given a room of his own puts his seal on it. A nation expresses itself in the towns and cities which it builds. The Dutch are reputed to be very clean in their habits, but all too often that cleanliness is limited to the individual's home and garden and does not extend to public areas. They take great care of their personal property but are more indifferent to the public domain. The same attitude reveals itself in the fact that they are rather parsimonious in the amounts they are willing to spend on public buildings. Italians, on the other hand, express a different attitude in the magnificence of their public buildings and the relative simplicity of their private dwellings.

Man comes to existence in expression. He expresses himself in many ways, in his countenance, his behavior, his words, his surroundings, the products of his labor and the creations of his art. In all of this he realizes himself. Existence and expression cannot be separated.

*Orientation of Expression to Our Fellow-Men.* Expression has also another aspect that deserves our attention. It is always an existing-for-the-others, it is always orientated to our fellow-men. In our speaking we address ourselves to other human beings. The artist expresses himself in matter to make himself known by others. Joyful or sorrowful behavior wants to find resonance in others. We want to be understood, to be appreciated, or to find sympathy.

Sometimes we address ourselves consciously and deliberately to others. This happens when man has reached a certain level of interiorization. By means of this interiorization we learn to speak internally. This internal speech may make us discover something which we want to communicate to others. Long before we consciously address others in this way, however, we are oriented to them in a way which we do not freely choose. When we consciously direct ourselves to others, we have, to a certain extent, control over our attitude toward them. This makes it possible for

205

us to pretend. For instance, a parent who is very happy that his son's engagement with a girl has fallen through, may still assume an attitude of sympathy and disappointment. Yet we have never full control over our expression. It easily happens that our real feelings penetrate through the assumed attitude and do not deceive one who sharply observes us. Moreover, below the sphere of expression which we control freely there is another sphere which escapes our control.

Expression as such should not be separated from its orientation to our fellow-men, for our existence itself is an existence for the others as well as through the others. Our existence is a co-existence. If we did not exist together, we would not exist as human beings. We are beings of innumerable possibilities. All our human possibilities, however, are actualized within our co-existence. By being together we learn how to act as human beings and to think. Within our co-existence with our fellow-men we develop our human tendencies and emotions and become aware of norms and values. We realize ourselves in everything within the context of our togetherness with others. Our life loses its meaning in utter aloneness. If no one appreciates us we can no longer believe in ourselves. One who is systematically distrusted by everyone around him loses also his self-confidence. One who is not accepted by anyone in the community may perhaps manage to "get by" by making himself feared, for being-feared still has some meaning. But to be "nobody" whatsoever, to be a "non-entity," is more than man can stand. He cannot live in such a condition.

Our life itself is existence and to be existent is to be orientated to others. Man's orientation to his fellow-men belongs to his inmost essence. If we mentally eliminate our being toward the others from ourselves, we eliminate also ourselves. One could object to this assertion from a religious standpoint and say that man can be orientated to God. That is true, but God also is an "other," "The Other" even. Moreover, it is through our being-together with others that we enter into our relationship to God.

Hence religion cannot be conceived separately from our connection with our fellow-men. We cannot divorce our orientation to our fellow-men from that to God.

Accordingly, the meaning of expression lies in this, that we are accepted by others. Without being accepted by them, we simply cannot live. Our expression therefore is a message addressed to other human beings. In this respect also we must not separate existence from expression, for our existence itself is a being-for-others. Thinkers often speak, and correctly so, of man's interiority. Yet interiority does not simply precede expression. On the contrary, our interiority is the interiorization of the world of expression. We arrive at interior reflection only after we have learned to think in the world of expression. We attain, for example, inner feelings of guilt because we see in the expression of other human beings that we have misbehaved. We address ourselves in our expression to other men, and they address themselves to us. Man's life runs its course in this wondrous interplay of expression.

*Manifold Forms of Expression.* But, one may object, isn't man a person? Of course, he is. Within and through his being together with his fellow-men this person learns to think and to be free. For this reason man's possible level of personal existence is dependent upon the level attained by his fellow-men. In a primitive society, in which the common level of life remains very low, it is not possible to lead a high level of personal existence. Man's personal existence actualizes itself and raises itself to a higher level by way of common sphere of life. In our era this common sphere has become very rich, and its wealth compels man to lead a personal existence—no matter what alarmed thinkers write about the modern mass society and its depersonalization. The sciences flourish in our modern society: there are many men who study and think for themselves, as appears from the veritable flood of scholarly books and articles that are published constantly. The world of our labor has become very rich and productive and therefore needs many people trained and educated to assume functions in it. Modern man reveals a striking critical attitude. He no longer accepts as a matter of course values that have been handed down to us from the past and is less inclined to follow accepted patterns of behavior simply because they are accepted. So much personal existence is demanded today that some people have difficulty in meeting that demand. Yet the demand must be met, for the wealth of our common sphere of life can continue to exist only if, and to the extent that, it is taken up and appropriated by human persons.

The preceding remarks show that the phenomenon of expression occurs in as many forms as our human existence itself. On this basis we can also understand the many different ways in which speech functions. We realize also that we acquire our forms of expression within society and that therefore we inherit them from the past. The past supplies us with our patterns of behavior, our forms of existence, our language and techniques of expression. We are persons because we take part in our own way in the common life of expression.

Experience teaches us that accepted forms of expression can become antiquated, lose their meaning. People often feel that it is impossible for them to continue to live in the accepted forms of expression. How does it happen that we are no longer able to exist in forms of expression in which past generations felt entirely at home? One could point to man's critical sense, to his increasing insight and understanding. These play a role, of course, but they do not offer an adequate explanation. Man's critical sense makes him understand, or rather feel, that certain forms of expression are antiquated, but why are they antiquated? A kind of "objective" antiquation seems to precede our insight and understanding of the situation.[2]

---

[2] This point is of importance in connection with the liturgical renewal that is taking place in some churches. We must not forget that it is possible for liturgical forms of expression to become objectively antiquated. When that happens it does not mean, as we have said before in a similar case, that man has become too bad for the liturgical expression but that the liturgical expression has become too bad for man.

The explanation must probably be sought in the fact that man's expressive life assumes many forms. Man develops himself as well as his world and therefore also compels himself to exist in a new way in a new kind of world. Consequently, he also compels himself to find new forms of expression. Such a renewal always proceeds in a piecemeal fashion. For this reason it can happen that man's expressive life in one realm advances beyond that of another realm which has not yet been adapted to the new situation. Life then is no longer harmonious because the different realms do not fit together. New forms of existence and expression create a new man, and this new man no longer fits into the old frames. The result is that the old frames of life become antiquated and fail to arouse interest in man.

*The Influence of Technology.* The most profound renewal occurring in contemporary life in the West is the renewal of the methods and means of working and consequently also of the products of work. We have started to live as technical men in a technical world. The technical world is permeated with the light of the exact sciences, for these sciences have made this world possible. The renewal in question has taken place at a very rapid rate. Thus it should not surprise us that it has rendered certain forms of expression antiquated. The modern world of technology demands efficiency and speed in thinking and acting. It makes life businesslike. It develops our intelligence in a certain direction. In a word, the technical world has a style of its own. Not all forms of expression current in the past fit in with this technical style. Much of the past appears grotesque and bombastic to us. Instead of long-winded speeches, we like to come directly to the point. Even politicians shorten their talks and go more immediately to the core of the questions.

Of course, we do not want to claim that in our technological era everything must become technical. Nevertheless, the forms of expression must be such that modern man, living as he does in a technical world, can exist in them. The positive gains made in technical life may not be disregarded in the other forms of existence. For technique has become an essential component of modern life and influences everything else. This influence can assume two forms—one negative, the other positive. It is positive insofar as technique imposes its sphere on other realms of life, and negative insofar as man reacts against the one-sidedness of the technical sphere of life.

## 2. THE VARIOUS FUNCTIONS OF LANGUAGE

Speech undoubtedly is the most important means of expression. The "matter" used in this means, however, is related to the importance of speech in an inverse ratio. It consists in the expulsion of air while the throat and the mouth are in a certain position, so that a series of sounds results. This "matter," then, is almost nothing, but it is perhaps precisely its rarified nature that allows it to offer such great possibilities for expression. The more matter is massive and solid, the more resistance also it offers to man's attempts to shape it.

With respect to verbal expression, attention must be paid not only to the material content of speech, to that which is said, but also to the tone of voice used by the speaker. This tone is an essential aspect of speech. When, for example, a parent calls his son by pronouncing the latter's name, the youngster often knows from the tone of his father's voice what the general nature will be of his words. Depending upon the way they are pronounced, the same words can express a serious reproach, a threat or a humorous remark. Moreover, speech is accompanied by all kinds of epiphenomena which constitute a single whole with it; for instance, gestures, physiognomy and bodily attitude. To understand someone we must pay attention to the whole of the speaking man rather than only to his words. In practice there is little difficulty involved in this matter, but the complexity of the whole makes a theoretical analysis particularly difficult.

Because speaking occupies the central position in our expressive existence, it stands to reason that all our relationships with our fellow-men will manifest themselves in speech. Language functions in innumerable ways to express these relationships. Since it is not possible to present a complete and detailed enumeration of all the ways in which language is used in our speaking, we will restrict ourselves here to a few of the most important uses.

*Speaking in the Indicative Mood.* Theoretical analyses usually draw attention to the type of speech which intends to acquaint others with facts or speculative truths. This type of speech is speaking in the indicative mood. The one-sidedness of which mention was made at the beginning of this chapter consists in the emphasis we have laid on the indicative mood of speaking. Nevertheless, such a one-sided emphasis occurs quite naturally. Only theorists discuss language in a reflective way and it is the theorists who have developed speech in the indicative mood. They have become accustomed to state facts in a critical fashion and to formulate insights; they are the ones who teach, write articles and publish books. In all these matters they use sentences in the indicative mood. In the realm of science language has become the means *par excellence* to express objectively what man and the world are. Scientific publications rely on sentences in the indicative mood and grammatical analysis draws attention to them. In school the children are told about the subject, the predicate, the direct and indirect objects of these sentences; and their readers illustrate these grammatical analyses with appropriate stories.

Speech in indicative sentences undoubtedly is of the greatest importance. Through it man has developed as a seeker of truth, through it he gives rise to the light of evidence. Man's ability to do this is one of his greatest gifts. He is orientated to knowing his situation, for his being is a being conscious. By developing the indicative mood of speech, we develop ourselves as consciousness of life and of the world. Through it we are able to situate ourselves, for knowledge is power. Man is ill equipped for life, but he possesses the gift of equipping himself, guided by the light of his knowledge. Western man has attained great power precisely because he has developed the indicative way of speaking. So-

211

called underdeveloped nations will have to take over this way of speaking if they want to advance on the road to progress.

When man wants to speak indicatively, he assumes a certain attitude. It is the attitude in which messengers delivered news in former times, in which town criers announced the news, in which newscasts are made over radio and television. It is the attitude also which in the realm of science has become scientific objectivity. This attitude is present also, at least implicitly, in ordinary conversation, for people have always communicated facts and views to one another.

*Speaking in the Affective Mood.* Observing ordinary conversation, we notice that the above-described attitude is hardly ever present in it in all its purity and that it is only one of many possible attitudes. Speech functions also in many other ways.

Speaking is, for example, one of the existential forms of affective feeling and emotion. If we dislike each other, we can have recourse to arms. In our civilized society, however, it is no longer fitting to fight one another with our fists or clubs. We do it with words. People living in the slums develop a most colorful vocabulary of abusive language. Children fight with words and call one another names. More civilized grown-ups usually abstain from coarse forms of abusive language, but even they have more refined forms of fighting others with words. They use indicative sentences to communicate things for the avowed purpose of hurting or dismaying others. It is possible to go against a fellow-man with seemingly perfect objectivity. A speech which presents itself as the embodiment of truth is often really a terrible weapon. The news sent out over radio and television has become a most important instrument to battle against the enemy. Something is gained, of course, when antagonists delay having recourse to armed force and decide to sit down at a conference table. Yet their relationship does not automatically become normal by the very fact that they speak with one another, for speech also can be the embodiment of the most bitter enmity and even increase

212

the opponents' feelings of hatred. Even scientific publications can have the fundamental intention to harm others.

Fortunately language can also embody entirely different affections. In and through language man can bring about his affective unification. While speaking with a friend, one can sometimes experience a feeling of strong unity. There are two human beings, each with his own outlook upon the world, yet these two outlooks seem to merge into one. They speak to each other, but there is hardly any question of exchanging views because the two views merge in such a way that the one seems to express the view of the other. The two merge so much that it is no longer of any importance to distinguish what each of them has contributed to the whole. Both appear to speak when one of them says something. This marvelous unity becomes a reality in and through speech. It did not exist before they spoke to each other, and sometimes it is impossible to recover it when the conversation is finished.

Only those who have personally experienced such a unifying colloquy will understand its value. In it, the two raise each other to higher levels and make each other realize themselves. It can make them reach a level of understanding and a depth of feeling which they may be unable to reach again later when they are alone. A classical example of such a colloquy is that of St. Augustine with his mother at Ostia, shortly before her death.

Children become friends in their talking together. Their talks sometimes communicate hardly any truth. Children do not speak about their interiority but about the world in which they live together. They do not speak about that world in an objective way, for word and world, life and speech are still fused in an undifferentiated manner. Children fully exist in their speech, and there is no question yet of a distance between word and existence, between word and world. Adults are no longer familiar with that undifferentiated fusion and for this reason find it difficult really to participate in children's talk. The latter's mutual relationships also exist fully in their speaking, so that the rapid changes occurring in these relationships find direct expression in their speaking.

213

Speech functions in a very special way when lovers attain an apex in their experience of mutual love.[3] In their case apply Merleau-Ponty's words that silence is an integral part of speech.[4] At such moments there is hardly question of speaking in sentences. Usually there are only isolated words which silence joins into an eloquent whole. Words, gestures, regard and the body's attitude are in perfect harmony. Words are no longer the embodiment of truth but the embodiment of what the lovers are for each other. They are the channel through which flows the lovers' existence for each other, they are filled with a wondrous affective and emotional fullness, which it would be very difficult to express in a theoretical way.

*The Living Speech of Daily Life.* In the living speech of daily life grammatically complete sentences are used only rarely. It would be wrong, however, to conclude that therefore ordinary speech is incomplete or awkward. Everyday speaking is integrated in a concrete whole in which gestures, physiognomy, bodily behavior and man's oneness with a situation play a role. Speech is not something apart from all that which therefore does not need full sentences. Such sentences occur when man cultivates speech separately, when he makes it a special pursuit upon which he centers his attention. Such a pursuit is present when he delivers an address or writes a book. In such a case his speaking is no longer complemented by other aspects of his expressive existence and therefore has to be made complete in itself. This kind of speech constitutes a special sector of culture. We need to be educated in it, and this education places us to some extent outside the ordinary stream of life. A sign of this is that people who move easily in ordinary life, always find the right word to say and show themselves quick-thinking, sometimes are completely at a loss for words when a special occasion compels them to speak

---

[3] Cf. L. Binswanger, "Liebe und Sprache," *Grundformen und Erkenntnis menschlichen Daseins,* Zurich, 1953, pp. 192–196.

[4] Concerning the interplay of speech and silence see also J. H. van den Berg, "Het Gesprek," *Persoon en Wereld,* pp. 137–138, and Max Picard, *Die Welt des Schweigens,* Frankfurt a.M., 1959.

in full sentences. Others, on the other hand, move with ease in the world of cultured speech, can speak readily without much preparation or write a well-conceived article, yet they can handle themselves only with difficulty in ordinary conversation.

The ordinary kind of speaking, which is integrated in many other aspects of expressive life, must not be regarded as an inferior type of speech, as the first awkward beginning of genuine speech. Everyday speech and cultivated speech do not function in the same way. Ordinary speech requires a distinct kind of intelligence of the person who wants to take part in it. It requires, for instance, that one knows how to meet others and how to deal with them. One must have the ability to become part of the conversing group, to understand that which is said and that which is left unsaid, and especially have a feeling for the tone of the conversation. The right word has to be spoken at the right time, and this word need not be a full sentence but may be limited to a single word. All this requires a special intelligence, which is not the same as theoretical intelligence. People whose theoretical intelligence is well developed and who can speak with ease in complete sentences may nonetheless be ill equipped to move around in ordinary life. Theoretically well-educated people sometimes fail when they assume a practical function. For this reason a transition period is needed after theoretical training and during this period they must learn how to handle themselves in practical life. In the world of business, politics and in general all professions in which one must deal with many human beings, that kind of practical skill plays a decisive role.

*Function of Speech in Radio, Television and Film.* It is rather striking that certain characteristics of ordinary speech now occur again in new forms of culture. It suffices to pay attention in this matter to the function of speech in television newscasts. In newspapers and on the radio speech has to be self-sufficient because there can be no question of visual images. The word has to present the whole picture. Television, on the contrary, offers also a visual image, it presents matters both by sound and by sight. For

215

this reason words have to be spoken in such a way that they integrate themselves in the visual event. They may no longer aspire to completeness. A television reporter who would try to be complete in his spoken words would bore us to death. Some reporters do not seem to realize the difference between radio and television reporting and continue to paint the whole event with spoken words.

A similar phenomenon occurs in the world of film. A sound motion picture uses a special kind of language, consisting largely of incomplete sentences which, taken in themselves, are disjointed. We do not even notice that when we watch a film because its language is disjointed only if it is divorced from the visual image. Taken together with this image, the language is complete. Motion picture language and television language are strikingly similar to so-called "ordinary language." In them we find again the multiple aspects and integration proper to ordinary life. People who have specialized in the separate culture of the word, who have cultivated speech in rounded sentences, may be annoyed by the disjointed character and the seemingly incompleteness of the language used in film and television, but their annoyance is wholly out of place.

*Speech as Influencing Others.* As we have stated before, our expressive life is essentially directed to our fellow-men. This orientation applies *par excellence* to speech. By speaking we want to attain the others. Our existence is an existing through and for the others. By speaking we want to be something for our fellow-men; for instance, we want to communicate something to them, to acquaint them with something. Let us add that speech is rarely wholly disinterested, for our self-esteem is likely to increase by the fact that we know something which the others do not know and are able to enlighten them. Sometimes we speak to make others laugh and to amuse them, sometimes we talk simply to please them or to do them good; for instance, when someone whom we like is sad. Although our speaking in these cases may not be entirely disinterested, nonetheless we may say that our

216

existence for others predominates or at least that it occupies the center of attention.

Often, however, it happens also that through our speaking we want to make others exist for us or for the ideals which we pursue. Our speaking is then an exercise of influence or power, although we must add at once that as a rule there is a reciprocal influence. People influence each other's way of being.

The extent to which speech is an influence exercised on others manifests itself very clearly in the life of children. They are still largely unformed and have not yet assumed a definitive way of life. Through the speaking of their parents children gradually develop their form. This formation does not result primarily from speeches addressed explicitly to them. That type of speaking does not suit children very well and, moreover, may not be in harmony with the everyday, situated way of the parents' speech. The primary role in the formation of children is played by the parents' situated speech. In the latter type of speech meanings and values become evident, the everyday world of life makes itself manifest, things and human beings assume a fixed place.

Children are formed also through the speaking of other persons with whom they have frequent contacts, including other children. The power of speech over children reveals itself sometimes very strikingly when they are trained by excellent educators. A single teacher may be able to impress his stamp on an entire class.

Adults are already formed and therefore no longer as easily influenced as children. Yet even on them speech can exercise great influence, although its power will be largely limited to particular sectors of life. Adults are usually set in the little world of their daily life. The farmer has his own ideas about work on his land, the shopkeeper about his store and the craftsman about his workshop. They go their own way in those little worlds and distrust the advice of others. Nothing is more difficult than to persuade the traditional farmer to change his methods or to try "new-fangled" machinery. As a rule, however, the adult has his own set and independent ways only in the little world of every-day life and work.

This little world is interwoven with a world at large. The adult knows that his little world depends in many ways upon that larger world and he realizes in an obscure fashion that he does not know much about the world at large. He remains very much subject to influence when there is question of that large world, that great sphere of interests which encompasses his own little sphere. People who want to exercise power over him tell him that the world at large is badly organized, that it threatens his own little sphere of interests and that, to safeguard his own little world, it will be necessary to reform the world at large. In this way it is possible to sway large masses of people and to organize them in popular movements. The power of speech is behind all such movements. Whatever one may think about Hitler, for example, it is unquestionably true that his speaking was extremely powerful. He was able to convince people that their little interests would be safe in his plans for the world at large. Marxism likewise pretends to do justice to the labor of the little man within its social and political system.

*The Language of Power.* There is no reason to be surprised that at present the power of speech is greater than ever. Large sections of the world have merged into a single sphere of interest, and we may even say that the entire world is gradually fusing into a common sphere of interest. The little interests of adults are more and more compenetrated with a world at large which they cannot fathom. People desire more than ever before to arrive at some understanding of that world, they need theories and ideologies about it. Speech, therefore, has more opportunity than ever to exercise its power.

If we observe people who speak the language of power, we notice that they always claim to dedicate themselves to the service of others, to see to it that justice is done to the others. They plead and struggle for the others' interests. Yet their words usually conceal the intention to gain the others for themselves. He who

218

speaks the language of power wants to make the others his followers, he ultimately wants to make them exist for himself. Hitler claimed to live and fight for the interests of all Germans. Most of them believed him but arrived belatedly at the conclusion that in reality they existed for the sake of Hitler and of Nazism. The language of power rarely presents itself nakedly as it is. One who wants to seize power finds it more useful to present himself as a benefactor of mankind.

One who speaks the language of power has made the world his field of meaning. He has done it in such a way that a place in it is assigned to other human beings. By speaking he wants to make that field of meaning a field of significations. He wants the others to occupy the place which he has assigned to them in his field. Of course, he does not present matters in this way, it is even possible that he himself does not exactly know the true state of affairs and thinks that he is really speaking in the interest of the others. At any rate, he wants them to occupy the place he has assigned to them and presents it to them as the best place for them, as the place which simply coincides with their own interest. Through his language of power he reduces the others to chessmen in his world.

Even among children one can observe examples of such language of power. A boy with authoritarian inclinations may have decided how his group will have to spend the free afternoon. Since he needs the others, he has to convince them that his plan will help them have "lots of fun." If the boy in question is a born leader, the others will believe in him. They will begin to exist in his sphere. The language of power leads men to existence in the sphere of the one who can speak the language of power.

Those who speak that language do not really want any dialogue or discussion. Objections are overruled as irrelevant or as examples of ignorance and stupidity. Better still, they are ridiculed. "To make things ridiculous" is a constituent part of the language of power. It may heap ridicule upon something that is not ridiculous at all, for that is the best way to make it wholly unacceptable and removes competition for the speaker's view. Ridicule is a powerful weapon of the language of power. Those who use that language may succeed even in reaching the point where no one dares to contradict them for fear of being ridiculed. They like to addresss people who like to laugh. If one manages to speak to them when they are alone, their self-assurance sometimes disappears completely. For this reason they will try to avoid such private discussions, for they realize that their language of power is more convincing when it is spoken in the presence of many.

The language of power occupies also an important place in political negotiations and business. Through this language the politician and the businessman know how to present their own interests as something that is "really" in the interest of all. For this reason politics and business lie largely in the sphere of force—not that of physical weapons, however, but the force exercised by the language of power. Once a person has managed to organize a part of the world through his language of power, this language becomes even more powerful. He has so many means at his disposal that he has less need to use them in preference to his language of power. He will use other weapons only when he has to deal with groups which are unwilling to listen to his word of power. Hitler, for example, accomplished much with words and resorted only to war when his words proved unable to give him everything he wanted.

We meet here one of the reasons why disarmament alone is not enough to make the world a suitable dwelling place for man. The real disruption of interhuman relationships lies much deeper. Those who speak the language of power and address themselves to their fellow-men mostly in terms of that language treat the others simply as chessmen in their own world. There are many people who do this, especially in the world of politics and business. One's fellow-man is not accepted there in the full sense as a fellow-man. He is "pushed around," given a right to existence only insofar as he is willing to occupy the place assigned to him in the other's world of meaning. He is reduced to a "subman." Long before people have recourse to arms; they often "push one another around" in the world of speech. Paradoxical as it may seem, there are people who battle for peace in that fashion. They constantly talk about peace and disarmament without giving the others an opportunity to say anything. They practice what they profess to combat.

Man often uses speech, which is orientated toward his fellow-men, against this fellow-man. Here lies the deepest ground of the disease of which war is a symptom. While it may be useful to combat this symptom, it leaves the disease itself untouched. As long as man continues to let the world of material interest be dominated by the language of power, as long as we do not accept one another as fellow-men in the full sense of the term, no essential progress can be made.

*Magic Words.* Words sometimes also have a magic character. Magic words are a kind of language of power, but in a different sense from the one we have discussed above. Man has always realized that the field of meaning which he understands clearly is limited, that it is surrounded by the unknown and that this unknown exercises influence upon him. He speaks therefore of "occult powers," that is, powers which influence his field of meaning but remain hidden. Some people pretend to have mysterious connections with these occult powers and to know the secret word by which the action of these powers can be effectively directed. If that word is spoken, the powers begin to operate, either for good or for evil, in the human field of meaning. The magic word therefore embodies power over unknown forces and indirectly also over other human beings. The latter are not addressed directly in the magic word, but they experience its results.

For this reason primitive man was extremely afraid of magic words, a fear which continued to be felt by many people even long after they have left the primitive stage. Influences coming from the world one knows could be evaded or counteracted at least to some extent, but the influence of hidden forces were un-

221

predictable. Thus those who pretended to know magic words exercised great power over the others. They often were more powerful than the official rulers. Because it controlled mysterious forces the magic word often had a mysterious and strange sound, for it belonged to a secret language unintelligible to outsiders. The magic word still plays a role in fairy tales, where it is no longer dangerous.

*The Religious Word.* The magic word and the religious word sometimes are closely connected,[5] for the latter is regarded to be coming from, or addressed to, the hidden power called "God." A distinction should be made between the religious word and man's rational speaking about God. A thinker can raise the question whether God exists and, when he does, he speaks of God. However, in this way he tries to make God a knowable reality within the field of human significations or to deny that God is a real signification. In these efforts he speaks the accepted language of philosophical thought, but not a religious word in the strict sense of the term. Human speech becomes really religious only when it claims to put us in contact with God. This contact can arise in two ways. First, God can address Himself to man through the intermediary of some human being. In this case this human being speaks words of revelation, which believers consider to be the word of God. Secondly, man can address himself to God. In that case the human word becomes a word of prayer.[6] The language of revelation and that of prayer have a distinct character which sets them apart from other usages of languages. They speak to and from the Unknown. They use words that are connected with man's worldly field of meaning, but they want to transcend this field. They make present to us that which cannot

---

[5] Protestants claim that the Catholic's religious words sometimes have magic undertones, which is one of the reasons why they object to certain Catholic practices.

[6] It would be interesting to make a special study of the language of prayer as it is used in accepted Catholic or Protestant devotional prayer books and official books of prayer. One of the characteristics of the language of prayer is that it does not develop as fast as ordinary speech. For this reason the past lives longer in the language of prayer.

be made really present. They point to the Unknown. The word becomes a symbol in religious language. It has a known significa-tion, one which fits into our field of significations, but it points to something beyond its ordinary signification. The religious word evokes its ordinary signification but at the same time denies it. It makes the ordinary signification a stepping stone in its trans-cendence of this signification. He of whom it really speaks can-not become a signification in our field of significations. We make Him present in significations which point to Him without being identical with Him.

The magic word and the religious word, we have said, some-times are very close to each other. For man can misuse the reli-gious word in a magic way. He does this when he thinks that, by speaking the religious word, he can compel God to produce a certain effect in the world. Man speaks and his word makes God do something in the world or in man. The religious word used in a magic way is not a prayer. For prayer is a supplication and leaves God free. Man cannot claim to compel God. Yet the reli-gious and magic sometimes come very close to each other.

As should be clear from the preceding considerations, the reli-gious word has its own function, its own mode of existence, only for those who believe in God as one who speaks to them and to whom they can speak. For a believer the religious word is not ultimately encompassed by the worldly signification evoked by it. Any one of our words has a signification belonging to our ordinary field of significations. For the religious man that signifi-cation is both presented and transcended by the religious word. For this reason we should refer to the religious word as a symbol. When there is question of a symbol, there is always something that is made present, something material belonging to our ordi-nary world, such as a piece of cloth with white and red stripes and white stars in a blue field. The importance of this symbol lies not in its material composition but in what it symbolizes. This symbol we call a flag. It indicates a value that cannot be pointed to but which, nonetheless, is a reality for us. This reality cannot be made

223

present in any other way except by symbols. One who does not know and accept the value which it represents sees nothing but a piece of multi-colored cloth and does not understand the respect people show to it.

In a similar way the atheist sees in the religious word nothing else but the common signification (comparable to the cloth of the flag) evoked by it. He does not transcend this common signification and it does not point to anything else for him. He examines the significations evoked by religious language, analyzes them and finds nothing else but the wordly reality known to him from other forms of language. At most there is an added illusion of his fellow-men who believe that there is something mysterious hidden behind those significations. For the religious man, however, as we have seen, the situation is different; and therefore religious language does not have the same character for him as it has for the atheist. This special character of religious language exists only for one who believes in God.

In the preceding section we have considered a few examples of the many forms in which language is used. We have seen that language can function in many different ways. It was not our intention to offer a complete enumeration of all these ways; for instance, we have not spoken about the remarkable way in which language functions in certain forms of poetry.[7] Moreover, there are many other forms of word usage which we have not discussed. Yet what has been offered should suffice to make us suspect the untold riches of language.

## 3. The Central Form of the Use of Language

Man gives meaning in many ways, so that meaning exists for us in many fashions. There is, however, one way of giving meaning—namely, speech—which encompasses all the others, for all meanings can be made a topic of speech. Nevertheless, as we have

---

[7] For some interesting remarks about this matter, see Stefan Andres, "Ueber die Sendung des Dichters," *Offner Horizont, Festschrift für Karl Jaspers,* München, pp. 357–367.

seen, the "spoken" meaning may not be made the absolute norm of all meaning, for not every meaning can be adequately put into words. It often happens that the meaning which is put into words can be understood only on the basis of our experience of it. By putting a meaning into words, we project a field of significations. This field is not the absolute norm of our field of meaning.

*Progressive Interiorization and Absolute Norm of Meaning.* A similar phenomenon occurs also within speech itself. Language is used in many ways. Among the many forms which the use of language can assume there is one which extends to all others. This all-encompassing form is the so-called "objective language of science." All forms of speech can be discussed in a scientific way. Man can speak scientifically about all significations which owe their origin to his speaking in the realms of poetry, love, emotion, religion, and everything else.

We see therefore that Sartre speaks correctly about man as an "interiorization." Man appropriates meaning on different levels. The first of these appropriations occurs within our "lived" giving of meaning. Next, we make a meaning our own by transforming it into a signification, that is, by putting it into words. On the third level we can subject the "spoken" meanings, the significations, to a scientific investigation. In this way we arrive at a progressive clarification of the original meaning. A fourth level can be added to these three. Although our scientific investigation throws light on the meaning transformed into a signification by making it a signification in a new way, that scientific investigation is not entirely uniform, for the scientific consideration of the various spheres of signification gives rise to different sciences. For this reason one can propose a new level of interiorization by demanding that the many sciences be considered in a philosophy of the sciences. Man is a marvelous possibility to interiorize.

In spite of all the advantages of this progressive interiorization, there are also great dangers. Because the stages of interiorization result in progressive clarification, one could think that each subsequent stage is the norm of the preceding stage: the "spoken" meaning would be the norm of the "lived" meaning; the scientifically "spoken" meaning would be the norm of the ordinary signification; and the philosophy of the sciences would be the norm of man's entire pursuit of the sciences. For, after all, meaning is progressively clarified, and this clarification is at the same time a critical purification since each subsequent level determines what is genuine and what is not genuine on the preceding level.

Although analytic philosophy does not express itself in the terms we have used, it appears that it holds such a view. Everything that enlightens us is supposed to owe its origin to language; hence a radical critique of language and its possibilities must disclose what truths can exisit for man. Analytic philosophy claims to be such a radical critique and, therefore, also that it is the norm of all meaning.

*Reciprocity of "Spoken" and "Lived" Meaning.* Phenomenological philosophy takes an entirely different view. It does not deny that there is a progressive clarification on the above-mentioned levels and that this clarification offers many advantages. At the same time, however, it wants to emphasize that the clarified ways of meaning cannot be understood in and by themselves. The "spoken" meaning can be understood from the standpoint of the "lived" meaning, and for this reason the latter has a special function of its own which cannot be dispensed with. The "spoken" meaning is a critical refinement of the "lived" meaning and in this sense has the character of a norm. However, one can also say that the "lived" meaning is a norm of the "spoken" meaning, for the latter is genuine only insofar as it gives expression to the former. In evaluating the "spoken" meaning we must base ourselves also on the "lived" meaning.

The same applies to the subsequent levels of interiorization. Scientific speaking has a normative character with respect to meaning as "lived" or "spoken" in ordinary speech, but at the same time the latter function also as norms of the former. A similar relationship of reciprocity exists between philosophy and the sciences. If the normative character is exclusively and one-sidedly attributed to the more clarified ways of thinking, the rich variegation of life and speech would ultimately be resolved in the poverty of a monotone. We would fail to do justice to the wealth of variety existing in our world of meaning and signification.

Phenomenological philosophy does not like to use the terms "higher" and "lower" with respect to the above-mentioned levels. For these terms are easily understood in the sense that everything contained in the "lower" level is found also and in a better way in the "higher" level. This is certainly not the case. The so-called "lower" has a light and a value of its own, which are lost in the so-called "higher." The world of "lived" meaning has a wealth of shades to which speech cannot do full justice. Non-scientific speech likewise has riches which are to some extent lost in the monotony of scientific language.

Phenomenological philosophy pleads for the recognition of the "lived" world, for the recognition of its distinct character with respect to the field of scientific thinking. This distinct character, however, does not take away the fact that there is a progressive interiorization. Man can always ask himself in a new reflective way what meanings he possesses. By means of that reflection he makes those meanings also exist in a new way. No matter how critical this new way in which meaning exists may be, it must not be considered as an absolute norm. For man can always transcend the many forms of his existence and speaking and arrive at a higher unity. This higher unity is a clarification but at the same time an impoverishment. Only a very relative value can be attached to the term "higher" in this matter. It would be better to abstain entirely from using it, but it is almost inevitable that we have recourse to that familiar metaphor.

# CHAPTER NINE

# Man and Language

In this last chapter we will consider the relationship between man and his language. We want to show how man's speaking reveals the proper character of man, the fundamental lines of his intentionality, his possibilities. Speech is a revelation and an unfolding of being-man. In the preceding chapters the relationship between man and his speech has already been considered to some extent, but mostly by way of incidental remarks. The importance of the topic demands that a special chapter be devoted to it.

## 1. Speaking as Totalization

*Man as Totalization of the World.* The term "totalization" is borrowed from Sartre, who uses it regularly in his *Critique de la raison dialectique.* He knows how to create terms that are very meaningful and offer considerable aid in throwing light on man and the world. Several of the new terms coined by him have become part and parcel of the contemporary philosophical vocabulary. The way, however, in which he uses those terms does not permit the same general admiration. Despite the concreteness of the themes considered by him, he is a thorough rationalist and therefore often ascribes too much explanatory power to his categories.[1] All this, however, does not mean that his newly invented terms are not very useful.

---

[1] Speaking about Sartre, Merleau-Ponty refers to "his accursed lucidity." *Signes,* p. 33.

Sartre calls man the "totalization of the world." Man is, indeed, a being who makes himself the center of the world as his field of existence. He makes everything around himself meaning for himself. He makes the world a synthesis, and of this synthesis he himself is a part. He is the center of the whole which he projects, but this center does not lie outside this whole. The totalization projected by man can be very primitive and even queer. A person who is psychologically disturbed sometimes gives evidence of having arrived at a queer kind of synthesis, which nonetheless constitutes a coherent whole. The world in which such a person lives hangs together, be it in a most peculiar fashion. His psychological disturbance permeates everything in his world. For this reason it is sometimes difficult to adduce reasons capable of upsetting his synthesis. Whatever argument one brings forward is immediately taken up and interpreted in a way that fits in with his distorted world.

*Intentional Attitude and Speech.* The totalizing character of man's existence reveals itself most strikingly in his speech. There are several reasons for this. Speech itself is a kind of living "symbiosis" of man and the world.[2] For living speech cannot be divorced from the speaking man and from the reality of which he speaks, but is the living unity of both. In and through speaking, man makes himself someone who is centered upon a certain reality. In this way he assumes a certain intentional attitude. It would be wrong to think that man first assumes his intentional attitude and then begins to speak from that attitude. On the contrary, in and through his speaking the intentional attitude comes into existence.

For instance, a student who learns the first principles of a particular science does not yet have its intentional attitude, but makes an effort to become acquainted with the way this science speaks about reality. By learning to speak its language, he gradually also learns how to assume its attitude. The Ameri-

---

[2] "Le phénomène central du langage est l'acte commun du signifiant et du signifié." Merleau-Ponty, *Signes*, p. 119.

can and German boy are not born with the intentional attitude of the American or the German. But they learn to speak and think in American or German and thus, without knowing or willing it, also assume the intentional attitude of the American or the German. We cannot divorce speech from the speaking man for the simple reason that this man himself is formed in and through his speaking.

Neither can speech be separated from the reality of which it speaks, for in and through his speaking man aims at this reality. Speech makes this reality be for man in a certain way. Materially speaking, it is true, of course, that speech and the reality of which we speak are not identical. Speaking is, as we have seen, a pointing-at something; and pointing-at cannot wholly coincide with that which is pointed-at, for a certain distance between these two is a basic condition for the possibility of pointing at something. Nevertheless, it is impossible to divorce the two, for pointing-at and that which is pointed at depend upon each other for their existence. If there is nothing that is pointed-at, pointing-at is not pointing-at; and, through my pointing-at, that which is pointed-at is pointed-at. That which is spoken of begins to be for us through our speaking, and the way in which it begins to be for us, its mode of appearing, depends upon our speaking.

Speech brings to light. If we try to divorce speech and the light which it brings, speaking loses its meaning, its inner character, and sinks into darkness. To understand this, we must abandon the illusion that the light brought by speech exists independently from our speaking. Speech gives rise to light. We are inclined to take this light so much for granted that we conceive it as a reality which exists in complete independence of us. However, if we do this, we regard speech as an external and incidental indication of this light. We fail to do justice to the true character of both this light and speech. Speech and that which is spoken of are insolubly connected. This statement is in harmony with the general thesis of phenomenology that the intentional attitude and that which is brought to light by it cannot be separated. It is not possible to divorce, for example, the visible world appearing to us from our seeing. Our seeing itself draws the world from concealment and makes it a field of seeing.

However, our seeing makes us take this field so much for granted that we are inclined to regard it as an "in itself," as something existing as brute reality. As a result, we regard seeing itself, which is the source of the field, as an accessory something by which we become acquainted with this field. That is an illusion which has been unmasked long ago by philosophical reflection. In the same way we must abandon the illusion that the reality of which we speak can be divorced from our speaking. We must insist upon this point although it has been mentioned several times already. One who fails to understand it is blind to the true sense of speaking.

Accordingly, through his speech man assumes a certain intentional attitude, and reality becomes in a certain way meaning for him. Speech, then, is a living "symbiosis" of man and the world. In and through speech both man and the world are given form in a mutual essential dependence. This is the reason why speech possesses the power of which we have spoken above. One who succeeds in controlling the speaking of a nation controls this nation and its world. In this respect, then, speech really is totalization, unification of man and the world.

*Speech and Coherence in the Field of Significations.* There is another sense also in which speech is a totalization. The speaking man seeks, of course, coherence in his speech. He dislikes very much to affirm something at one moment and then to deny the same at another. Yet it happens sometimes that he catches either himself or others in doing it. Speech tends to eliminate its own incoherences. Its search for coherence is facilitated by the fact that speech itself implies a kind of reflection, a placing oneself at a distance. Our speaking is bound to the world, but this bond implies a certain distance, which is not the case in many other forms of action. Other actions occur in semi-darkness, but in speech this darkness is to some extent overcome. By the fact that man began to speak he attained a higher form of consciousness, so that his tendency to coherence became also more explicit in his speaking.

The reality of which man speaks is inseparably connected with his speech. Speaking makes reality become a field of significations. Because speech tends to inner coherence, it creates the same coherence in this field of significations. It transforms the field into a coherent world. A nation's "universe of discourse" contains something that is more or less a systematic whole. Of course, we do not mean that it is rigidly organized like a scientific system, but nonetheless the fundamental lines of a systematization are present. One can observe it even in ordinary conversations with simple people living in a world that is not too complex. Their speech reveals a coherent world as well as the fact that this world is narrow and one-sided. Efforts to overcome this narrowness and one-sidedness are not always successful, for these people do not show themselves open to viewpoints which do not fit in with their coherent world. They tend to deny such viewpoints or, as happens more frequently, are unable to absorb them. This is one of the reasons why people whose lives run their course within a narrow horizon prefer to read a local newspaper rather than a national one. They are interested in news which fits in with their horizon of existence, their "universe of discourse," and tend to disregard wider perspectives. Our speaking is the totalization of the world. It makes the world a field of significations and creates coherence in this field.

*Disruption of an Existing Totalization.* Man's speech is disrupted when new elements penetrate into the existing totalization, so that the latter can no longer be maintained as a coherent whole. Until a few decades ago the accepted Catholic way of speaking about reality constituted a coherent whole, whose fundamental lines were known to anyone who received a Catholic education. In the past few decades, however, new elements have penetrated into the coherent whole of Catholic speaking and these elements do not fit in with that whole. This has given rise to uneasiness, for man's speech naturally tends to coherence. Efforts have therefore been made to create a new coherent whole. An example of these efforts is the work done by Teilhard de Chardin. A similar uneasiness exists also in the world of Protestant speech.

Another example. The communist world tries to prevent disrupting elements from penetrating the accepted communist way of speaking. One of the means used for this purpose is the "iron curtain." Any accepted form of speaking which has established a coherent whole is always inclined to surround itself by such a kind of curtain. For the speaking man always tends to remain faithful to the coherent whole which he has created. It gives him a feeling of having accomplished something definitive and he dislikes the idea of having to start all over again. It should be kept in mind, however, that speech is a group phenomenon. It is the group which tries to protect the coherence of its way of speaking by establishing a kind of iron curtain. Any significantly separate group tends to do so.

Monastic groups, for instance, such as the Trappists or the Benedictines, have a certain way of speaking and through it possess a coherent universe with which their entire way of life is connected. They tend to erect an "iron curtain" around their way of speaking, for they feel disturbed when their accepted way is threatened. The same applies to a certain extent also to the way of speaking of all other orders and congregations, of priests in general, as well as ministers and rabbis, to the speech of any religious group or political organization. Man's speech is a totalization because it creates a coherent field of significations, a coherent world.

For the same reason also any established science is inclined to conservatism. At first any developing science—or philosophy for that matter—is inventive and creative. As soon, however, as it matures, it constitues a coherent universe which it does not like to abandon. Once a way of speaking has become current and created a coherent world, it always inclines to conservatism. Not even science or philosophy can escape from this tendency. Speaking inherently tends to petrification.

It remains possible, of course, to break through this petrified shell. Experience offers us many examples of it. Nevertheless, a certain self-denial is needed to make man succeed in overcoming the petrification of his speech. He feels, and correctly, that by rupturing the petrified shell of speech he has to give up himself and his world. It is not merely a question of human respect which makes him ashamed that he has to take back what once he asserted with so much confidence. Undoubtedly this factor also plays a role, but the main reason is that man wants to retain the coherent picture which he has created of himself and his world. Those who accuse others of conservatism would do well to keep this tendency in mind in connection with their own way of speaking and their own world.

*Totalization and the Autonomous Culture of the Word.* Accordingly, speech manifests very clearly that man is a totalization of the world. It contains a tendency to coherence, to forming a system, although the latter term should not be taken too rigorously as long as there is question of speaking below the scientific level. Combining the idea of "symbiosis," mentioned at the beginning of this section, with that of the tendency to coherence, we must say that man's coherent "universe of discourse" likewise is a "symbiosis" of life and the world. The speech adopted by a group contains at least an implicit view of life and the world. The way a people or a group speaks implies a hidden view of life and the world. For this reason their way of speaking, even if the people in question are primitives, extends also to the hidden sources of their existence. It also has a religious character.

All this implies that the tendency to totalization will manifest itself more clearly when speech begins to be cultivated for its own sake, when an autonomous culture of the word comes into existence. The first beginnings of such a culture are present when a people gives a fixed form to its myths and passes them on to their successors. Myths possess very strikingly a totalizing charac-

234

ter. The autonomous culture of the word exists, of course, also in a nation's literature. This literature, for instance, the Greek drama or the novels of Dostoevski, manifestly displays a vision on the whole of reality. It is not formulated in a theoretical way but is present in the actions and words of the characters portrayed in the drama or the novel.

Finally, the autonomous culture of the word assumes a form in man's sciences, philosophy and theology. These theoretical forms of knowledge are always dominated and will always be dominated by a tendency to a total view. It is true, of course, that theoretical knowledge is at the same time very critical. Those who pursue it often express skepticism regarding the possibility of arriving at a total view. Nevertheless, even these forms of relativism and skepticism contain the tendency to a total view as one of their positive constituent elements. For precisely because the possibility of such a view is explicitly denied, this denial can be called "relativism" or "skepticism." If the very idea of totalization was absent from the theoretical level, there could be no question at all of relativism or skepticism.

*Totalizing Speech as a Contemporary Problem.* In our time totalizing speech has become a great problem. We do not mean that man's speaking has given up its totalizing tendencies. On the contrary, totalizing visions play an important role in our life. The totalizing view of Marxism, for example, controls a great part of the world and has been put into practice there. And the totalizing view of Teilhard de Chardin appeals to many of our contemporaries, who have made it one of the most discussed questions of our time. The sciences likewise constantly present us with new totalizing views regarding the origin and growth of the material universe. It is almost fashionable to offer a total perspective upon human history.

On the other hand, there has been a great increase in analytic knowledge, and the pursuit of science has given a highly developed critical sense. Metaphysical thought experiences a period

235

of crisis partly because man's former metaphysical visions have been overtaken by new forms of consciousness. All this has greatly increased the skepticism of many regarding total views. Nevertheless, as experience confirms, man is unable to give up his tendency to totalization, which, as we have seen, is inherent in speech itself. We cannot give up that tendency without doing violence to the inmost nature of speech.

Our era commits, perhaps, the mistake of imposing on totalizing speech all the demands made by the rigorous pursuit of science.[3] It demands a metaphysical synthesis which satisfies the requirements of the most rigorous science, we may perhaps even say, of exact science. Such a demand is impossible, as is evident from the fact that a total view has to take into account forms of knowledge which are in principle unable to satisfy that demand. As we have repeatedly pointed out, man's speech and consequently also man's knowledge have many forms. In many instances we really have knowledge, even though it will never be possible to justify that knowledge according to the methods of exact science. For instance, we taste food, we appreciate beauty, we have a feeling for values, we understand one another's words and actions, and the believer has the awareness of a real contact with the transcendent reality of God. In all these cases there is question of genuine light, of real knowledge, but this knowledge cannot justify itself in the way exact knowledge does or sometimes thinks that it does. Yet the total vision, the metaphysical totalization must take into account also these genuine forms of knowledge. How, then, can one impose on it demands which are in principle beyond the reach of these forms of knowledge? If

---

[3] In his *Critique de la raison dialectique* Sartre refuses to submit totalizing thought (which he calls "dialectical" thought) to the demands of the analytic sciences. The reason is that the latter do not know the dimension proper to the historical event which encompasses everything and in which everything is connected with everything else. Nevertheless, he imposes rigid demands upon totalizing or dialectical knowledge. This knowledge may not be satisfied with facts but has to show their necessity. It is questionable, we think, whether Sartre himself satisfied his own demands in the development of his vision.

metaphysics experiences a crisis, the reason lies in part also in those unreasonable demands.

Some metaphysicians are too sensitive to these demands and in consequence fail to do justice to the proper character of their own pursuits. This is a deplorable weakness.

The tendency to totalization is inherent in speech and becomes more emphatic according as speech reveals its own character more clearly. Since speaking and thinking are essentially interwoven, our thinking also tends to totalize. Sartre stresses this point in his *Critique de la raison dialectique.* Man is a totalization not only in the thinking that is put into words but in all aspects of his existence. Work and play, as well as art, also totalize. However, we have restricted ourselves here to the totalization which manifests itself in man's speaking.

## 2. THE ONE-SIDED EMPHASIS ON SPEECH IN THE WESTERN WORLD

*Culture of Work and Culture of the Word.* In a preceding chapter we have made a distinction between grasping and pointing and we have showed there that these two intentional attitudes give rise to two spheres of culture, namely, the culture of work and that of the word. According to Marxist ideology, the evolution of work culture is decisive for the development of history. For man is a user of the world, so that his existence is inconceivable without a usable world. To the extent that man has a usable world at his disposal, that is, a world adapted to his human needs, he is able to exist as a human being. Because man's work makes the world usable, the evolution of work determines man's progress. If work improves the usable world improves, so that there is also more human use of the world and consequently improvement in man's life as such. In this way Marxism thinks it possible to prove that the development of work dominates history.

237

This line of reasoning would be conclusive if the development of work could be conceived as an autonomous whole, as something that is independent of other factors. However, if we consider the evolution of work, we are struck by a remarkable and strange fact. During many centuries man's work developed only very slowly, but the past century has witnessed a tremendously accelerated rate of development. One can say that in one century we have made more progress in this respect than in all the thousands of years before that. This fantastic upsurge in the curve of development is not self-explanatory but raises a problem. Marxism wants to explain history through this curve, but the explanatory factor to which it appeals itself demands an explanation.

It seems to me that the evolution of work during the past century can be understood only on the basis of our culture of the word, the intervention of the sciences. As soon as the sciences began to occupy themselves intensely with the means of production, the culture of work, the latter developed at an accelerated rate. For this reason the Marxist thesis attributing primacy to the culture of work is extremely doubtful. Man is able to work because of his reason. This idea finds expression even in a famous myth narrated by Plato. When the deity had formed animals and man, it proceeded to the distribution of special gifts such as wings, claws and fangs. In this distribution man's turn came after all others, when the deity's treasury of gifts was empty. It therefore decided to give him something of itself, namely, reason. What the myth wants to say is that nature has not equipped man's body fully for life, but has provided him with something better, viz., the ability to take care of his own needs by using his reason. Man takes care of his needs through his work, but he is enabled to work by his reason.

Man's way of working improves in direct ratio to the light which reason throws on his work. Even primitive man made use of reason in his work. But the reason enlightening him in his work was not separated from this work itself. Primitive man

238

was guided by understanding-in-action or practognosis. Western man has learned to let his work be guided by his speaking reason, especially in the form of scientific reason. The latter has become the light guiding his work and this is the reason why his way of working has made so much progress.

Work is power but speech also is power, for by speaking we bring reality to light in a new way, we make ourselves familiar with it in a new fashion. Thanks to this new light and this new familiarity, we are able to manipulate reality in a new way. Which power, one may ask, is more important: the power of work or that of the word? It seems to us that the power of the word is more fundamental and more important, for this is the power which has enabled the power of work to develop in an enormous way during the past century. Western man has seized control of the world in an entirely new way by virtue of his way of speaking in his sciences.

Here lies the reason why speech occupies such a primary position in Western civilization and why it is so important for man's work. Never before have so many human beings devoted themselves to mathematics and physical science. Never before has there been such a wide-spread diffusion of science in general. Never before has there been such an enormous quantity and variety of books and publications. We find it perfectly normal that all children finish at least grade school. For many of them that is not the end of their schooling; they go on to high school and in increasing numbers to colleges and universities. The purpose of all this schooling is to enable them to occupy a position in modern society by making them familiar with our scientific way of speaking about reality.

Our era is not the first one in which people are trained in speaking for the purpose of occupying a practical function. In ancient Greece and Rome anyone who wanted to participate in political life had to be a trained speaker and therefore there existed a kind of educational system. However, this education or training in speaking was needed only for a limited number of

239

functions and remained the privilege of a relatively small number. There was not yet, nor could there be, question of education for all. In our time, however, the entire world of labor, the entire field of practical pursuits, is approached to a greater or lesser extent in the light of theory, of science. For this reason education, which introduces children to our way of speaking, has become general. Modern society can no longer tolerate illiteracy, for we live in an order in which speaking about reality is a fundamental prerequisite of all practical pursuits. Our society is characterized in all its aspects by the power of the word.

*Positive Value of the Word Culture.* In this section we want to draw attention to the one-sidedness of this evolution of speech, but before doing this, draw attention to its enormous positive value. Thanks to this development of speech, Western man has created a new way of life, destined to become the accepted way of life of all mankind. Man has the task of making his own life possible. If he fails in it, he suffers want. To fill his needs, man must acquire power over the world, which supplies him with the necessary means. Western man has acquired this power through his way of speaking about the world. He can fill his needs in a way which surpasses by far anything that former ages could imagine. For his control of the world he needs energy. Western man's speech as embodied in his sciences has placed untold sources of energy at his disposal and constantly adds new ones to them. These sciences have also given him productive tools which enormously increase the productivity of his labor. All kinds of goods are at the disposal of the large majority of people in the West, partly also because the new methods of production demand many consumers. In our society the masses must become consumers, otherwise the system of production cannot function. Advertising therefore artificially creates the need for the manufactured products. In this way we have acquired many needs. Once a need exists, Western man organizes giant systems of production to satisfy this need. Thus he has developed a way of life which would have been unthinkable in former ages. He hardly

240

knows what it means to lack sufficient food, clothing, shelter, heat or water. There is an abundance of medical supplies, and anyone suffering from illness does not have far to seek to find a skilled physician. Thanks to our power, we can live together in comfort even in a relatively small area.

All this has become possible because our way of speaking, especially in science, has placed power at our disposal in our practical pursuits. We have risen above the level of bare necessities and make our existence secure. In this way we have solved one of the basic problems with which man has always struggled. It is Western man who has succeeded in doing this. We do not mean, of course, that all our problems have been solved. On the contrary, the most profound problems of being-man come into the foreground only after he has satisfied his most urgent wants. Once he has been liberated from the grip of these wants, he has to face the question of what to do with his freedom. Nevertheless, Western man has found a solution for his elementary material needs thanks to the power given him by his way of speaking. There are parts of the world where people have not yet reached the solution and continue to live in want. To overcome their want, they will have to take over the solution discovered by the West. In this respect the Western way of life will become the way of life adopted by all mankind.[4] The whole world will have to take over Western science and Western ways of doing things. Otherwise it will be impossible for the increasing world population to secure the necessities of life.

There is a certain amount of aversion to the West, the reasons are not difficult to understand. First of all, the flourishing condition of the West is bound to give rise to envy. Western affluence sharply contrasts with the poverty and want of other parts of the world. Secondly, Western man's prosperity is based in part on his exploitation of the rest of the world. He made other coun-

---

[4] The achievements of the West, however, do not have to be taken over in the same way as they exist in the West, but may be adapted to the character of the other peoples.

241

tries supply his raw materials and sometimes even his labor force. He increased his own affluence without letting the others share in the wealth their natural resources and labor helped produce. These and other reasons explain why these other countries sometimes do not like the West. Disliked and reproached, Western man occasionally becomes the victim of a feeling of inferiority.

All this, however, does not take away from the fact that Western man has created a way of life which makes it possible for all mankind to rise above poverty and want. This creation is decisive for history. Man now stands on the threshold of an era in which starvation and want will be overcome. The fundamental possibility of this victory is already given, thanks to the sciences of the West. Mankind has every reason to be grateful to Western man for making this victory possible. It is unfortunately true, of course, that the West has partly misused its creation to seek self-glorification and excessive power. Yet this misuse does not remove the world-wide importance of its creation. Before reproaching the West too sharply, it is good to recall the general ambiguity of human history. It has never happened yet that an important discovery was from the very beginning used only in an ideal way.

*One-Sided Rationalization.* In the light of all these considerations it should not be difficult to understand that at present speech plays a one-sidedly prevalent role in Western existence. Especially the form of speech that is important for the Western way of life exercises a dominating and controlling function. The life of the West is largely controlled by the sciences which make technology possible. Our time is an era of rationalization, for we have made rational knowledge the guiding principle of our life. Rationalized forms of speaking occupy a very prominent place in our entire life. A few examples will suffice to illustrate this point.

Let us begin with the way in which our children are trained and educated. After a first rudimentary training at home, the school becomes the main factor in the formation of our children. This educational institution is primarily geared to rational knowledge, to the development of theoretical reason. In many countries the child's affectivity and emotionality, its bodily development, sportiveness and artistic inclinations are not sufficiently taken into consideration. Many people are now becoming aware of this one-sidedness, but relatively little is done to overcome it.

In the world of work likewise many people have to occupy themselves with speech. Not only those who earn their living by teaching but also many others, for Western man has expressed his entire world of reality in the world of speech. One could say that he has duplicated his world in such a way that it exists now both in reality and on paper. The name of each one of us is carefully recorded in many places; it is inscribed on the registers of our employers, suppliers, insurance companies, political party, social security, religious denomination, clubs and every other possible kind of organization. The duplication of our real world in the world of the word written down on paper is an important aid in helping us to control the real world. We find ourselves in a certain situation in the real world, unable to survey the whole of it or to be present everywhere. By putting the world on paper we get a grip on it and are able to control it.

The world has to be expressed in words, put on paper, to make modern ways of working possible. The small businessman and craftsman of former times knew exactly who their customers were without having to write it down. They were able to remain familiar with their financial position without extensive systems of bookkeeping. As soon, however, as the sphere of work and operations expands, it becomes necessary to reproduce everything on paper. Customers have to be inscribed in registers, transactions recorded, and a system of bookkeeping is needed to know one's financial situation. Anyone who today wants to establish a business has to be able to duplicate the world of his operations. Our tax system likewise is based on the paper duplication of our world.

It stands to reason therefore that today many people earn their living in the world of the word. Enormous office buildings are filled with innumerable workers recording facts and figures in

243

writing. How important this duplication of the world on paper is became evident during World War II. In some parts of occupied Europe the underground forces resorted to the destruction of certain archives and records, and the result was that the Nazi conqueror was greatly hampered in his efforts to control the sectors of life to which they referred. The paper world sometimes becomes excessive. It grows out of all proportion to reality. People feel hampered in their freedom by the world of paper. They would like to move and act without control, but are not permitted to do so. Before anyone can act in the world of reality, he has first to come to terms with the world of paper. He cannot build a house, remodel his store, acquire a new car or even an old jalopy without first clearing the matter with the world of paper. Nothing is permitted to happen in the world of reality unless it is duplicated in the world of paper.

Although undoubtedly there are excesses in this matter, in general there is no reason to complain about it. Thanks to the duplication of the world on paper, Western man has been able to seize control of his world in a new way. It would be unthinkable that he would give up the gains made in this fashion. Increasingly large numbers of people spend their working hours in this paper world. Their work keeps them busy in a rational sphere, the sphere of rationalized speech and rationalized writing.

*The Danger of Duplicating the World on Paper.* There exists a danger that the duplication of the world on paper will be made a norm of the real world. Because this duplication has made it possible for man to obtain a comprehensive picture of reality, those who work in the world of paper will be inclined to look at the real world in the mirror of the paper world. As a result they may not have a sufficient feeling for reality itself. People who are closer to reality itself can easily come into conflict with the world of paper. This conflict, as we have said, sometimes arises from an unreasonable desire for uncontrolled freedom. Certain individuals revolt against the idea that they have to live and work in a world which in many respects is controlled by others. However,

244

the conflict can also have a sound basis. Officialdom can become blind to the world of reality and impede its progress with paper requirements. In that case it frustrates the very purpose of the paper world, which is to control the real world and to make it progress in a systematic way.

*Separation of Planning and Execution.* The paper duplication of the world has integrated the so-called "white collar worker" in the labor order. It looks as if he occupies a permanent place in it, for his functions continue to increase. As in the production of material goods, so here also work becomes more mechanized. Numerous modern inventions see to it that the duplication of the world on paper is made more effective than man alone would be able to do it.

The rationalization of labor should be understood in the light of the modern paper world. Primitive man also was guided by reason in his work, but for him planning and execution were not separated from each other. Their unity still survives where there are small farmers. After milking his cows in the morning, the small farmer will decide what he will do during the rest of the day and his decision will be influenced by the weather. If the weather is suitable, he will work outside; if not, he will busy himself with work in his stable or barn. If during the course of his work he notices that something else needs attention, he will act accordingly. In his case one and the same man both plans and executes the work that is to be done. In our modern complicated labor order, however, planning and execution are separated. The planning is done in the world of the word, on paper. It precedes execution and the two are not performed by the same people. Work is planned with the aid of scientific reflection and governed by a more rigid rationality than in the world of thinking-in-action.

*"Passive Activity."* Those who execute the planned work labor within a framework laid down for them by others. With Sartre, one could say that their work is a "passive activity." The worker is active, of course, but his activity runs its course within a frame-

work which is not his own. His activity therefore is permeated with passivity. Many forms of work leave hardly any room, even none at all, for the worker's own activity. There remain, of course, types of work which cannot be subjected to such a rigorous planning and in which the worker himself to a greater or lesser extent determines how he will perform his work. Rigorously planned work prevails in many factories. What "passive activity" means one can see by visiting a plant in which everything is planned, down to the last details, in the world of paper. The power of speech, written down in the world of paper, controls the workers of such a plant. Human beings are active there, but their every move is fully planned by others without leaving them the slightest room for private initiative. Such people are sometimes called slaves of machines. Superficially speaking, this may be true, but we should not forget that behind every machine we find the reason of its inventors. The worker is the slave of the creative reason of others, of the power of human speech embodied in their creations.

The creative mind revealing itself in machines has thought only in terms of productivity. Man has entered into the picture only as one of the producing factors. His possibilities have been taken into account insofar as they affect production, but much in the same way as the strength of the foundation on which the machines are to be based or the strains and stresses of the material of which they are composed. Man has not been taken into account as a human being, that is, as a self-project. In this respect there is no room provided for him in the modern process of production. He is expected to be diligent and reliable, but this condition is fulfilled if he does what the machines require at the prescribed rate of speed. This "passive activity" is inhuman because it disregards man as a self-project, it fails to do justice to him precisely as a human being. A labor situation is human only if it leaves room for man as a self-project. This room should be relative, of course, to the individuals involved, for not all men can handle the same amount of room for self-project. Anyone,

246

however, who is genuinely human needs some room to be himself.

The objection is sometimes raised that many people would not want to work in conditions where much would be left to their own initiative and responsibility. This may be true and is not surprising. If people work for many years without any opportunity to express themselves in their labor, they unlearn to make their work a self-project. While it is true that man makes the structure of labor in which he works, it is also true that this structure makes man. The modern structure of labor has made the worker a human being who no longer wants a different structure. Yet this does not take away from the fact that the modern structure contains an evil. On the contrary, it reveals how far-reaching the evil is and how deep it has penetrated. It has given birth to a new type of man. This new man is deprived of his human character to such an extent that he himself no longer realizes his privation and does not even want to overcome it.

Man's work has made progress, it has become powerful, because it is controlled by the power of speech in the form of science. Man himself is in danger of becoming the victim of his own power. The word of science plans our world, our own existence even and our own occupation. Its planning sometimes goes so far that there is no longer room for man as a self-project, as a genuinely human being. Like a cancerous growth this neglect has deeply penetrated into the modern process of production. Yet this process was planned by man's creative reason.

*The Dehumanization of Man.* Must we say, therefore, that creative reason has not been rational in its planning? It was rational, of course, exceedingly rational even, but its rationality was one-sidedly directed to the productivity of labor. Labor had to be profitable, produce as much as possible as cheaply as possible. Almost nowhere else does the rigid rationality of creative reason manifest itself as clearly as in certain sectors of the labor process. However, creative reason regarded the laborer one-sidedly not as a self-project but as a production factor, a factor in a profit-making process. This evil cannot be undone by raising the worker's wages or improving the external surroundings of his work. Work, for example, does not become more human if it is accompanied by music. Realizing its mistakes, creative reason now tries to improve the situation by making such incidental corrections. The latter, however, leave the root of the evil untouched. Of course, it would be impossible to make at once the necessary essential correction, for the evil is incorporated in the entire process of production, a process so costly and complex that it cannot be transformed at once. Nevertheless, this practical difficulty is no reason why one should try to bury the evil instead of honestly facing its reality.

Our world is dominated by speech. On the basis of our duplication of the world in words and on paper we give shape to the real world. Although in itself this duplication is a good because it gives us control over the world, it also contains great dangers. For, by giving shape to our world through our speaking, we also shape man himself. Man's life and work are inseparably united with his world, so that our speaking about the world also shapes our life and work. They, too, are in the grip of our speech. Man can become the victim of his own creations. To prevent it, the creative planning of our reason must base itself also on the human character of man.

The planning of man's work itself reveals that it is possible to take this character into account. The design of the product to be manufactured is based on the user or consumer, the one who will have to pay for it and who has to be induced to buy it. Everything possible is done to satisfy his wishes. A motor car, for example, will be designed in such a way that the user enjoys comfort, has sufficient elbow room, and does not have to do too much work— or too little—in driving the car. If he wants to smoke there is an ash tray within reach as well as a lighter. A twist of a button and he can enjoy music, roll up the windows, have heat or air-conditioning. Everything is thought out with the future user in mind.

The designers do their utmost to anticipate his wishes. The labor process would have been planned quite differently if a little of that attention had also been bestowed on the human beings who have to manufacture the products. They have been regarded only as producing factors. The evil does not lie in the very nature of the process of labor or in a technical necessity, but in the one-sidedness of man's planning reason.

This one-sidedness should not be called inevitable. It happens sometimes that man makes mistakes because he did not foresee, and even could not foresee, certain aspects of reality. No one can blame man for not knowing everything. It often happens that in designing a product legitimate wishes of its users are forgotten. If that happens, the mistakes are corrected with the greatest possible dispatch. But the situation is entirely different with respect to the one-sidedness of the production process. This process has been deliberately willed in a one-sided way. On the basis of a one-sided economic attitude, its planners refused to see the worker as a self-project and wanted to regard him only as a production factor. They were to blame for their lack of respect for their fellow-men. We have not yet managed to overcome their mistake. One can claim, of course, that at present this situation is an economic necessity and that it cannot be eliminated all at once. Yet we should not forget that this necessity is of our own making. We are confronted with the results of our own planning. Man himself has become the enemy of humanity.

Similar phenomena can be observed also in other realms. Dwellings, for instance, are more rigidly planned than ever. Their plans are drawn on paper down to the last details. Man, of course, is taken into consideration in this planning. All his needs are foreseen and provided for. Anyone entering such a house knows at once where each piece of furniture is supposed to fit, for the architect's rationalized design has fixed the function of each little space in the whole. The only thing that has been forgotten is that the man who will dwell there is a self-project. In the modern house, everything has been projected for him, he need no longer be a self-project but merely a good user of the house. He cannot adapt the house to himself but has to adapt himself to the design of the architect. If he doesn't, he makes "mistakes" in the use of the house that are evident to anyone who enters it. An attempt to use his own initiative in his dwelling looks ridiculous in the light of its design. Man's dwelling is fully planned and fixed in the world of paper. Similar remarks could be made about other aspects of the modern world.

*The Quasi-Autonomy of the Paper World.* We have emphasized here the one-sided emphasis which the modern Western world places on speech. We have seen how Western man duplicates his world in the realm of speech by putting his world down on paper and how he plans his real world on the basis of his paper world. The term "duplication" has been chosen intentionally. Some may dislike the term because speech is an expression of the real world and not its duplication. While this is true in a certain sense, it is also true that man's speaking can begin to lead a life of its own, a quasi-autonomous life. It becomes the basis on which the real world is increasingly planned. Precisely because of this quasi-autonomy, we may say that the world of paper is a kind of duplicate of the real world. There is a real danger that this verbal duplicate of the world on paper will impose itself as the norm of the real world. The numerous jokes about bureaucracy have in common the idea that the paper world is made to serve as the norm of the real world. They are humorous because they exaggerate this idea out of all propotion. It would be foolish to claim that ridiculous bureaucratic formalism is a necessary phenomenon in the modern world. The attitude and action of many officials shows that that is not the case. Yet, who has not on occasion met with situations in which bureaucracy appeared to have lost contact with the world of reality and tried to cling to its paper replica? In other words, the danger of making the paper world the norm of the real world is a real danger.

The paper duplication of the world, however, has its advantages and cannot be discarded. But man must be on guard against a one-sided rationality which is blind to certain aspects of human reality. The man who speaks in the paper world must understand human reality in the full sense of the term.

If modern man wants to participate in our world, he needs to be educated for this purpose. If he is destined for a function in the sphere of speech, that is, in the sphere in which the real world is duplicated in spoken or written form, his education will introduce him especially to this duplicated world. A result of this education can be that he does not acquire a sufficient sense of reality. In the West it is almost inevitable now to regard the world of reality through the mirror of the spoken and written word. Western man realizes that this approach has made him powerful. Yet he must be on guard against the danger of one-sidedness with respect to the real world and real life. This danger needs to be pointed out to the young people who prepare them-selves for their task in the world of the word. This is one of the reasons why we have dwelled rather long on this point.

## 3. THE SCOPE OF SPEECH

In the first section of this chapter we have seen that the totaliz-ing character of our existence manifests itself especially in speech. For our speaking tends to an inner coherence of its own and there-fore seeks to find coherence in the "spoken" world, in the field of significations. In the second section we have seen that Western man has placed his realms of action under the control of the light given by his speaking. The result has been great progress and a way of life which eventually will become the accepted way of life for all mankind. Nevertheless, this Western approach is not without dangers. When the rationality proper to the word descends to the realm of action, it can easily happen that life be-comes rationalized one-sidedly. It can also happen that the lives of many are forced into rational schemes planned by others. As a matter of fact, this has happened with respect to certain forms of work. We must be on guard against letting life and work become the mere execution of plans created by others. Such a loss of freedom undoubtedly exists in the situation of many laborers. It is not a typical phenomenon of capitalism, however, for the same situation occurs also in the Marxist way of life: there also a few plan the life of all. Paradoxical as it may seem, Marx was the first thinker who clearly analyzed the unfreedom in question, yet the movement which arose from his thinking has brought about this same unfreedom in a new way.

In the third section of this chapter we must now consider the scope of totalizing speech. By asking about its scope, we are asking at the same time about its possibilities.

*The Many Dimensions of Speech.* The many dimensions of our speech reveal themselves in our speaking. First of all, it extends to the present, the past and the future. That we speak about the present is hardly surprising, but it is remarkable that we speak also about the past and the future. We do so even in ordinary prescientific ways of speaking. We often discuss past events and appear able to reconstruct them. People who meet after a long time usually begin by reconstructing the past together. We discuss the future, as is exemplified by farmers who argue about the weather of the coming day. In scientific speaking we try to approach the past and the future in a more systematic way. All kind of historical sciences try to give us a picture of the past and even to reconstruct the evolution of the earth and of the universe. Modern man is very curious also about his own past, although that curiosity is not really new, for even man's oldest myths bear witness to his curiosity in this respect.

Our speaking extends also to the many dimensions of the universe. We have developed sciences about the stars and the planets and created new means to observe what happens far away so that we can discuss it. We speak about the hidden depth of the oceans and the earth. By means of our speaking we manage to penetrate into the inner composition of matter—with marvelous results. Our speech tries to throw light on the organic and psychical life of animals. It endeavors to discover man himself. We have

252

developed many sciences of man. We speak about our own organism, our psyche, our spirit, our social and economic life. We even speak about our speaking.

Finally, we have metaphysical and religious forms of speech. Although these two differ essentially, they tend in the same direction insofar as both try to penetrate into the most profound depth of all reality, the ultimate origin of everything—God.

*The Mysterious Character of the Scope of Speech.* This multidimensional character of speech is very mysterious. In the preceding chapters we have repeatedly discovered reasons why man's speech causes us to wonder. We wonder that man is able to bring things to light by speaking. How is it possible that, by placing our throat and mouth in a certain position to produce a succession of sounds, we make these sounds have meaning, bring clarity and enlightment? The philosophy of language points to this mystery but does not solve it. When we see a painter busy and observe how meaning gradually develops under his strokes on the canvas, we wonder at this marvel. But it is just as marvelous that a succession of sounds becomes meaning for us. The philosopher reflects upon this wonder but cannot explain its mystery. He is likewise unable to explain the scope of our speech.

For instance, we cannot explain that we are able to reconstruct the past, to penetrate into it with our gaze, to explain that we are beings who can recall things. We are so used to it that we are annoyed if occasionally our memory fails. Yet we should be greatly surprised that we are able to remember anything at all.

Likewise, how is it possible for us to go far beyond our own personal past and ask questions about the origin of man's organism or that of the earth? Similar questions can be asked about all dimensions of our speaking. In reply one can describe, of course, the method we follow and the fundamental experiences from which we proceed in penetrating into these dimensions. Such replies, which are given by, e.g., the philosophy of science, are very illuminating, but nevertheless we always end up with the

253

fact that we have this or that ability and cannot further explain why we have it. The same happens with respect to any of our human abilities.

We cannot explain, for example, why we are able to see, hear, taste or smell, why we appreciate beauty and humor, why we are sensitive to values, why we are able to love and hate, why we have an ethical sense. Ultimately we always have simply to admit that we *find* ourselves having all those abilities. We find ourselves as we are. Even the attempt to find an *a priori* explanation of what we are and are able to do is absurd. Of course, we must try to understand ourselves, but this attempt is always an effort to penetrate into what we find given. Man's existence with all his abilities is a primordial fact. In the light of this primordial fact and thanks to it, other facts appear to us, but we cannot explain this primordial fact itself. Hence we cannot explain that we speak, that by speaking we bring things to light. We cannot give an ultimate explanation for the fact that our speaking encompasses certain dimensions, but have to accept ourselves and our abilities as a gift.

It would be dangerous therefore to deny certain dimensions of our speech on the ground that their possibility cannot be demonstrated. For ultimately we cannot demonstrate *a priori* any human possibility whatsoever. We cannot explain that we are able to see, that our organism can rest or go forward on two relatively small feet, that the full weight of our body can rest on the skin of our soles without causing discomfort. One who wants to accept a human possibility only if he can justify it *a priori* in a rational fashion, will ultimately have to reject every human possibility, which would, of course, be absurd. We know our possibilities from what we actually do and not vice versa. While we have every right and duty to examine our activities, to reflect critically upon them and to improve them, we must realize that any form of critical and scientific reflection is based on the acceptance of the possibilities and abilities which we discover in ourselves. The

254

old saying that "from the fact one can conclude to the possibility" contains a profound truth.

*The Possibility of Religious and Metaphysical Speech.* For the same reason there is no justification for rejecting the possibility of religious and metaphysical speech on the ground that this possibility cannot be demonstrated. We do not mean that there are no reasons why some people are inclined to question their possibility. First of all, metaphysical and religious speaking are the most mysterious dimension of speech, for in them man wants to attain the absolute origin of everything. Secondly, in the course of history man has constructed the most fantastic systems of metaphysics and religion, which later he had to reject as fictions or projections of his own mind. For these reasons one can understand that some people are suspicious about metaphysics and religion and inclined to consider them as pure fictions.

A third reason why metaphysical and religious speech are rejected is that in these matters man goes beyond the realm of experience. According to the religious man, God transcends the world and therefore does not lie in the realm of our experience. On the other hand, a justified way of speaking is always based on an experience preceding speech, for, as we have said, an experience of meaning always precedes our speaking. But with respect to the transcendent God there is no experience upon which our speaking can be based. Therefore, such a speech belongs to the realm of fiction. For this reason one can understand why some people impose upon metaphysical and religious speaking the obligation to demonstrate first its own possibility.

However, such an obligation cannot be imposed, for the simple reason that man is unable to satisfy this demand with respect to even a single one of his fundamental possibilities. Note that we say "fundamental possibilities," for with respect to more concrete possibilities it is often possible to derive them from their roots in other possibilities. For example, before a technician actually constructs a new type of apparatus, he will first demonstrate its possibilities. Before one undertakes a voyage of discovery, one will investigate its possibilities. Ultimately, however, we will always end up with fundamental possibilities which we simply find given and whose possibility we cannot demonstrate. For this reason it is wholly excluded that we can ever demonstrate the possibility of metaphysics and religion, for these two are fundamental aspects of human existence.

Sometimes it is possible to demonstrate that something is impossible for man. Our being-man is an actual datum, something we find given, and it may be possible to show that this actual datum does not include this or that particular possibility. For example, given the actual weight of our body, we are not able to rise in the air by means of our bodily forces alone. The arguments presented in the preceding paragraphs also really want to show that religion and metaphysics are impossible for man. However, they fall short of that goal. That man in his speaking attains the Transcendent is indeed mysterious and astonishing, but there are many marvelous possibilities in man. It is true, of course, that there have been many fictions in metaphysics and religion, but shouldn't these fictions be regarded as primitive forms of a fundamental intuition whose inmost essence transcends the fictitious elements? It is possible that man attains the Transcendent, that he tries to give expression to the correlate of this intentional attitude, but that in his attempts he makes use of primitive representations which subsequently he learns to overcome.

Regarding the objection that religious and metaphysical speech are not based on experience, one can reply that this remark simply is not true. For there are many people who bear witness to religious and metaphysical experience. It happens sometimes that real experiences are denied by theoretical thought. For example, we experience one another as subjects, as persons, yet the claim has been made that our immediate experience does not go beyond knowledge of one another's bodily exterior.

It is in principle impossible to demonstrate the possibility of religious and metaphysical speech. Their impossibility likewise has not been demonstrated.[5] Nevertheless, we are faced with the fact that some people accept this kind of speech while others reject it. Is there, then, no way to justify our standpoint, so that we have either blindly to accept or blindly to reject the possibility of religion and metaphysics? Our reply is that man knows his fundamental possibilities in his actual pursuits. Religion and metaphysics demonstrate their right to existence by their actual existence. But, one will object, it is not at all excluded that the metaphysician and the religious man think that they are in contact with reality while they merely pursue illusions. This reproach is actually made and the number of people who make it has greatly increased in our time. The metaphysician and the religious man do not remain insensitive to this reproach. They speak with greater hesitation and less self-confidence than formerly. It often happens that those who believe in God have to struggle against doubts.

It is not our intention to plead here in favor of irrationalism, for we do not deny that man in his thinking can raise his mind to God. However, he can do this only by way of thinking metaphysically. One who denies the possibility of metaphysical thought, denies also that man can raise his thinking to God. There are many today who doubt the entire field of thought in which man finds his way to God. Personally I accept the possibility of metaphysical thought, but for the reasons explained above this kind of thinking cannot be justified *a priori*. It has to prove its right to existence in its actual existence.

The metaphysician and the religious man take comfort in the fact that the metaphysical and religious questions continue to present themselves in spite of all doubts and denials. Several times in history it has happened that the conviction of man's

---

[5] Some scholastic metaphysicians rigorously want to demonstrate the possibility of metaphysical thinking. In our opinion it cannot be done. All we can do is point to the possibility. The case of metaphysics is not in any way special, for, as we have said, ultimately none of man's fundamental possibilities can be rigorously demonstrated. It appears to us that the philosophers in question have been too much impressed by the reproaches addressed to them and have fallen into an exaggerated form of rationalism.

inability to rise above his worldly horizon gained ground and became widely accepted as a philosophical standpoint. Yet every time metaphysics and religion have survived to bury their undertakers. Why, we must ask, did this happen? Why do metaphysics and religion always overcome these doubts and denials?

Man is in a situation, but in such a way that the situation is known to him. His life runs its course within certain boundaries, but in such a way that these boundaries are known to him. The most striking example undoubtedly is that man knows the limits of his own existence. We know with absolute certainty that our life extends from our conception to our death, but, in knowing it, we look beyond these boundaries. We affirm our own finiteness and thereby look beyond it. We live in a psychical, social and historical situation, but are able to regard this situation and its influence as such. We realize the relativity of everything that is connected with this situation. We are individual persons but able to look at things from the standpoint of human beings who are different from us. Surprising as it may seem, we can think and speak from the standpoint of others. If there is a situation of conflict, we are able to plead for our view on the basis of our own situation and nonetheless also feel how the others look at the matter and envision his view and his evaluation. We find ourselves as actually given, we experience our existence as a gift and as a task. At certain moments we feel intensely grateful that we exist as human beings, we experience the riches of being-man and rejoice that we are permitted to live in its untold possibilities, for we know that we do not owe our existence and possibilities to ourselves.

Even our speaking transcends our particularity. The one who speaks is always an empirical *I*, but this empirical *I* speaks in a universal fashion. If it did not, science would not be possible. For, if the teaching man did not know that his speech is valid also for his listeners, he would not speak. Discussion is the search for a way of speaking that is common. It is so on principle. Our speaking originates in our empirical subjectivity but transcends it. Otherwise it would be meaningless. We transcend ourselves in our speaking. For this reason we are a question for ourselves in our speaking. The questioning *I* asks questions not only about the non-*I* but also, if it reflects, about itself. It is astonishing and mysterious that we can speak in such a way. No one is able to account *a priori* for these facts, yet they belong to the very character of being-man. These marvelous possibilities reveal themselves in our actual speaking.

*The Mysterious Character of Metaphysical and Religious Speech.* These and other similar experiences give rise to metaphysical and religious speech. Man begins to see himself as a manifestation, a form of appearance of, a participation in, an absolute reality. He regards his own word as a sharing in an absolute *Logos* which is the origin of man and the world. From his empirical *I* the religious man rises to the recognition of an absolute Subject. He is no longer able to understand his own existence without God. His existence finds meaning and fulfillment in God. The religious man and the metaphysician are able to meet the doubts and denials of others with considerable empathy, for they are very much aware of the mysterious character of religious and metaphysical speech. They see this mystery in all the ambiguity of being-man as he is actually is.

Nevertheless, it should be kept in mind that the metaphysician and the religious man cannot be expected to justify themselves in the rigidly rationalized way of the sciences. He cannot account for his contact with the Transcendent in that fashion, for no form of meaning or value can be rationalized in that way. We cannot rationally justify in the way of the sciences that the beautiful, the humorous and the ethical are, that we are able to see, laugh and speak. Not one of man's fundamental possibilities can be accounted for in that fashion.

Man simply has to accept with gratitude the many dimensions of his existence and of his speech. We have to be satisfied with the fact that we are a source of wonder for ourselves. We constantly discover new possibilities of man, new dimensions of speech. Parapsychology, for example, is now recognized as a science. Scientifically investigated experiences show that some people can speak about dimensions which are altogether inaccessible to others. They speak about things lying beyond the horizon of ordinary experience. Formerly talk about such phenomena was simply rejected as absurd. It is certain that many alleged cases are based on illusions and fancy. But it is also certain that not all such phenomena are without foundation. There is no reason to be surprised by these new discoveries, for man does not know all his possibilities. Any new mode of scientific speech reveals a new human possibility, many new sciences have arisen in the past century. Experience has made us wiser and we now proceed with more circumspection before we make the claim that it is impossible for man to do this or that thing which was hitherto unheard of. The same prudence should be shown also with respect to religion and metaphysics.

## 4. The Tendency of Speech to Clarity

*A Decisive Aspect of Speech.* What does man want to attain in and through his speech? As the preceding chapters have shown, no simple answer can be given to this question. Practically all human attitudes can be embodied and realized in speech. Love and hatred, confidence and distrust, desire and aversion become existent in speech. In our speaking we open ourselves to one another, but we also seek to overpower the other through it. Speech can be an attempt to break out of isolation as well as the embodiment of a self-satisfied man's exhibitionism. Man can seek the most diverse values in and through his speech.

Nevertheless, there is one value that dominates here, namely, the clarity, the evidence, the light of truth. In his speaking man reveals himself as someone who endeavors to attain understanding. Is it possible to assign a privileged position to this value, to consider the tendency to it as something that is more intrinsically connected with speech than other tendencies are? We believe that an affirmative answer must be given to this question. The more man's speaking detaches itself from the whole of life, the more it purifies itself in a critical way, the more also it reveals man's tendency to clarity. We may even say that in these more refined stages the tendency to clarity manifests itself as the factor which dominates speech entirely. Especially in the sciences man's passions, affections and emotions are no longer allowed to influence his speaking; his tendency to achieve power or to exhibitionism are not permitted to play a role. The one aspect which stands in the foreground here as the most crucial aspect of speech is man's search for clarity.

Why does man try to find clarity in speaking? This question needs to be asked, for all kinds of practical aims can be involved in the search for clarity. Man has to live in the world which is his field of existence. The situation which he needs is not given to him ready made. He has to situate himself, that is, to plan his own situation. For this reason he must create clarity in his field of existence. As we have pointed out repeatedly, our knowledge, even our scientific knowledge, has also a practical function.

Nevertheless, this reply, no matter how realistic it is, does not suffice. For man seeks clarity also for its own sake, as should be evident from the fact that our search for it goes far beyond the requirements imposed by the needs of our field of existence. We have created sciences concerning realities which have no practical importance at all. We try to look beyond the sphere of our practical interests. We even expect such an "unpractical" interest from one another, for we dislike anyone whose interests do not go beyond himself. Science and literature, as well as many "ordinary" conversations, do not make sense unless we pay attention to man's desire for clarity.

*Reality as Meaning-for-Us.* There are people who dislike the phenomenological philosopher because he refers to everything that is for us, to everything that we know, as meaning-for-us and because he calls everything that appears to us a correlate of human intentionally. This thesis is met with distrust and resentment. We suspect, however, that a misunderstanding plays a role in this distrust. When there is question of meaning-for-us, attention should be paid to all dimensions of human subjectivity. Man stands in the world as a needy subject, and anything that satisfies

261

his needs is a value for him. For this reason value belongs to meaning-for-us. Many of man's needs are individual needs only. With respect to them meaning-for-the-subject does not go beyond an individual character. However, as we have seen, the speaking subject can speak also in the name of others. If he does, then the meaning-for-us has an intersubjective character. Science endeavors to find intersubjective meaning. Man is also a being who seeks clarity. He seeks clarity not only about his worldly field of existence but also about himself, about his empirical reality, whose factual and contingent character is known to him. This clarity also is meaning-for-us. One who takes into consideration all the dimensions of human subjectivity and therefore realizes the many senses which the expression "meaning-for-us" can have will see no reason to protest against the use of this expression.

Those who protest against it attribute to the expression a narrow sense which is rejected by the phenomenologist himself. All the phenomenologist wants to claim when he uses the expression is this: man cannot affirm any dimension of appearing reality without affirming at the same time that the subject tends to this dimension; hence this dimension of appearing reality is the correlate of a human attitude or intention. It is not possible for man to transcend this correlation of subject and meaning. He who wants to affirm a dimension lying outside this correlation contradicts himself. For he implicitly affirms that he tends to this dimension, that it is a correlate of his intentional attitude.

*Intersubjective Character of the Tendency to Clarity.* The tendency to clarity is the driving force of human speech. It accounts for the fact that man is never satisfied with his speaking, that he always realizes the relative character of what has already been said and endeavors to express reality in a better way. The tendency to clarity is an intersubjective event. For we take over the clarity which others have brought and from their achievements we actively go forward toward greater clarity. We make our own the clarity achieved by others by taking over the current way of speaking, by reading and listening. We can also consult the past, for in his search for clarity man continues also to seek inspiration in the great thinkers of the past. Bringing things to light through speech is an intersubjective event. The search for clarity is intersubjective also for a different reason. We are very much aware of the fact that whatever clarity we find through speech is not destined only for ourselves. This is the reason why we speak with others and write books. We seek to attain clarity together with the others and for the others.

Strange as it may seem, in this search for clarity we participate in a social event and, at the same time, each one of us, as a totalization, contracts this common event into something that is his alone. Each man is in his own way a synthesis of the universe, a synthesis of mankind. Everyone is both a part of mankind and himself a totalization of the world. It is as if in our empirical reality we discover a dimension which exceeds this empirical reality. The truth of this statement manifests itself in the paradox that we speak also about ourselves, that we seek to obtain clarity about ourselves, and recognize our own relativity and contingency.

Is the subject which recognizes its own contingency wholly identical with the subject whose contingency is recognized? Is the subject which recognizes its own finiteness wholly identical with the subject whose finiteness is recognized? Is the subject which speaks about itself wholly identical with the subject that is spoken of?

These and other similar paradoxes made Plato say that man is a participation in eternal and infinite Ideas. They made St. Augustine speak about a divine light that is active in us. They induced Hegel to regard empirical subjects as forms in which the unique and absolute subject appears and through which it becomes itself. They lead the religious man to the conviction that man is a participation in God, an image in which God manifests Himself. We cannot develop these questions here in detail, although they are connected with our speaking. Our speaking is a manifestation, a realization of the mystery which we are.

263

# Epilogue

HAVING arrived at the end of this study, we realize very much how correctly Merleau-Ponty describes man's pursuits as a "slipping grasp" (*prise glissante*). One who begins to write about a topic is driven by the desire to grasp this topic and to put it into words. We had wanted to discuss the phenomenon of language. Now we see how much our work is not more than a "slipping grasp." It still remains an astonishing mystery that we human beings bring light in a succession of sounds. The author still does not know how words proceed from his lips, combine into sentences and are full of meaning. After his reflections upon this mystery, it seems even more mysterious to him than before. Many readers will perhaps share in his wonder. Language is perhaps a more mysterious reality for them now that they have read this work than before its reading. If this is so, the author has not entirely failed. It is important for us, it makes us more human, if we become more aware of the mysterious wonder which we ourselves are. Man's wonder about himself helps him to become fully human.

# Bibliography

I. Abramczyk, *Platos Dialog Kratylos und das Problem der Sprachphilosophie,* Breslau, 1928.

*Actes du Colloque International de Phénoménologie,* ed. H. L. Van Breda, O.F.M., Bruxelles, 1952.

H. Adank, *Essais sur les fondements psychologiques et linguistiques de la métaphore affective,* Genève, 1939.

G. W. Allport and Ph.. E. Vernon, *Studies in Expressive Movement,* New York, 1933.

Hermann Amman, *Die menschliche Rede, Sprachphilosophische Untersuchungen.* Two vols., Schauenburg, 1925 and 1928.

Stefan Andres, "Ueber die Sendung des Dichters," *Offner Horizont, Festschrift für Karl Jaspers,* München, 1953.

K. O. Apel, "Sprache und Wahrheit in der gegenwärtigen Situation der Philosophie," *Philosophische Rundschau,* Vol. VII (1959), pp. 161–184.

P. B. Ballard, *Thoughts and Language,* London, 1934.

E. Benveniste, "Nature du signe linguistique," *Acta Linguistica,* Vol. I (1939), pp. 23–29.

Ludwig Binswanger, *Grundformen und Erkenntnis menschlichen Daseins,* Zurich, 1953.

"Zum Problem von Sprache und Denken," *Ausgewählte Vorträge und Aufsätze,* Vol. II, pp. 346–362.

M. Black, *The Importance of Language,* Englewood Cliffs, 1962.

M. Blondel, *La Pensée,* Paris, 1934.

Leonard Bloomfield, *An Introduction to the Study of Language,* New York, 1914.

*Language,* London, 1935.

K. Borinski, *Der Ursprung der Sprache,* Halle, 1911.

A. Bricteux, *Essai sur l'origine du langage,* Liège, n.d.

K. Britton, *A Philosophical Study of Language (communication),* London, 1939.

W. Bröcker and J. Lohmann, "Vom Wesen des sprachlichen Zeichens," *Lexis,* Vol. I (1948), pp. 24–33.

L. Brunschvicg, *Héritage de mots, héritage d'idées,* Paris, 1945.

B. Brus, "De taal bij Merleau-Ponty," *Ned. Tijdschrift v. Psychologie,* (1958), pp. 26–80.

K. Büchner, *Platons Kratylos und die moderne Sprachphilosophie,* Berlin, 1936.

E. Buyssens, "La nature du signe linguistique," *Acta Linguistica,* Vol. II (1940–1941), pp. 83–86.

Frederick J. Buytendijk, *De psychologie van de roman,* Utrecht, 1961.

Dorion Cairns, "The Ideality of Verbal Expressions," *Philosophical and Phenomenological Research,* Vol. I (1940), pp. 453–462.

R. Carnap, *Logische Syntax der Sprache,* Wien, 1934.

A. Carnoy, *La science du mot. Traité de sémantique,* Louvain, 1927.

Ernst Cassirer, *Language and Myth,* New York, 1946.

*Philosophy of Symbolic Forms,* New Haven, 1953.

*Wesen und Wirkung des Symbolbegriffs,* Oxford, 1956.

St. Chase, *The Tyranny of Words,* New York, 1938.

Malcolm Clark, "Meaning and Language in Hegel's Philosophy," *Revue Philosophique de Louvain,* Vol. LVIII (1960), pp. 557–578.

Macdonald Critchley, *The Language of Gesture,* London, 1939.

Czech, *Versinnlichte Denk- und Sprachlehre,* Wien, 1836.

A. Dauzat, *La philosophie du langage,* Paris, 1912.

H. Delacroix, *Le langage et la pensée,* Paris, 1930.

*Psychologie du langage,* Paris, 1933.

J. Delanglade, "Essai sur la signification de la parole," *Signe et Symbole (Etre et Penser),* Neuchâtel, 1946.

J. M. De Petter, "Impliciete Intuïtie," *Tijdschrift voor Philosophie,* Vol. I (1939), no. 1.

Alphonse De Waelhens, "De mens en de cultuur," *De mens,* Utrecht, 1958.

"De taalphilosophie volgens M. Merleau-Ponty," *Tijdschrift voor Philosophie,* Vol. XVI (1954), pp. 402–418.

A. Dondeyne, *Contemporary European Thought and Christian Faith,* 2nd impr., Pittsburgh, 1963.

*Faith and the World,* Pittsburgh, 1963.

W. Doroszewski, "Quelques remarques sur les rapports de la sociologie et de la linguistique: Durkheim et F. de Saussure," *Journal de Psychologie Normale et Pathologique, Vol.* XXX (1933), (*Psychologie du langage*), pp. 82–91.

M. Dufrenne, *Language and Philosophy,* Bloomington, 1963.

Ferdinand Elner, *Das Wort und die geistigen Realitäten,* Wien, 1952.

K. Erdmann, *Die Bedeutung des Wortes,* Leipzig, 1922.

H. Feigl, "The Mind-Body Problem in the Development of Logical Positivism," *Revue Internationale de Philosophie,* Vol. IV (1950); reprinted in H. Feigl and May Brodback, *Readings in the Philosophy of Science,* pp. 612–626.

I. Fónagy, "Ueber die Eigenart des sprachlichen Zeichens, Bemerkungen zu einer alten Streitfrage," *Lingua,* Vol. VI (1956), pp. 67–88.

Victor E. Frankl, *Der unbewusste Gott,* Wien, 1949.

O. Funcke, *Studien zur Geschichte der Sprachphilosophie,* Bern, 1927.

A. Gardiner, *The Theory of Speech and Language,* Oxford, 1951, 2nd. ed., (1932).

L. Geiger, *Der Ursprung der Sprache,* 1869.

I. Goldberg, *The Wonder of Words,* New York, 1938.

E. Grassi, *Ueber das Problem des Wortes und des individuellen Lebens,* Berlin, 1942.

Josephus Gredt, *Elementa philosophiae Aristotelicae-Thomisticae,* Freiburg im B., 1937.

G. Gusdorf, *La parole,* Paris, 1953.

Peter Hartmann, *Wesen und Wirkung der Sprache im Spiegel der Theorie Leo Weisgerbers,* Heidelberg, 1958.

*Das Wort als Name, Struktur, Konstitution und Leistung der benennenden Bestimmung,* Köln, 1958.

S. I. Hayakawa, *Language in Thought and Action,* London, 1952.

Martin Heidegger, *Hebel der Hausfreund,* Pfulligen, n.d.

*Einführung in die Metaphysik,* Tübingen, 1958, 2nd. ed., (1953).

*Sein und Zeit,* 7th impr., Tübingen, 1953.

*Unterwegs zur Sprache,* Pfulligen, 1959.

*Vom Wesen der Wahrheit,* Frankfurt a.M., 1949.

L. Hjelmslev, *Langue et Parole,* Genève, 1942.

Peter R. Hofstätter, *Vom Leben des Wortes, Das Problem an Platons Dialog "Kratylos" dargestellt,* Wien, 1949.

Hans Heinz Holz, *Sprache und Welt, Probleme der Sprachphilosophie,* Frankfurt a.M., 1953.

R. Hönigswald, *Philosophie und Sprache,* Basel, 1937.

Edmund Husserl, *Ideen zu einer reinen Phänomenologie,* 3 vols., Den Haag, 1950 ff.

Karl Jaspers, *Von der Wahrheit,* München, 1947.

O. Jespersen, *Language, its Nature, Development and Origin,* London, 1921.

*The Philosophy of Grammar,* London, 1935.

F. G. Jünger, *Sprache und Denken,* Frankfurt a.M., 1962.

W. N. A. Klever, *Anamnèsis en anagogè,* Assen, 1962.

Gerhard Krüger, *Grundfragen der Philosophie,* Frankfurt a.M., 1958.

Remy C. Kwant, *Encounter,* Pittsburgh, 1960.

*Het Arbeidsbestel,* 4th impr., Utrecht, 1962.

*Mens en Kritiek,* Utrecht, 1962.

*The Phenomenological Philosophy of Merleau-Ponty,* Pittsburgh, 1963.

*Philosophy of Labor,* Pittsburgh, 1960.

*Subject en zin,* Utrecht, 1961.

*De wijsbegeerte van Karl Marx,* Utrecht, 1962.

L. Lechance, *Philosophie du langage,* Ottawa, 1943.

Eric H. Lenneberg, "A Note on Cassirer's Philosophy of Language," *Philosophy and Phenomenological Research,* Vol. XV (1954–1955), pp. 512–522.

J. Linschoten, "Over de humor," *Tijdschrift voor Philosophie,* Vol. XIII (1951), no. 4.

Hans Lipps, *Die Verbindlichkeit der Sprache,* Frankfurt a.M., 1958.

J. Lohmann, "M. Heideggers 'ontologische Differenz' und die Sprache," *Lexis,* Vol. I (1948), pp. 49–106.

J. B. Lotz, "Sprache und Denken, Zur Phänomenologie und Metaphysik der Sprache," *Scholastik,* Vol. XXXI (1956), pp. 496–514.

J. Maritain, "Signe et symbole," *Quatre essais sur l'esprit dans sa condition charnelle,* Paris, 1939.

Karl Marx, *Zur Kritik der politischen Ökonomie,* Berlin, 1958.

Maurice Merleau-Ponty, *Les aventures de la dialectique,* Paris, 1953.

*In Praise of Philosophy,* Chicago, 1963.

*Humanisme et terreur,* Paris, 1948.

*Phenomenology of Perception,* New York, 1962.

*Sens et non-sens,* Paris, 1948.

*Signes,* Paris, 1960.

*The Structure of Behavior,* Boston, 1963.

Eugène Minkowski, "Phénoménologie du langage," *Encyclopédie Francaise,* Vol. XIX, 10–12 to 12–2.

Charles Morris, *Signs, Language and Behavior,* New York, 1946.

G. Nuchelmans, "De kritiek op de metaphysica," *Wijsgerig perspectief,* Vol. III (1963), no. 3.

C. K. Ogden and I. A. Richards, *The Meaning of Meaning, A study of the influence of language upon thought and of the science of symbolism,* New York, 1930, 3rd. ed., (1923).

Edmond Ortigues, *Le discours et le symbole,* Paris, 1962.

E. Otto, *Wirklichkeit, Sprechen und Sprachsymbolik*, Reichenberg, 1943.

R. Paget, *Speech as a Form of Human Behavior*, 1939.

G. Paloczi-Horvath, *De schrijver en de kommissaris*, Gravenhage, 1962.

B. Parain, "Le langage et l'existence," *L'Existence*, Paris, 1945.

*Recherches sur la nature et les fonctions du langage*, Paris, 1942.

J. Piaget, *Le langage et la pensée*, Neuchâtel, 1923.

Max Picard, *Der Mensch und das Wort*, Stuttgart, 1955.

W. Porzig, *Das Wunder der Sprache*, 2nd ed., Bern.

H. J. Pos, *Keur uit de verspreide geschriften van Dr. H. J. Pos*, Vol. I, Assen, 1957.

"Phénoménologie et linguistique," *Revue Internationale de Philosophie*, Vol. I (1939) no, 2.

"De taal als symbolische functie," *Uitdrukkingswijze der Wetenschap*, Groningen, 1934.

*Problèmes actuels de la phénoménologie*, ed. H. L. Van Breda, O.F.M., Colloque International de Phénoménologie, Bruxelles, 1952.

Jean Przyluski, "Le langage, la langue et la parole," *Journal de Psychologie Normale et Pathologique*, Vol. XXXVII–XXXVIII (1940–1941), pp. 29–38.

Geza Révész, "Thought and Language," *Archivum Linguisticum*, Vol. II (1950), pp. 122–131.

*Revue internationale de philosophie*, Vol. XVI (1962), no. 59. Various articles about "L'expression."

Paul Ricoeur, "Travail et parole," *Histoire et vérité*, Paris, 1955.

Richard Robinson, "The Theory of Names in Plato's Cratylus," *Revue internationale de Philosophie*, Vol. IX (1955), pp. 221–236.

Jean-Paul Sartre, *Critique de la raison dialectique*, Vol. I, *Théorie des ensembles pratiques*, Paris, 1960.

"Qu'est-ce que la littérature?" *Situations*, Vol. II, Paris, 1947.

H. Schmalenbach, "Phénoménologie du signe," *Signe et Symbole*, Neuchâtel, 1945.

Alfred Schuetz, "Language, Language Disturbances, and the Texture of Consciousness," *Social Research*, (1950), pp. 380–382.

Wilhelm Seelberger, *Hegel oder die Entwicklung des Geistes zur Freiheit*, Stuttgart, 1961.

H. Spiegelberg, *The Phenomenological Movement*, 2 vols., The Hague, 1960.

Julius Stenzel, *Philosophie der Sprache*, München, 1934.

C. F. P. Stutterheim, *Het begrip Metaphoor. Een taalkundig en wijsgerig onderzoek, Inleiding tot de taalfilosofie*, Antwerpen, 1949.

W. L. Thieme, *Spraak, taal en rede. Proeve eener redelijke ontwikkeling van het taalbegrip,* Bussum, 1941.

Colin Murray Turbayne, *The Myth of Metaphor,* New Haven, 1962.

W. M. Urban, *Language and Reality. The philosophy of Language and the principles of Symbolism,* London, 1939.

J. H. Van den Berg, "Het Gesprek," *Persoon en wereld,* Utrecht, 1953.

Louis Van Haecht, "Le langage et la philosophie," *Revue Philosophique de Louvain,* Vol. LVIII (1960), pp. 135–164.

"Phaenomenologische analyse van het menschelijk lichaam naar Edmund Husserl," *Tijdschrift voor Philosophie,* Vol. VI (1944), no. 1–2.

*Taalphilosophische beschouwingen,* Leuven, 1947.

D. J. Van Lennep, "Psychologie van het chaufferen," *Persoon en wereld,* Utrecht, 1953.

Andrew G. Van Melsen, *Science and Technology,* Pittsburgh, 1961.

C. A. Van Peursen, "L'horizon," *Situation,* Utrecht, 1954.

J. W. M. Verhaar, *Some Relations Between Perception, Speech and Thought,* Assen, 1963.

*Speech, Language and Inner Form (Some Linguistic Remarks on Thought),* Preprints of Papers for the Ninth International Congress of Linguists, Cambridge (Mass.), 1962, pp. 377–382.

F. Von Schlegel, *Philosophie der Sprache,* 1830.

K. Vossler, *Idealismus und Positivismus in der Sprachwissenschaft,* Heidelberg, 1904.

*Gesammelte Schriften zur Sprachphilosophie,* München, 1923.

Jean Wahl, *Etudes Kierkegaardiennes,* Paris, 1938.

*Traité de métaphysique,* Paris, 1953.

F. Waismann, *Philosophy and Language,* London, 1939.

H. Weber, *Herders Sprachphilosophie. Eine Interpretation in Hinblick auf die moderne Sprachphilosophie,* Berlin, 1939.

J. L. Weisgerber, *Muttersprache und Geistesbildung,* Göttingen, 1929.

E. Wezel, *Sprache und Geist. Der Zusammenhang von Spracherziehung und Geistesbildung im Spiegel der Philosophie der Gegenwart,* Leipzig, 1935.

B. L. Whorf, *Language, Thought and Reality,* New York, 1956.

W. Wundt, *Sprachgeschichte und Sprachpsychologie,* 1901.

# Index of Names

271

# Index of Subject Matter

Meaning (*cont.*)

*Homogeneity;* as intrinsic and
extrinsic to speech, 46 f.; man's
possibilities revealed by giving
of, 55 f.; the "other" revealed
by giving of, 57 f.; field of, see
*Field;* pointing gives new mode
of being to, 61 ff.; to signification from, 69 ff.; reality, signification and, 72 ff.; reason
and, 76 f.; dependence of
spoken, on pre-given, 80 ff.;
signification and, 99 f.; lived
forms of, 190 f.; progressive
interiorization and absolute
norms of, 225 f.; reciprocity of
spoken and lived, 226 f.; reality
as, 261 f.

Metaphysics, crisis of, 45.

Opinion, group, 124 ff.; personal
and public, 138 f.

Orthodoxy, collective light and,
158 f.

"Other(s)," revelation of the,
through giving of meaning,
57 f.; orientation of expression
to, 205 ff. speech as influencing,
216 ff. See also *Dialogue.*

Paradoxes of speech, 47 ff., 132 ff.

Passivity of speech, 133 f.

Person, the speaking, 136 ff.; collective enlightenment and,
150 ff.

Phenomenology, positivism and
existential, 20 f.; meaning and,
21 ff.

Platonism, Christianism and,
177 f.

Playfulness in speech, 110 ff.

Pointing, speaking as, 55 ff., 63 f.;
space, field of meaning and,
59 ff.; gives new mode of being
to meaning, 61 ff.; primacy of,
65 ff.; culture of, 65 f.

Positivism, existential phenomenology and, 20 f.

Power, of speech, 106 ff.; common
speech's conservative, 119 f.; no
escape from common speech's,
122 ff.; of man over speech,
134 f.; language of, 218 f.

Powerlessness, of speech, 106 ff.;
over speech, 135 f.

Practognosis, 169 ff.; theory and,
171 f.; importance of, 172 f.

Presuppositions of language, 6 f.

Rationalization, one-sided, 242 ff.

Realism of language, 11 f.

Reality, meaning, signification
and, 72 ff.; faithfulness to,
140 f.; as meaning for us,
261 f.

Reason, meaning and, 76 f.

Reflection, thinking and speaking
inseparable in, 194 ff.

Relativity of worded knowledge,
199 f.

Saying, seeing and, 141 ff.

Science, freedom and, 87 f., 94 ff.;
necessity of, 97 ff.; relationship
between world view and,
129 ff.; common field of existence and, 155 f.

Seeing, saying and, 141 ff.

Seriousness in playing with words,
110 ff.

Signification, from meaning to,
69 ff.; reality and, 72 f.; field
of, see *Field;* meaning and,
99 f.; coherence in field of,
231 f.

Situation, spoken word as aspect
of human, 143 ff.

Space, pointing and, 59 ff.; lived,
79 ff.

Speaking, as pointing, 55 ff., 63 f.;
talking and, 139 f.; spoken
word and, 142 ff.; understand-

ing and, 145 ff.; goes beyond knowing, 148 ff.; light and darkness in, 161 ff.; not simply identical with thinking, 169 ff.; in reflection inseparable from thinking, 194 ff.; in indicative mood, 211 f.; in affective mood, 212 ff.; as totalization, 228 ff. See also *Speech, Language, Word.*

Speech, as non-creative of meaning, 10 ff.; uprooted, 31; proper character of, 31 f.; crisis of metaphysics and, 45; ambiguity of, 46; meaning as intrinsic and extrinsic to, 46 f.; as contact with, as distance from, meaning, 47 f.; as approach to, and distance from meaning, 47; critique and, 48; communication, isolation and, 48 f.; distinction between language and, 50 ff.; poverty of, 53 f.; analytic and synthetic character of, 69 ff.; expression and, 82 f.; new mode of freedom in, 84 f.; lack of freedom in scientific, 87 f.; relative freedom in free, 90 f.; life and free, 92 ff.; power and powerlessness of, 106 ff.; seeming unimportance of, 107 ff.; playful misuse of, 107 f.; ideological hypocrisy of, 109; group conformity and, 112 ff.; censorship and, 114 ff.; no escape from power of common, 122 ff.; paradoxes of, 132 ff.; authentic, 136 ff.; darkness in, 164 f.; thought and, 167 ff.; manifold forms of, 201 ff.; living daily life, 214 f.; as influencing others, 216 ff.; intentional attitude and, 229 ff.; coherence in field of significa-

tions and, 231 f.; contemporary problem of totalizing, 235 ff.; Western one-sided emphasis on, 237 ff.; scope of, 251 ff.; many dimensions of, 252 ff.; possibility of religious and metaphysical, 255 ff.; mysterious character of same, 259 f.; tendency to clarity, 260 ff. See also *Speaking, Language, Word.*

Spirit, existent, 193 f.

Talking, speaking and, 139 f.
Technology, influence of, 209 f.
Theory, practognosis and, 171 f.
Thinking, existential character of, 174 ff., 187 f.; reasons for, 189 ff.; in reflection inseparable from speaking, 194 ff.; many existential forms of, 197 ff. See also *Thought, Knowing.*

Thought, language and, 4 ff.; speech and, 167 ff.; views about relationship between speech and, 168 f.; not identical with speech, 169 ff., 173 f. See also *Thinking.*

Tolerance, freedom, truth and, 102 ff.
Totalization, speaking as, 228 ff.; disruption of existing, 232 ff.; autonomous culture of word and, 234 f.
Truth, speech and, 47 f.; many field of, 100 ff.; freedom, tolerance and, 102 ff.; deceptive concealment of, 109 f.

Understanding, speaking and, 145 f.; personal character of, 152 ff.
Universe of discourse, collective light and, 159 ff.

275

Use of language, central form, 224 ff.

Value(s), common speech and human, 120 ff.; lived form of, 189 f.

Vision, collective, 153 ff.

West, one-sided emphasis on speech in, 237 ff.

Word(s), seriousness in playing with, 110 ff.; speaking and spoken, 142 f.; spoken, as aspect of human situation, 143 ff.; relativity of knowledge expressed in, 199 ff.; magic, 221 f.; religious, 222 f.; totalization and autonomous culture of, 234 f.; culture of work and of, 237 ff.; positive value of culture of, 240 ff.

Work, culture of, 237 f.

World, duplication of, on paper, 244 f.; quasi-autonomy of this paper, 250 f.

World-view, science and, 129 ff.